Designing and Prototyping Interfaces with Figma

Learn essential UX/UI design principles
by creating interactive prototypes for mobile,
tablet, and desktop

Fabio Staiano

BIRMINGHAM—MUMBAI

Designing and Prototyping Interfaces with Figma

Group Product Manager: Rohit Rajkumar

Publishing Product Manager: Kaustubh Manglurkar

Senior Editor: Aamir Ahmed

Content Development Editor: Feza Shaikh

Technical Editor: Saurabh Kadave

Copy Editor: Safis Editing

Project Coordinator: Rashika Ba

Proofreader: Safis Editing

Indexer: Sejal Dsilva

Production Designer: Vijay Kamble

Marketing Coordinator: Elizabeth Varghese

First published: February 2022

Production reference: 1100222

Published by Packt Publishing Ltd.

Livery Place

35 Livery Street

Birmingham

B3 2PB, UK.

ISBN 978-1-80056-418-3

www.packt.com

To my family, to whom I owe everything.

*Special thanks to Gerel Burgustina, Fabio Di Corleto, and Alessia Saviano
for their precious contribution to the project.*

– Fabio Staiano

Foreword

More than 10 years have passed since Fabio was my student. Since then, he hasn't stopped growing. I was able to see a lot of this evolution because Fabio was always at my side, first as a university lecturer, then as my right-hand man.

It's a great opportunity to have someone with you who, like Fabio, makes you feel that no project is too big or too difficult to deal with. Now, my academic career has taken me away from him and, from everything I see, Fabio continues to evolve.

When he told me he wanted to write this book, I immediately thought it would be a text that would enrich and enlighten many people, including me. When he then asked me to write this foreword, I was both honored and a little frightened. The reason why I was honored is quite clear; the reason that I was scared – and I still am a bit scared – is that this book is about software (Figma) that is the competitor of Adobe XD, and I, in various ways, have always collaborated with Adobe. But let's get rid of any misunderstanding immediately: Figma is a fantastic tool, just like Adobe XD is, but beyond the tools, we all know that what really matters is how you use them. More than that, to say something more specific to our field, much depends on our design ability. And this is exactly what this book excels at: covering how to combine the tool with the correct vision and design of a digital product. Fabio, in fact, does not stop at the tool itself but embellishes this book with principles and best practices that he himself has applied in the real world over all these years, best practices that have distinguished him as an incredible leader of digital productions.

When you complete the wonderful journey of *Designing and Prototyping Interfaces with Figma*, many of you will probably feel ready to face the challenges that the world of UI/ UX will put before you, but maybe keeping this book on the bedside table will give you that comforting sense of security I mentioned before: no project will be too big or too challenging to deal with.

Italo Sannino

UI/UX professor at Accademia di Belle Arti and Adobe Community Professional

Contributors

About the author

Fabio Staiano is an experienced interface designer and Figma Community Advocate from Italy. After having been part of the creative agency Geko for several years, he later became a partner, creating digital products for well-known brands and running local events for the creative community. He then began his career in education in 2016, at The Guru Lab, teaching students about user interface and web design. In 2019, he decided to face new challenges by deepening his development skills at the Apple Developer Academy, where he specializes in frontend development and publishes various apps and boilerplate. Currently, he works as a consultant for IT projects and teaches at private design schools.

About the reviewer

Reony Tonneyck has been a designer since 2008. Currently, he's working on design systems at Khan Academy. Previously, he led the product design of QOMPLX's cybersecurity app, and spearheaded their design system. Before that, he led the creation of the first design system at AmWell. Where it all started was when Reony first read *Atomic Design* by Brad Frost.

Figma is where he found a new home within the design community. Eventually, he co-founded Figma's DC area community group for his "passion project," and proudly became a Figma Community Advocate.

Notably, the rest of his time is taken up by:

- Being a fun dad and loving husband
- Appreciating good food
- Being an avid PC gamer
- Advocating for electric vehicles
- Doing yoga and hiking

Table of Contents

Part 2: Exploring Components, Styles, and Variants

5

Designing Consistently Using Grids, Colors, and Typography

6

Creating a Responsive Mobile Interface Using Auto Layout

7

Building Components and Variants in a Collaborative Workspace

8
User Interface Design on Tablet, Desktop, and the Web

Part 3: Prototyping and Sharing

9
Prototyping with Transitions, Smart Animate, and Interactive Components

10

Testing and Sharing Your Prototype on Browsers and Real Devices

11

Exporting Assets and Managing the Handover Process

12

Discovering Plugins and Resources in the Figma Community

Index

Other Books You May Enjoy

Preface

Being a driving force in the design tools market, Figma makes everything easier by bringing unique innovations and opening up real-time collaboration possibilities, so it comes as no surprise that so many designers decide to switch from other tools to Figma.

In this book, you will be challenged to design a user interface for a responsive mobile application by researching, understanding user needs, and mastering all this in a step-by-step fashion by exploring the theory first and gradually moving on to practice. Your learning journey will cover the basics of user experience research with FigJam and the process of creating a complete design using Figma tools and features such as components, variants, auto layout, and much more. You will also learn how to prototype your design and expand your possibilities with Community resources such as templates and plugins.

By the end of this book, you will have a solid understanding of the user interface workflow, be able to manage the essential Figma tools, and know how to properly organize your workflow in it.

Who this book is for

This book is for aspiring UI/UX designers who want to get started with Figma, as well as established designers who want to migrate to Figma from other design tools. This guide will take you through the entire process of creating a full-fledged prototype for a responsive interface using all the tools and features that Figma has to offer. As a result, this Figma design book is suitable for UX and UI designers, product and graphic designers, and anyone who wants to explore the complete design process from scratch.

What this book covers

Chapter 1, Exploring Figma and Transitioning from Other Tools, serves as an introduction to Figma and its mission, explains the main differences between its desktop and web apps, explores the Figma welcome screen interface, and provides guidance on how to migrate to Figma from Sketch and Adobe XD.

Chapter 2, Structuring Moodboards, Personas, and User Flows within FigJam, is about how to work in FigJam, an additional tool implemented in Figma, using it to collect and analyze data in the early stages of design work.

Chapter 3, Getting to Know Your Design Environment, provides an overview of Figma tools in the toolbar, left and right panel functionalities, and instructions on how to start a new project from scratch.

Chapter 4, Wireframing a Mobile-First Experience Using Vector Shapes, focuses on defining the structure of the application and building its wireframe using Figma's shape and vector tools.

Chapter 5, Designing Consistently Using Grids, Colors, and Typography, dives into styles, a powerful feature that makes it easy to manage and reuse grids, typography, colors, and effects throughout a design project.

Chapter 6, Creating a Responsive Mobile Interface Using Auto Layout, introduces auto layout, one of Figma's advanced features, and provides guidance on how to best apply it using resizing and constraints.

Chapter 7, Building Components and Variants in a Collaborative Workspace, focuses on creating components and variants, both of which are crucial functions in Figma, as well as exploring other tools such as multiplayer, libraries, and version control.

Chapter 8, User Interface Design on Tablet, Desktop, and the Web, explores the basic principles of responsive design and focuses on how to adjust the interface design for different devices and screen resolutions.

Chapter 9, Prototyping with Transitions, Smart Animate and Interactive Components, explores various prototyping possibilities and functions in Figma, from basic to more advanced.

Chapter 10, Testing and Sharing Your Prototype on Browsers and Real Devices, covers all the ways to view and test an interactive prototype, as well as share it with others and work with feedback.

Chapter 11, Exporting Assets and Managing the Handover Process, focuses on preparing design project assets for further development, along with providing an overview of the Inspect tab in the right panel in Figma.

Chapter 12, Discovering Plugins and Resources in the Figma Community, covers the Figma Community and how to navigate it to locate the right files and plugins that can improve your design workflow.

To get the most out of this book

You will need any modern browser to use the web version of Figma, or alternatively, you can install the Figma desktop app on your computer. The book provides a step-by-step guide to designing an application interface, as well as recommendations for self-practice. To get the most out of the book, it is recommended that you follow the hands-on steps in the following chapters and devote some time to practicing your skills in Figma on your own.

Software/hardware covered in the book	Operating system requirements
Figma	Windows, macOS, or Linux
FigJam	Windows, macOS, or Linux

In *Chapter 10, Testing and Sharing Your Prototype on Browsers and Real Devices*, you will be asked to test your design on devices with smaller screens, and to do so, you will need to download the Figma app (available for iOS and Android) on your smartphone and/or tablet.

Download the color images

We also provide a PDF file that has color images of the screenshots and diagrams used in this book. You can download it here: `https://static.packt-cdn.com/downloads/9781800564183_ColorImages.pdf`.

Conventions used

There are a number of text conventions used throughout this book.

`Code in text`: Indicates code words in text, database table names, folder names, filenames, file extensions, pathnames, dummy URLs, user input, and Twitter handles. Here is an example: "Create a new text layer in auto-width mode (with a simple click) anywhere inside the Login frame and enter `Login`."

Bold: Indicates a new term, an important word, or words that you see onscreen. For instance, words in menus or dialog boxes appear in **bold**. Here is an example: "In the **Design** panel, you may have noticed a section not yet mentioned, namely **Effects**. This is definitely a tool that deserves an in-depth study, as with it you can apply various effects to elements such as **Inner shadow**, **Drop shadow**, **Layer shadow**, **Layer blur** and **Background blur**."

> **Tips or Important Notes**
> Appear like this.

Get in touch

Feedback from our readers is always welcome.

General feedback: If you have questions about any aspect of this book, email us at customercare@packtpub.com and mention the book title in the subject of your message.

Errata: Although we have taken every care to ensure the accuracy of our content, mistakes do happen. If you have found a mistake in this book, we would be grateful if you would report this to us. Please visit www.packtpub.com/support/errata and fill in the form.

Piracy: If you come across any illegal copies of our works in any form on the internet, we would be grateful if you would provide us with the location address or website name. Please contact us at copyright@packt.com with a link to the material.

If you are interested in becoming an author: If there is a topic that you have expertise in and you are interested in either writing or contributing to a book, please visit authors.packtpub.com.

Share Your Thoughts

Once you've read *Designing and Prototyping Interfaces with Figma*, we'd love to hear your thoughts! Scan the QR code below to go straight to the Amazon review page for this book and share your feedback.

https://packt.link/r/180056418X

Your review is important to us and the tech community and will help us make sure we're delivering excellent quality content.

Part 1: Introduction to Figma and FigJam

In this part, we'll introduce you to Figma and take the first step in using it by building your first wireframe. Also, you will explore FigJam, a collaborative space where you can run a whole design process.

In this part, we cover the following chapters:

- *Chapter 1, Exploring Figma and Transitioning from Other Tools*
- *Chapter 2, Structuring Moodboards, Personas, and User Flows within FigJam*
- *Chapter 3, Getting to Know Your Design Environment*
- *Chapter 4, Wireframing a Mobile-First Experience Using Vector Shapes*

1

Exploring Figma and Transitioning from Other Tools

Whether you are taking your first steps in design or already have some experience in the field, the tool you choose plays a big role in your day-to-day workflow. Of course, you need to know all the functions to use it professionally for your own purposes, but it is equally important to understand what ideology your design tool has, what benefits it gives you personally, and whether it develops and grows with you professionally.

Figma is one of the most advanced design tools out there and is constantly updating and releasing new features and capabilities. As a result, it has become not only a tool but also an irreplaceable assistant for many designers. In this chapter, you will discover how Figma manages to consistently push the boundaries and maintain its reputation to be many designers' favorite tool.

Figma is open to everyone and very flexible in many ways. It offers a variety of plans, including a free one, which is perfect for beginners in design. Figma also has web and desktop applications, each of which has its own benefits. This chapter contains detailed information about all of these and will help you to make your own choices. Here, you will also learn how to switch to Figma from other tools, namely Sketch and Adobe XD.

After that, we will look at how Figma presents you with the welcome screen, where you will explore all the buttons, toolbars, and areas, such as drafts, teams, Projects, and Community. It may seem overwhelming at first, but don't worry, we'll go over all the topics step by step. So, by the end of this chapter, you'll be ready to start putting Figma into practice!

In this chapter, we are going to cover the following main topics:

- Introducing Figma and its mission
- Difference between the desktop and web apps
- Transition to Figma from Sketch and Adobe XD
- Everything about the welcome screen

What is Figma?

If you are not a total newbie in UX/UI design, you have probably heard about Figma, a powerful real-time collaborative tool that can easily replace several design applications. If you're new to this design tool, get ready to learn what Figma is and what you need to know before using it.

Figure 1.1 – Figma's logo

One of the most amazing benefits of Figma is its facility of access. With the starter plan, you can use most features of the tool at no cost; all you need to do is to go on `figma.com` and create a personal account. You can download the Figma desktop app on your computer, but it also runs just as perfectly in a modern web browser, allowing you to use it on any operating system: Windows, Mac, Linux, or even ChromeOS. For now, Figma doesn't (officially) run on iPadOS but since the latest iPad has an M1 processor, the same you could find on new Macs, it might become possible in the near future.

Since Figma is cloud-based, you need to be connected to the internet to keep the auto-saved changes in your file. However, if you lose your internet connection and continue working, Figma will store every edit in your browser's local cache. So, once you are back online, all the changes in your file will be synced immediately.

Why Figma?

There are many design apps available on the market right now that can be used to solve any kind of creative challenges. But Figma is one of many designers' favorite tools and is becoming more and more popular. There are many good reasons for this. Let's talk about some of them.

First, Figma allows designers and other teammates to work simultaneously in real time, which takes the collaborative workflow to a whole new level. This powerful feature makes Figma stand out among other tools because it improves not only design work but also the team collaboration process itself. "Collaboration is hard. We make it easier" is one of Figma's fundamental principles.

Second, Figma has succeeded in bringing together a whole suite of design tools to provide an all-in-one solution. Figma covers just about everything you need to create a complex interface, from brainstorming and wireframing to prototyping and sharing assets. In addition to this, Figma goes beyond the design side of building a product and generates CSS, iOS, and Android code for developers to use.

Finally, Figma is not only a design app but also a community and platform for sharing ideas and solutions. Designers from all over the world use Figma not only for creating interfaces but also for vector illustrations, graphic design for digital media, and team-building activities. You can even play board games in Figma; how crazy is that? Yes, the Figma Community can definitely inspire you with tons of creative design works, but it can also help you simplify your workflow by providing plugins created by other community members. You can even develop your own plugin and share it with others!

Now you can see why Figma is a really great tool built for designers who want to stick to a fast and efficient workflow. However, keep in mind that neither Figma nor other tools will magically turn you into a good designer. Mastering a tool is not part of design, but it can save you time that you can reinvest into research and UX problem solving.

Excited enough? Time to jump in and see it in action!

Creating an account

The first thing you need to do before using Figma is to sign up at `figma.com`. On the home page of the site, click the **Sign up** button and create an account with your email address and a password of your choice or simply register using your Google account. That's it.

Figure 1.2 – The welcome popup

After registration, a few popup messages might appear with suggestions for creating a team. We will talk about teams later but for now, just skip it and go straight to the welcome screen.

Choosing the right plan

As mentioned earlier, you can use almost all of Figma's features while staying on the free Starter plan. This plan allows you to have unlimited cloud storage for your Figma and FigJam files, unlimited files in your drafts, unlimited viewers and commenters, plus some additional advanced features, such as one team project and 30-day version history. This is more than enough if you are just making your first steps in UX/UI design or working on your own. You can be sure that there will be no hidden fees and you won't be forced to sign up for an expensive premium service.

If a **Starter** plan is not enough for you, Figma offers two upgrade options: **Professional** and **Organization**.

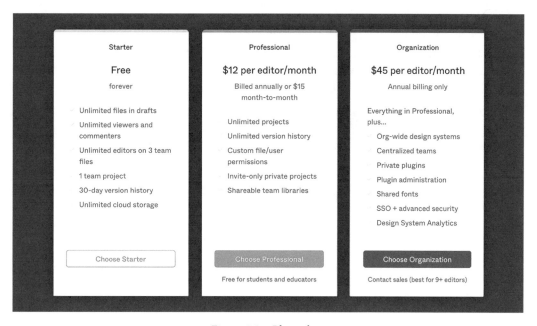

Figure 1.3 – Plans chart

The Professional plan is perfect for small- to medium-sized teams and allows you to have unlimited team projects, unlimited version history, shareable team libraries, and custom file permissions. It can be billed monthly or annually, your choice. The Organization plan is suitable for larger or multiple teams and, in addition to all the benefits of Professional, it provides advanced security, private plugins, shared fonts, and design system analytics. This plan is billed annually only.

> **Note**
> If you are a student or an educator, you can apply for a free Figma professional license here: `figma.com/education`.

Once you've created your account, you can immediately start using Figma from any web browser you have. Google Chrome, Firefox, Safari, or the new Microsoft Edge—all of those work great with Figma. So, you can continue to use it on the web or download the desktop app if your computer is running on Windows or macOS. We'll see more about the differences between the two in the next section.

Desktop app versus web app

In fact, there are no particular technical differences between Figma's desktop and web applications—both of them give you almost the same experience. Figma won't open when you're offline, whether you're using a desktop app or a web app. So, what's the point of downloading the application instead of using it in your favorite browser?

Figure 1.4 – Web app and desktop app

If you prefer to keep the environment less distracting while working on projects, you can go for the Figma desktop app. In addition to the clean and precise interface of the app, you don't have to worry about all the open tabs you might have, which could cause some crashes or slowdowns. Plus, with an actual native app, you can access the features of your operating system, such as setting up custom shortcuts or, on a Mac, quickly switching between apps using *Cmd + Tab*, or *Alt + Tab* for Windows.

Setting up Font Installer

Before we move on, let's talk about one crucial difference in the desktop app. Once you install Figma, you can use all of your local fonts in it. You can install your own fonts, or even use Adobe Fonts if you have an active Creative Cloud subscription and get a whole new set of fonts.

In the web app, you only get access to Google Fonts (also available in the desktop app through the **Preferences** menu), but you won't find your local fonts in the list. Fortunately, there is a workaround.

To set up access to your local fonts in the Figma web app, go to `figma.com/downloads` and simply download and install the macOS or Windows version of Font Installer. With this quick and easy move, you will be able to use all your favorite local fonts in the web app too.

> **Note**
> If you are using the Figma desktop app, there is no need to install anything additional to access your local fonts.

Obviously, once you've installed the app on your computer, you can still access the Figma web app through your account and freely work with your files there. Figma will automatically save and sync all your changes across both apps. This allows you to work on your projects even if you ever want to open them outside of your personal computer.

Whether you have chosen a web browser or the desktop app, it is time to give it a try, which you will do very soon. But if you already have some design files in other tools and you would like to transfer them to Figma first, you can follow the instructions you will find in the next section.

Transitioning to Figma from Sketch and Adobe XD

This part of the chapter will be useful if you are not new to design and you are thinking about switching to Figma from other tools. Switching to a new tool can be tricky and stressful, even if the transition seems smooth or your previous tool looks similar to the new one. Nobody likes to sacrifice an already established and familiar routine for the sake of something risky and unfamiliar, something that will have to be explored and mastered all over again. But being a digital designer means adjusting to new technologies, tools, and specifications every day. In this part, you will find detailed instructions on how to switch from Adobe XD and Sketch to Figma as painlessly and quickly as possible. So, let's start without any hesitation.

Coming from Sketch

Sketch was a revolutionary tool that changed the design workflow. It managed to combine everything that designers needed to create a UI in a simple and fast way. Designers used whatever tools they installed to create the UI, such as Corel, Illustrator, and Photoshop. Sketch was completely focused on the UX/UI creating process, getting rid of everything unnecessary, providing a clean, simple, and ultra-fast tool.

Figma has taken it a step further by offering real-time collaboration and speeding up just about any challenge a designer might face. Be assured that you are making a great choice, having decided to give it a try!

So, now you may be wondering, how difficult is it to go from Sketch to Figma? The good news is that you don't have to worry about seeing a completely unfamiliar interface in the new tool. Once you first open Figma, you can easily identify most of its features. Of course, there are still major differences between Sketch and Figma. Some of them will be completely new to you, but you will learn everything step by step in this book.

So, let's say you have a ton of projects created in Sketch. How do you transfer all the data from one tool to another? Unfortunately, Sketch doesn't have a magic button that says "Export to Figma"—no one wants users to leave their ecosystem. But don't worry, you have an import function in Figma, right in the welcome screen!

Figure 1.5 – Import function

Just click on **Import file**, select a .sketch file on your computer, and you're done. Instead, if you've already opened a new design file, access the menu bar on the top left, by clicking the Figma logo, then click **File | New from Sketch File**.

The loading time estimate will change depending on the size and complexity of the file. But after this simple operation, you will end up with a converted, fully working Figma file with all your Sketch pages, components, and layers. Nevertheless, no software automation is error-free, so the results of this transition may not be perfect. If you convert simple shapes, vectors, and texts, you'll find everything as it has to be in Figma. But if your source file contained a complex interface, or even a complete design system, it can take some time to create a satisfying Figma file. Sketch symbols will be converted into Figma components without any additional manipulation. But you will need to recreate styles and then apply them to your Components to restore the original library. It is also better to double-check the entire file, clean up, reorganize layers, and so on.

> **Note**
>
> Copy-pasting individual layers or artboards also works if you prefer to migrate manually, or you just need a few elements from the source file.

Coming from Adobe XD

After Sketch's revolution in the process of creating UIs, similar design tools began to come up in the market. Adobe upgraded Photoshop with artboards and additional interface design tools, but that still didn't help it gain popularity among interface designers. Therefore, the company released Adobe XD, an essential and simple tool built specifically for UX/UI. In fact, XD's standout line was its commitment to experience design.

The competition between Sketch and XD was quite intense from the beginning. Adobe XD did not have the same wide range of features as Sketch. But it was constantly updated and, most importantly, was included in the Creative Cloud subscription. It also became connected with other Creative Cloud software, such as Illustrator and Photoshop, and working with vectors and images became really simple and fast.

When Figma was released, it managed to simplify everything from the ground and speed up the workflow with collaboration features, variants, advanced prototyping, and auto layout. Now Figma is a driving force among design tools; it sets trends and introduces new ones.

So, now you may be wondering how easy it is to migrate all your files from the entire Adobe ecosystem to Figma. Well, this can be tricky since Figma doesn't have an import function for your .xd files like there is for Sketch. The complexity of the transition from XD to Figma really depends on the content of the source file. If you don't need to transfer components, styles, or even raster images (JPEG, PNG, and so on), the fastest way is to copy and paste artboards individually from XD to Figma, or export elements in SVG format to import them into Figma.

The end result of these manipulations will be visually similar to the content from the original file, but the functionality from one tool to another will not be transferred. In most cases, this is not enough, and you will have to spend additional time manually rebuilding the base, renaming and organizing layers, creating components and styles, and prototyping your interface.

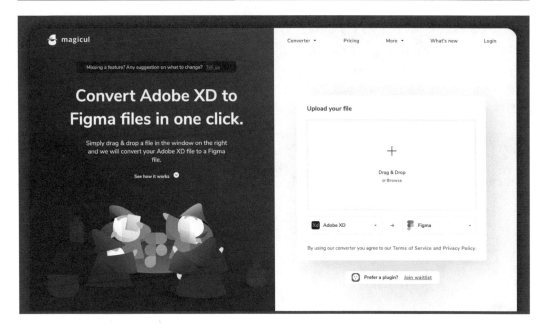

Figure 1.6 – XD to Figma converter

If you can't just let your old projects go, or you don't have time to rebuild the file to make it correct for use in Figma, there is an unofficial workaround. Go to `xd2sketch.com` and select the **from XD to Figma** option in the converter. After uploading the `.xd` file to the website, you will have a working `.fig` file with styles and components, ready to be imported into Figma. Sounds cool, but the service is not free. You will have to pay for each file you want to convert. Is it worth it? Up to you, but it surely is a time-saving solution.

A quick final thought

Transferring your designs to Figma may not always be easy, but with the right amount of time and patience, it is certainly doable. On a long-term project, you won't regret your transition, because Figma will allow you to recover all the losses, improving your daily tasks with more unique features available.

However, migration is not always the only and most convenient solution. Switching to a new tool does not mean transferring everything that you have done until today. You don't have to say goodbye to Sketch and Adobe XD forever. Instead, you can keep them beside Figma, ready to open up your old projects for quick changes if needed.

Now that the tricky transition is done, it's time to focus your attention on Figma and take a closer look at it!

Exploring the welcome screen

Whenever you open Figma, the first thing you see is the welcome screen. This is your control center, a personal hub with a huge amount of information and functions. It may take some time to learn everything that is presented on this screen, but at the end of this section, you will know all about its functionalities.

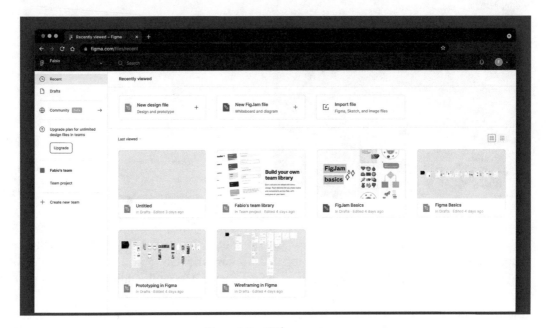

Figure 1.7 – Welcome screen

Recent and Drafts

If you have already used Figma before or you have just transferred some files from another tool, you'll see all of your most recent Figma and FigJam files. If you are just starting Figma for the first time, you may be confused by some files already appearing in there. Don't worry, no one hacked your account, those are simply some pre-existing example files provided by Figma itself.

As a rule of thumb, **Recent** in the left sidebar shows you all the files and prototypes that you've recently opened or edited. This area includes files and prototypes from your drafts, teams, and any files you opened. You can only see recent files from the account you are currently using, not ones from other Figma accounts, if you have more than one.

Let's now take a look at **Drafts**. Despite the obvious title, this page is more than just a collection of all your drafts. According to the plan chart, drafts are not limited to pages, even on the starter plan. This way, you can create as many drafts as you like and keep all your projects stored in the cloud.

The main difference between Drafts and a regular team folder is access restrictions. This means that no one can view your draft files until you share a personal link with them. As your personal space, Drafts lets you play with Figma, draw mockups, and test ideas without worrying about others seeing them. When you're done with the design file in Drafts, you can immediately convert the draft to a team file. This action unlocks multi-editor capabilities for your file.

Community

Figma's Community feature is a space for all creators who want to publish their design files and plugins with other designers. This is a huge topic that definitely needs to be explored in more detail. So, we'll come back to this in the last chapter of the book and take a closer look at it. For now, let's focus on the standard features.

Teams and Projects

Figma wouldn't be Figma without its collaborative core. It succeeded in understanding the designer's struggle and came up with a brand-new way of working with others. Since the beginning, its focus was to simplify this experience, making a team work as easy as being in the same room, editing the same file.

As stated earlier, Drafts is a safe place where you can freely follow your inspiration and test your ideas. But when that folder starts to get messy, which happens very soon, it's time to move on to teams, where you can better organize your design files. Moreover, teams, unlike drafts, are about collaboration. You can invite an unlimited number of viewers to your file in Drafts, but not editors. Once you create or move your file in teams, you can add as many editors as you want, and you can all work on the same file in real time.

To better understand the difference between drafts, files, projects, and teams, let's create a functional workspace:

1. In the left column, click on **Create new team**. This will lead you to a multi-step window.

2. First, you have to enter a name for your team. You can call it `Personal` since it won't be shared with anyone, but you can choose any name you like.

3. Next, you'll be prompted to add collaborators to the team. Collaborators can instantly view, open, or edit any new file you create. They can also create new files themselves unless you manually change the permissions. Eventually, you can skip this part and add people to your team whenever you want.

4. The final step is choosing a plan between the free Starter one, Professional, and Organization. For now, pick the Starter plan. You can upgrade it whenever you face some limitation, if needed.

So, your team is set up and you should now see it on the left bar of the welcome screen, ready to be used. If you click on it, you will see an area with a lot of details, such as any projects, the members on the team, and the limitations of your current plans.

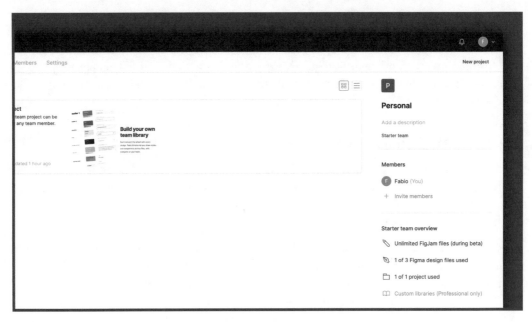

Figure 1.8 – Team description

On the Starter plan, you can create only one project per team. A project in Figma represents a team's shared folder, where you can store up to three design files in one project on the free plan. Teams don't have to be shared. You can use them privately, but plan limitations will still be the same. Since you invite someone to your team, each file you create inside it will be visible to others. You can have unlimited editors on this plan but only for three design files. Each file also has a limit of three pages. You can still create as many Starter teams as you like.

If the free plan doesn't cover your needs, or you want to collaborate with others on multiple projects and files, there is a Professional team option for you. By choosing this plan, you can have an unlimited number of projects, files, and viewers, plus shared libraries in one team. You will need to pay for each Professional team you want to create but the libraries still cannot be shared between different teams.

Figma also has an option for companies that have multiple products offering an Organization plan. Every Organization team has access to Professional teams' functionality, as well as an unlimited number of teams and shared libraries across all these teams. Companies on this plan will have their Figma account linked to the organization's email address. Every file including drafts created by members of this team will be owned by the organization. Moreover, Organization teams have access to other extra, advanced features, such as private plugins, shared fonts, and library analytics.

Figma and FigJam files

In this section, you will learn about two types of files that you can create right from the welcome screen in Figma: design files and FigJam files. FigJam is a brand-new collaboration tool recently introduced in Config 2021. It is basically a whiteboard that you can use with your team to brainstorm, build flows, organize your ideas, and even play games! It's a very helpful tool, but especially for working on the early phases of a project.

Figure 1.9 – New file options

Before the release of FigJam, most designers were using specific tools for digital whiteboards and diagrams. Some of them used Figma itself for these purposes but it was not very handy for that. Since Figma already managed to get us to ditch a lot of tools by bundling everything into a single solution, the introduction of FigJam seemed like the right way to fill the last gap. However, adding to Figma a whole new set of tools was certainly not the best idea in terms of performance and ease of use, and neither was creating a separate software a great solution. FigJam became a different space with a completely unique interface and new features. Plus, it is still a part of Figma, and it makes it very easy to switch from one file to another as if they were one big environment.

Figure 1.10 – FigJam file

We'll briefly introduce FigJam and you'll learn more about it in the next chapter. For now, let's take a look at one more thing on the welcome screen.

Account and notifications

It seems that every function placed on the top toolbar of the welcome screen is easy to understand. However, there is still something to clarify before moving on to practice.

Starting from the top search bar, Figma's search functionality is a very powerful one, as it can search through your personal and shared files, even within file content, as well as Community templates and plugins.

In the top-left corner, you can see your account email address. By clicking on it, you can switch between your workspace and other ones to which you are added. There is a bell icon in the opposite corner of the top bar. This is where you will see all of your personal notifications about invitations to shared files and so on. It's important to always keep an eye on this. Finally, by clicking on your avatar, in the top-right corner, you can access all settings, add accounts, log out, and more.

Now, can you say that you are familiar with the welcome screen? If so, you are finally ready to sail.

Summary

As you can see, Figma is a revolutionary design tool that allows many creators to take their workflow to the next level. It covers every need a designer could ever have. Therefore, it is equally perfect for individual workers as well as teams of small and large companies. Through this approach, Figma is gaining popularity among designers all over the world. Now you can become a part of this community, exchange experiences, and contribute to its growth. No other tool has achieved this level of user loyalty!

In this chapter, we learned about the ideology of Figma and its benefits over other tools. You also created an account and found out about Figma's plans and the difference between its desktop and web applications. Perhaps you even managed to switch from another tool! We also explored Figma's welcome screen, so now you know about some primary buttons and sections and what stands behind those.

In the next chapter, our journey will be even more exciting! We'll learn how to use FigJam in practice by structuring personas there and creating user flows for your first project in Figma!

2
Structuring Moodboards, Personas, and User Flows within FigJam

Now that you have an understanding of Figma as a design tool, and you already know about some of its basic functionality, you are ready to dive into learning by doing. This is a reasonable and logical next step, since the best way to learn is to practice as much as possible. As mentioned earlier, Figma now consists of two types of files – design and FigJam. You will start your practice with the second one, although it is a recently released brand-new feature. You might think that FigJam is Figma's complementary tool, but let's take a look at the reasons why you should start with it.

First of all, FigJam is much easier to use; consider it as a warm-up before you start practicing with more complex tools in Figma. Its functionality doesn't even come close to what the design editor has, since it was created for a different purpose, which we will talk about later. Secondly, it's important to study all stages of the design process, many or even most of which are not related to the creation of screens or even a wireframe. Before doing this, you must go through several brainstorming sessions with your team, collect and analyze data, get to know your user, and so on. You will learn about all these topics in this chapter, and you do not even need to leave Figma because you will practice absolutely all the stages of research in FigJam.

This chapter may seem tricky and confusing to you because it is filled with a lot of information, and of course, it can be overwhelming, especially if you are new to design. But you should know that the deeper and better you understand the basic principles of research and analytics in design, the easier it will be for you to get started with the user interface. So, there is no doubt that this chapter deserves your attention, and by the end, you will have a clear idea of what to consider when working with a real prototype.

In this chapter, we are going to cover the following main topics:

- Gathering and analyzing data using FigJam
- Creating a moodboard and designing user personas in FigJam
- Building a functional user flow with FigJam tools

Exploring ideas and collaborating in FigJam

You were briefly introduced to FigJam in the previous chapter, but now it's time to learn how to use it and for what purposes. You will be guided through a complete workflow of collecting, analyzing, and processing data. This is a necessary part of a designer's work before building any prototype. All designers, freelancers, and those who work in agencies or in-house should devote a significant amount of their working time to the research stage. It will be a very challenging but interesting journey, and FigJam will be our main tool to successfully complete it. Before we gather any data, let's start with an overview of the interface of FigJam.

Exploring FigJam

As you already know, FigJam is completely different from Figma's design file, although it is still implemented in Figma itself, so we still don't need to install anything or create another account to start using it. It's a very easy-to-use tool that is as simple as using pen and paper while adding collaboration to it. Before diving together into FigJam, try to explore it yourself, and feel free to play with it in different ways to find your own unique approach, as if you were working on your personal notepad.

When you launch your first FigJam file – by clicking on **FigJam file** right under the **New file** panel on the welcome screen – you'll already have an idea of what this tool really is. Basically, it is a full-screen whiteboard that can be filled with ideas, notes, findings, images, and so on. It's that simple.

The entire interface of FigJam is intuitive and clear. You can immediately see all the available tools in its toolbar at the bottom of the screen. Each tool offers specific properties for customizing the output, but you will soon find out that FigJam doesn't have many options for colors, styles, and fonts. This is a conscious decision made by Figma designers because they don't want you to focus on polishing and wasting time choosing the right typeface instead of thinking about the underlying idea. The point is that FigJam is not a tool for designing, and this is the main reason behind its simplicity. Anyone from a team can take part in the initial stage of the project, participate in brainstorming, and show a different way of thinking, which certainly helps to conduct more effective research.

Let's now take a look at what each of these tools actually does:

Figure 2.1 – FigJam's toolbar

A – navigation

Select and move your elements on canvas with the selection tool – you can also access it with the *V* shortcut – or switch to the pan tool by clicking on the hand icon or pressing *H* on your keyboard to simply move around your work area. You can also quickly switch to the pan tool while holding down the spacebar on your keyboard.

B – marker

By clicking on the marker or pressing *M* key, you can choose between a set of different colors and two thicknesses. Use it to draw freehand on the canvas.

C – shapes

Fill the canvas with the already selected shape or just click on the right arrow to change the shape to something else, such as circles, rectangles, triangles or even more complex ones. Every shape can be resized by dragging its corner or side.

D – sticky notes

Stick these anywhere on the canvas, as if you were doing it on a whiteboard, to quickly add notes or comment on something.

Figure 2.2 – A shape and sticky note comparison

You may be wondering what the difference is between shapes and sticky notes. The confusion is understandable, since text can also be inserted into sticky notes and, when you use a rectangle shape with text inside, it might look like a sticky note. Sticky notes, however, have a fixed width, and their height will automatically be adapted to the length of the text you enter. Their text positions are different also – text in shapes can only be vertically centered. In addition, you may notice the author's name in the bottom left corner of the sticky note, which is automatically added as you type inside it. You can hide your name by clicking the element and toggling the last option with a signature icon from the menu. In contrast, neither rectangles nor any other shape have this functionality.

Next to the first skeuomorphic set of tools, you can find the next set, which has smaller icons but is no less important.

E – text

Use this to add any text to your canvas – titles, heading, body text, and even clickable links. The keyboard shortcut for this tool is the *T* key.

F – connector

Use this to connect any objects on the canvas. Drag it between text, shapes, notes, and components. Any element can be connected with this tool; moreover, it's magnetic and will always be attached to the object's side and follow after it. The keyboard shortcuts for this tool are *Shift + C* for elbow connectors and *L* for a straight line.

G – stamp

After clicking on this tool or pressing *E* on your keyboard, a selection wheel will pop up with two options in the center:

Figure 2.3 – The stamp and emote wheels

The bottom one, stamps, contains all kinds of stickers that let you visualize your reaction and feedback with permanently sticking upvotes, downvotes, and more. If you switch to the top one, emotes, you will see a set of icons that will help you to express your live reaction. Select an emote, click on the canvas, and express your feelings in real time. Keep it pressed to trigger a flood of emotes. All those emotes appear temporarily and stay on the canvas only for a few seconds.

Among emotes, there is one that is truly special – the chat bubble icon. This is not a simple temporary reaction but a fully functional live chat in FigJam, called **cursor chat**. By clicking on this icon or using the / key, you can activate cursor chat mode; you will recognize it by the empty bubble attached to your cursor on the screen. You can simply start typing your message and, without having to click anything to confirm sending, your text will be displayed in real time to all the users of the FigJam file at that time. After you finish typing, your message will stay for a few seconds and then disappear without leaving any trace, just like the other emotes. If you want your message to be visible for longer or communicate with someone who is offline at that moment, the best choice is the **comment** function. We will talk about this later in the chapter:

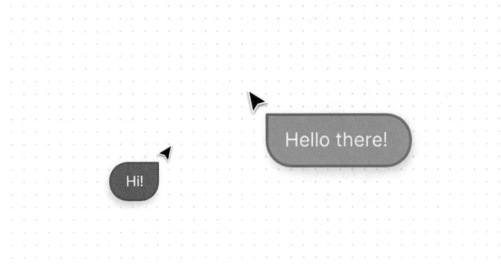

Figure 2.4 – Cursor chat

H – templates

From here, you can access a bunch of useful starting templates, such as research canvases, inspirational boards, team building activities and much more.

I – library

This is a diversified tool. Here, you can see a vast selection of complex shapes and illustrations to help you express and visualize your ideas on the canvas. But that's not all – you can publish libraries from your Figma files directly to FigJam. You will learn more about libraries later in this book.

J – more

All the basic tools are not enough? By clicking this element you will access a small set of extra functionalities, such as media importing (drag and drop on the canvas also works) or widgets and plugins, which you can use to extend even further FigJam's possibilities.

As you can see, FigJam offers you many ways to discuss ideas with your team, exchange reactions, and communicate as if you were all in the same room. All these tools are simpler than they may seem and soon you will learn how to use them in the best possible way to achieve a great project kickoff.

> **Note**
>
> FigJam is a separate tool within Figma that offers a free starter option but has a separate pricing plan, not included with Figma. Check out the official Figma website to discover more.

Brainstorming with others

Just like Figma, FigJam was launched as a collaborative tool. The advantage of FigJam is its simplicity and the ability to immediately get involved in the teamwork process. You can certainly enjoy FigJam on your own, but working together makes it extremely powerful. Sharing your file with someone else has never been easier. All you have to do is click the **Share** button in the upper right corner (*B*) and insert one or more email addresses of your collaborators. Be sure to provide the right permissions by switching between **can view** and **can edit**, depending on your intentions.

A less secure but easier way to do the same action is by clicking on **Copy link** and sending it to your collaborators. Depending on what you choose under the **Anyone with the link** drop-down list, the recipient can edit your file or just view it. Be careful, because if your link goes public, you risk having unwanted guests in your file.

Until your collaborators accept the invitation or follow the link, their names will stay grayed out in the share dialog box. As soon as they open your file, you will see their avatars appear in the top-right panel (*A*) and your guests' profile names change color.

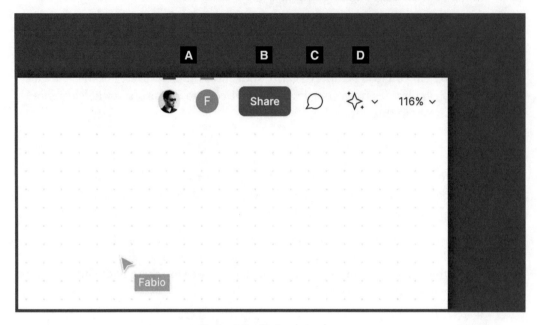

Figure 2.5 – FigJam's top bar

From now on, you and your colleagues will be able to see each other's cursors in real time while working together in the file. Be ready to discover a whole new world of amazing possibilities – brainstorming, design sprints, team building, workshops, moodboards, and so on. Nowadays, people get more and more involved in remote communication; our workflow speeds up and an agile approach is becoming standard, so it's not hard to see why FigJam is an essential tool that needs to be incorporated into our daily work.

We already know about emotes, stamps, and cursor chat. All these functions are duplicated under the **Collaborate** drop-down list in the panel in the upper right corner (*D*). This is implemented for quick access to these functions, and they are technically identical to those from the bottom toolbar. However, you can also see another feature that was later introduced with the FigJam update – the timer.

You might be wondering why and how to properly use it in FigJam. Actually, this tool is nothing more than a regular timer but becomes very powerful within FigJam, creating a strong synergy with other tools. Most team-building activities are timed, and it's also reasonable to want to track and limit the duration for design sprints and idea gathering. Once you activate the timer, it will automatically sync for all participants, and when time runs out, everyone will be notified:

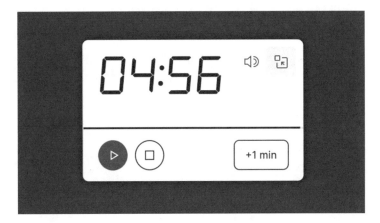

Figure 2.6 – The timer

Working with teammates in real time is great but not always possible. In this case, if you want to provide feedback, ask questions, or express an idea without editing the actual whiteboard elements, you can always use the comment function. You can see the icon right next to the share button. Clicking on it, you will see your cursor turn into a location icon, and you can click anywhere on the board to pin a comment. All those who have access to the file will receive a notification about your comment, both in-app and via email, by default.

> **Note**
> Currently, FigJam supports up to 50 participants (viewers or editors) at the same time.

Moving to the next step

Now that you know every FigJam feature, it's time to put together what you've learned and get some real work done. Let's say you just had a brainstorming session with your team. Generally, the result would be having a definition of the best idea, which then needs to be accepted by your potential client or your supervisor. Once approved, it's time to get a general idea of the upcoming briefing, so take your time and write down all your concerns, which you can discuss later with stakeholders:

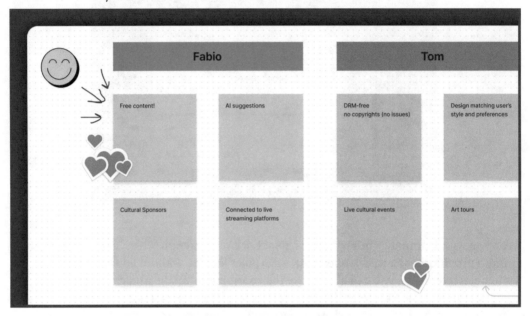

Figure 2.7 – Brainstorming

Remember that every project is unique, and you can approach it completely differently each time. Of course, learning a standard flow can help you avoid missing important steps, but only with hands-on experience will we master the process. You should also keep in mind that the UX working process is very time-consuming and, by consequence, needs the right budget. So, although it would be great to follow the best design path, you will not always have enough financial resources to cover all stages, and sometimes, you'll have to make some compromise between time and cost, while still achieving excellent results.

Let's keep it simple this time, starting a project with a brief that focuses on creating a brand-new streaming service filled with free documentaries and other cultural content, where you will be responsible for designing a fresh, modern, and intuitive interface for mobile, tablet and desktop. This is your starting point.

So, when you have formed an idea, it's time to move forward and explore it from every angle. In the next section, you will learn how to do this as easily as possible.

Creating moodboards and personas in FigJam

Getting inspired isn't easy, especially when you have to stick to tight deadlines. But if you follow proven strategies and stick to the right design process, you will definitely achieve amazing results in a short period of time. This section will focus on defining some of the most common best practices.

Research phase

Whether you are creating a landing page, a complex website, or an entire ecosystem for a product, the research phase is very important for structuring a functional design solution. After analyzing the brief and understanding your stakeholder's vision, you need to set up a mission statement. This is a short and affirmative description of the project's purpose that highlights the problem your product is going to solve. In our first project, the mission statement could be as follows:

Mission Statement

An easy-to-use, modern streaming service that allows users to browse a collection of culturally interesting content, such as documentaries and movies for entertainment and educational purposes, for free.

Setting up a mission statement helps you and your team always keep a product's purpose in mind, reducing the risk of going off the rails.

Let's take a look at a few examples. Here are some of the big brands' mission statements.

Apple: *"Apple strives to bring the best personal computing experience to students, educators, creative professionals, and consumers around the world through its innovative hardware, software, and internet offerings."*

Google: *"Our mission is to organize the world's information and make it universally accessible and useful."*

Ikea: *"To offer a wide range of well-designed, functional home furnishing products at prices so low that as many people as possible will be able to afford them."*

Once the mission statement is clearly formulated, the design process becomes much more integral. And now you can move on to the next stage – competitor research:

Figure 2.8 – Competitor analysis

Competitive analysis is important for many different reasons. When you deeply analyze the market, its participants, and how they present their product, you collect data on functionalities, design patterns, and conventions. Of course, you need to examine your competitors in order to understand all the positive aspects and then enter the market with at least a decent offer. But it is equally important to identify the negative sides of their products. This is perhaps even more useful because it allows you to create something that can fill a market gap or improve the user experience in a new way.

A study of competitors consists of exploring their products, taking screenshots, noting interesting solutions, and collecting your own notes and comments. FigJam is, of course, a perfect tool for this step. As you analyze your artifacts, try to figure out how they solve their users' problems by comparing all the results against your product's goal. Write down and mark everything, even small notions and concerns, which later on can stimulate your flow of ideas and analysis. All images, text, and comments can easily be gathered in FigJam. Plus, with its limited set of tools to choose from, you don't have to worry too much about styling.

Before proceeding, try to create a FigJam board yourself by compiling the mobile, tablet, and desktop interfaces of the main competitors in the streaming services sector.

Starting a moodboard

If you've ever created a moodboard for any purpose, you will understand that it is more than just a bunch of images and text. As you work on analysis, research, and so on, you will inevitably find a lot of interesting content along the way, some of which can greatly inspire you for the next stages of design. And this is where the moodboard comes into play – a digital space with everything that may be useful in the future:

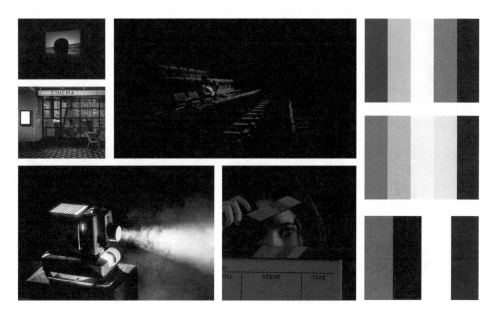

Figure 2.9 – A moodboard example

(Photos by Mike Simon, Jeremy Yap, Karen Zhao, Mason Kimbarovsky, Rock Staar on Unsplash)

In general, a moodboard can be useful in two early stages. You can create it in a brainstorming session, alone, or in a group, trying to put together content that can help you find inspiration. But also, most importantly, creating a moodboard is very helpful before building the flow and user interface. It's important to know that after you've created a moodboard, you can fill it out day after day by collecting anything that is currently getting your attention. You can find a lot of interesting and aesthetic content on resources made just for that purpose, such as Pinterest – a very special social network for creators. You might even discover something from your daily life and turn it into inspiration. Take your time and feel free to update this collection of your personally inspiring "items."

Try creating your personal moodboard in FigJam and start collecting everything inspirational for the phases to come.

Creating user personas

Now that you've set a mission statement, analyzed your competitors, and created a moodboard, it's the perfect time to define a target. It's not enough to understand a problem and determine how to solve it; you also need to know who your product is for. The shortest way to collect the necessary data and figure out this unknown variable is to interview and/or poll a group of people of different ages, genders, and backgrounds. As a result, you can understand what their needs are and whether your product – whatever it may be – can somehow satisfy them or solve their pain points in any way. Social media and website analytics are also great sources of valuable information, but of course, that's something more suited to a restyling project than brand-new product ideation.

Once you have collected enough raw data to analyze, you can start creating a user persona – a fictional description of a person who represents your typical user. From now on, you will use it as a guideline for each subsequent phase of the project.

Creating a user persona is useful not only for designers but also for the entire team working on the project. One of the most common mistakes when designing something is to forget who will be using your product, and you may end up following your personal preferences and tastes. Personas also can be used effectively by those who are keen to meet user needs, including stakeholders, marketers, and developers.

But how do we correctly create one or more user personas? There are no exact and strict rules but only general guidelines on what is useful to include and what is not. There is no doubt that when working on a persona, you should not trust your intuition or guesses but use an empirical method based on previously collected data. A careless and hasty user persona creation can lead to project failure, as well as undermine efforts made during the analysis and research phase:

Figure 2.10 – A user persona

Usually, to create a user persona template, you should fill in the following blocks of information:

- Name

- Photo

- Demographics (age, gender, relationship status, occupation, and location)

- A short biography

- Habits

- Goals, needs, and frustrations

Keep in mind that a persona should never, under any circumstances, represent people you know. Also, you should not use any personally identifiable information but rather rely on information from the general data collection. Obviously, if your data can identify different archetypes of typical users, it is highly recommended to create multiple user personas. In addition, depending on the type of project you're working on, you might find it helpful to add other fields to your personas' templates, such as personality traits, commonly used applications, or even some more specific additional data such as salary ranges.

For our sample project, it would be great if you can arrange an online survey – for example, using **Google Forms** – and send it to your group of friends. This way, you will learn how to best organize questions and collect data. This step may not be so easy the first time, since the survey needs to collect a lot of raw data to have any really effective results for analysis, so refer to our preceding user sample (*Figure 2.10*) if necessary.

Once you're done with your model, don't forget to share your user personas with anyone involved in the project to have a common reference when thinking about the product's target.

> **Note**
>
> Tons of user persona templates are available within the community for both Figma and FigJam. We'll cover that in more detail in *Chapter 12, Discovering Plugins and Resources in the Figma Community*.

You have completed most of the research phase of your project, and now you know more about your target audience. Now, let's explore the actions a user can take in your product to learn how to provide them with a clear and intuitive interface on every page of the application. That's exactly what you will learn to master in the next section.

Building user flow in FigJam

You already know that analysis and research are important stages in the initial phase of the implementation of any project, even small ones. The tools and processes used so far are part of the so-called **User Experience** (**UX**) research. Often, in the most professional environments, the UX and the UI are handled by different professionals. However, even if you are only responsible for the interface, it is better to know the basics of UX principles, as it may happen that you have to somehow figure it out yourself or, if you do not receive very precise instructions from the UX department on how to design your product, what style to use, and where to place each element.

Thus, the profession of a UX designer is far from being creative and much closer to subjects such as marketing and psychology. Both disciplines are essential in order to understand your users, analyze their behavior, and get a great product as a result.

The golden path

You already know the preferences and goals of your target audience, so the next step is to determine the typical path that a user will take when using the product, and FigJam is again the perfect place for this purpose.

You can create a new file or use a previously used one and dedicate a separate area for this. Feel free to choose your own way, depending on whether you prefer to collect the results of all stages of research and analysis separately or in a single file. However, with separate files, you can share each one with a different group of people – keep that in mind.

To build a navigation flow, you can use the classic flowchart. Select a rectangle from the shape tool and place it on the board. You can add others next to it just by repeating the operation, or, for a faster way, use the classic duplicate shortcut by holding the Option key (macOS) or the Alt key (Windows) and clicking and dragging an already existing shape. FigJam also makes duplication easier with a + button that appears on the sides of any shape on the canvas (**A**). When you click it, the same shape will appear next to the existing element with a connector between the two (**B**):

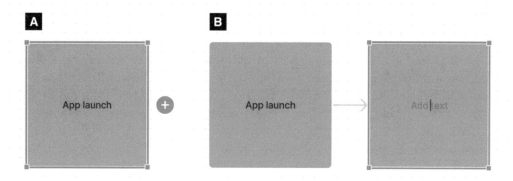

Figure 2.11 – Shapes and connectors

This way, you can first structure a horizontal diagram for our mobile app, which is simple but essential, that represents the golden path that leads the user from the starting point to the final point of the digital product, generally defined by the conversion goal:

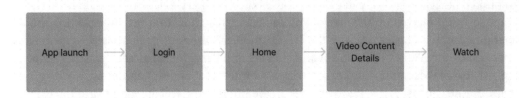

Figure 2.12 – A basic flow

This is a good start, but now it is necessary to add all the paths that users can take, also considering any direct or indirect choices they encounter along the way. To do this, you can take full advantage of the various functions that FigJam provides for creating diagrams. First, by selecting an existing shape, you can access its parameters at any time, having the ability to change its color, trace, and the shape itself. This allows you to distinguish between various parts of the diagram to represent different types of elements:

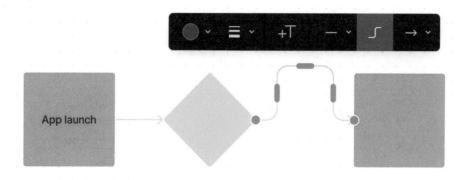

Figure 2.13 – The connector's edit mode

Now, let's take a closer look at the connectors between shapes, which can be customized as well. When you hover over any connector, you can see blue handles on it that allow you to manually edit curved lines. You can also see that a connector has two blue dots; these are its start and end points. By clicking on any of them, you can easily move and attach the connector to any other object on the canvas.

For now, you don't need to manually edit the lines – when you move items on the board, the connectors will automatically follow the ones they are attached to, but you still need to use the **Add Text** property, or just double-click on the center of the line, which allows you to add text exactly in the middle of the selected connector. This is a great feature for clarifying and making multiple paths more intuitive, as shown in the following example:

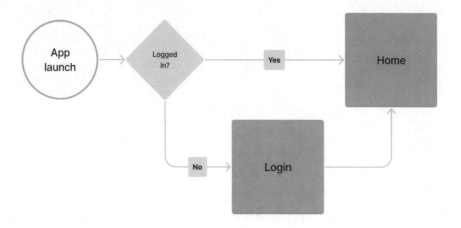

Figure 2.14 – A flow with variables

Here, you can see the first iteration of our mobile app login process. The diagram is made up of several different shapes and colors, so you can immediately understand the different meanings behind the blocks. Using connectors and associated properties, you can draw multiple paths to the variables.

In the current case, it should be assumed that when the application is launched on a device, the user may have already signed in before. Thus, it is possible that the user will immediately enter the home page after opening the application. Your flow should include these two cases – either the user creates an account for the first time or opens the home page directly.

It takes a lot of effort to structure the entire flow because you have to anticipate all the possible actions the user can take in the application. It is very easy to miss essential features such as login password recovery, so it is extremely important to test other real applications before working on your user flows. During testing, you need to break down and organize all the functionality into several paths and then make sure that your product does not miss anything. This is one of the most important steps in the transition from the early stages to the UI, as it provides clear navigational guidance from the beginning and, as a result, saves you from compromising all the work in the advanced design stages:

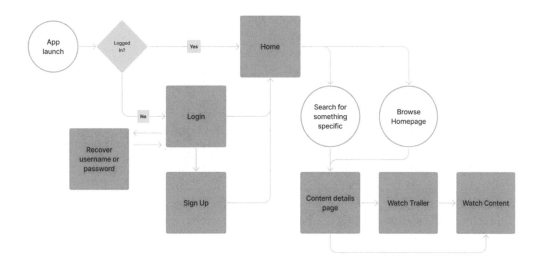

Figure 2.15 – A complex flow example

This second iteration (*Figure 2.15*) represents a more complete example of what our app could be, even though secondary paths such as all the category pages, user profile pages, and settings are still missing. In this diagram, you can clearly distinguish between user steps (circle-shaped) and application pages (rectangular-shaped) triggered by user actions. This is a fundamental difference between user flow and a more technical site map that only displays all the web or application pages.

> **Note**
>
> FigJam provides a bunch of shapes, colors, and styles, but if you need even more customization, remember that it's incredibly simple to copy and paste any sort of assets from the Figma design files.

Be the user

It is impossible to cover all the information about the complete UX process in a few pages, but now at least you have learned the fundamental part that every designer should know. If you wish, you can find specialized sources about UX and study this topic deeper. But for now, you will explore the UI and related tools. However, it does not mean that the UX research is complete. Design should never be confused with drawing. A good designer always remembers the purpose of a product and whom it serves at every stage of the project, with no exceptions. Therefore, a user-centered interface based on qualitative analysis will certainly achieve its intended goals.

Before moving on to the product wireframe stage, make sure that you have your content arranged. Interfaces are nothing more than custom-made containers adapted to present intended content. The most common mistake designers make is to start designing an interface without even having a vague idea of the actual content that the product will contain, which ultimately leads to them artificially inventing one. The famous *Lorem ipsum*, most commonly used as placeholder text, can be both useful and dangerous.

To give a practical example, let's take our streaming service project and imagine that you start designing interfaces right now with what you have. You've collected user data, built the flow, but you still don't know anything about the actual content of the service. How are you going to work on a detail page for individual video content without the slightest idea of what data to show to the user? Should you include information about the author, the director, and the duration? Of course, you can copy some content from competitors, but nothing guarantees that it will match the real data to be loaded onto the service. Therefore, without real content, there is always a risk of creating a beautiful container that is unsuitable for placing the final data in.

It is not always possible to obtain real and ready-made data at this stage due to the agreement with the stakeholders, but it is almost always possible to request a sample or demo information. In the case of a streaming service, you need at least one example of a detailed description to get started so that you know what data has to be presented on the interface.

Summary

It is clear how Figma tries to be more than just a design tool, providing everything you need at all stages of product design. FigJam is the perfect proof of this. Keeping all your artifacts in FigJam allows you to access them in two clicks without even leaving Figma. You can create and organize FigJam files as you like, dedicating some for team activities and others for your own templates to reuse in further projects. So, feel free to experiment with this tool to see how many amazing things you can do with it!

In this chapter, we covered the basics of the UX part of the design process, such as collecting and analyzing data for your project, defining a persona, creating inspiring moodboards, and building effective user flows. You've also explored all of FigJam's functional tools and learned how to use them and for what purpose. Now, you have a great set of artifacts that will come in handy in the next stages of our project. It's important that you do not forget the concepts learned in this chapter when working on your next projects. Remember that only with practice and experience will you be able to complete these initial steps as successfully as possible, making your professional life much easier.

In the next chapter, you will explore more Figma tool basics and set up your first design project. Get ready to continue your amazing journey!

3
Getting to Know Your Design Environment

In the previous chapter, you discovered the basic concepts of the UX process, which is without a doubt an essential part of any design project. As you work, it's best to keep all research results, analysis data, and other attributes nearby so you can always check if you're on your planned design path. Remember that the usability and clarity of your final user interface will directly depend on the quality of your UX work.

However, creating a user interface is also a tricky and time-consuming part of design work. You might have done some excellent research and collected enough relevant data, but your actual design work may not always be smooth and easy. In real life, anything can happen – maybe the chosen style will not be approved by the customer, or maybe your team decides to add a tablet version of your product. This book cannot anticipate all the challenges a designer might face, but you will definitely learn how to make your user interface work faster and more efficiently.

One of the key components of optimizing your workflow is knowing as much as possible about the capabilities of your design tool so you can get the most out of it. What basic and advanced features can it provide? Where can I find all the possible operations with elements? How to organize all layers and assets and get quick access to them? This and more is what you'll learn about using Figma in this chapter.

In this chapter, we are going to cover the following main topics:

- Starting a new project from scratch
- Overviewing the tools in the toolbar of Figma
- Learning the functionality of the left panel in Figma
- Exploring the right panel in Figma

Starting a new design project

In this chapter, you will temporarily step away from analysis and research work in FigJam files and instead discover Figma's essential tools and functions. You will find a lot of material to learn, and it's completely normal to feel overwhelmed by all this new information. But the good thing about this chapter is that you can refer to it from time to time when you're unsure of any of the basics of Figma. So don't worry about memorizing all the concepts of each function; you will see how everything works later on in the book, and each tool and feature will be explained in a more practical way.

Design files

You already know that Figma has two types of files – FigJam and design. You've learned about FigJam files in detail in the previous chapter. This time you will go back to the file selection and make another choice, namely to create a new design file.

To create a new blank design file, you have to open the welcome screen and click on **New design file** right on the top.

If you still have FigJam open with the previously created files, to go to the welcome screen, we just need to click on the Figma logo in the upper left corner and select **Back to Files** from the drop-down menu. Then, just proceed as previously described. However, if you are using the Figma desktop app, you can skip returning to the welcome screen and immediately press the + button to the right of the current file tab. Figma will prompt you to open a new project page where you can choose the type of new file – FigJam or design. You can also hit *Command + T* (macOS) or *Ctrl + T* (Windows) to quickly open a new tab, like in your browser, and you will be given a choice for your desired file type:

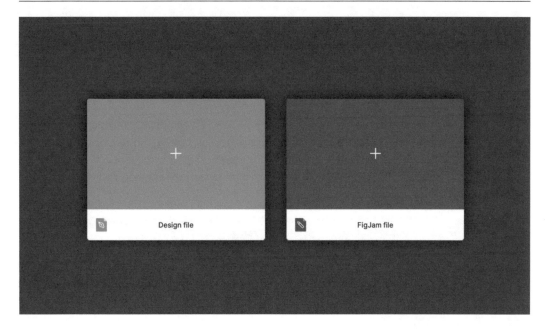

Figure 3.1 – A new file from the tab menu

Once you open a new design file, you can finally see Figma as it is, which is significantly different from what you had earlier with FigJam. It is a much more complex yet powerful working area that will allow you to create truly stunning masterpieces.

> **Note**
>
> Design and FigJam files can be easily recognized in the **Drafts** and **Recent** folders by their different colors and icons.

Frames and groups

When you first launch a design file, you see an empty gray space in front of you, framed by panels on either side and a toolbar at the top. At first glance, so many areas of different functionalities may seem complicated and almost intimidating. It is normal to feel that way because it is not a simple canvas but a place where you will create the entire interface of your project. Don't worry, you will explore all the sets of tools in Figma step by step. For now, the only thing you can interact with in an empty file is the top toolbar, which will be your starting point.

To start using Figma to its fullest, you need to create an artboard. You may be familiar with this concept from other design tools. However, Figma does not have standard artboards but rather something similar yet much more powerful – frames. While they share basic traits with artboards, frames differ in functionality. They can be nested, and also have auto layout, layout grids, and all prototyping functions set. You will learn more about this later, but for now, let's stop here.

What is a frame? In fact, it is a container. Your design must contain something, and it is frames that provide this opportunity. You can use custom-sized frames or choose practical presets for the most common standards, such as mobile devices, tablets, and desktop resolutions. So, it all starts with a single frame:

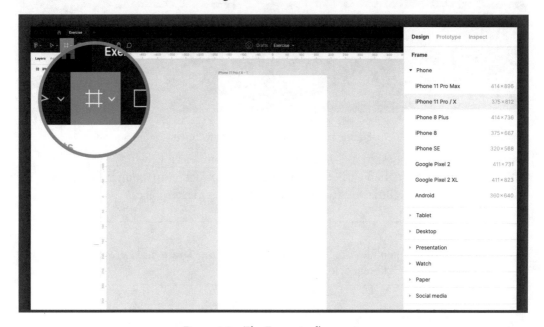

Figure 3.2 – The Frame tool's presets

To create a frame, you can use the **Frame** tool from the top toolbar (using the F or A shortcuts) and proceed in three different ways:

- Click any blank area on your workspace to create a default 100 x 100 frame.

- Click and drag with your cursor to create a custom-sized frame.

- Click on any preset size on the right panel to automatically create a frame of the appropriate size.

As you can imagine, the third option is most useful for immediately starting your design without having to search the internet for screen sizes of various devices. For example, clicking **Phone | iPhone 11 Pro / X** will immediately create a 375 x 812 frame. You can add more than one frame in your workspace, and no matter how many there are in your file, it is unlikely to slow down Figma.

But frames are not just artboards. They can act as containers as well, letting you nest as many elements or any other frame as you like. To quickly create a frame around one or more objects, simply select whatever you want to put together and press *Alt + Command + G* (macOS) or *Shift + Ctrl + G* (Windows). However, there is an alternative way to combine objects, and this method is called groups. Understanding the difference between frames and groups can be very confusing, as they share some basic functions, and you may think they are interchangeable, but this is mostly untrue. You will likely be using frames more often, since they offer a bunch of extra features, but there may be situations where you don't really need their advanced capabilities. Instead, you will be satisfied with something simpler, such as a group, that just combines several objects into one layer without flattening them and allowing you to maintain a fixed relationship between inner elements when scaling. If you want to create a group of objects, we just press *Command + G* (macOS) or *Ctrl + G* (Windows) after selecting the desired elements on the canvas. We can ungroup at any time by pressing *Shift + Command + G* (macOS) or *Shift + Ctrl + G* (Windows).

To visually understand frames and groups, combine two shapes into one frame and do the same with a group, and then try resizing the two containers. In the group, the shapes will be resized accordingly, while in the frame, what is scaled is only the frame itself, while the shapes retain their original size and position. Over time, as you progress through the chapters, you will fully understand the potential of frames, one of Figma's exclusive features, and this will lead you to have a clearer view of concepts that may now seem very complex.

Interface overview

Now that you've added the first frame on a gray backdrop, you may have noticed that the interface now provides you with a lot of new functions to explore. Now, it may seem more similar to many other design tools you may have used. However, compared to Adobe Photoshop, for example, Figma may seem like a tool that offers a rather limited number of features, and this may undermine your belief that Figma is still the best choice.

Of course, as mentioned earlier, it is also possible to create interfaces using Photoshop, but you will inevitably run into limitations, such as poor smoothness with numerous artboards and, above all, a lack of tools dedicated to prototyping. If you, for example, want to apply a watercolor effect to an image in your design, Figma will not be suitable for such purposes. However, it's important to emphasize that Figma has the essentials, and in most cases, that's pretty much all you need to create a complete interface. As a flexible collaboration tool, Figma can easily convert anything you create in it into web or mobile app development code, which is the point:

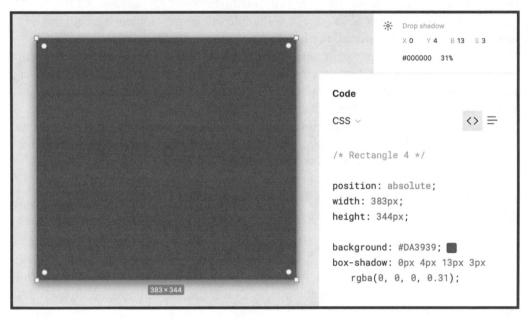

Figure 3.3 – Figma effects versus CSS effects

For example, if Figma allows you to apply a blur effect to an image, it's only because that effect can be applied in the same way with a CSS rule. However, there is no filter that can be applied with the code to apply the watercolor effect. This way, Figma guarantees that everything you design can actually be reproduced in code without much difficulty. Does this mean you can never apply a watercolor filter? Not at all. Without any problem, you can directly import an image that has been previously filtered into Figma. Adobe Photoshop, as well as Adobe Illustrator, are tools that can be perfectly combined with Figma to get more impressive results. However, using Figma as our main tool saves you from mistakes in design that can lead to problems in product development. As a result, you don't need to have any coding skills or worry about any technical constraints to create reliable layouts.

In addition, to make the experience even more user-friendly, Figma makes the most of a context-sensitive interface. This means that you will never see, for example, a left-align text icon unless you have selected text that can be aligned at that point. It is a methodology that more and more software has implemented in recent years, providing the user with the right tools and functions at the right time. Of course, for those of us new to this kind of UX, it can be difficult to find what they expect, but it really is only a matter of hours until you can no longer live without it:

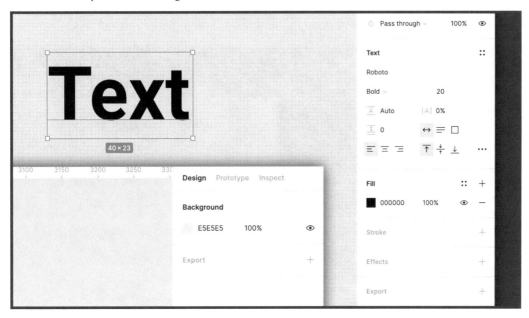

Figure 3.4 – An example of context-sensitive options

So, if you can't find a specific feature, it probably isn't available to you at the moment. In such cases, you should check whether you missed any steps or selected the wrong element. Everything becomes extremely simple and clear, and errors are minimized as much as possible.

Now, let's get down to exploring the interface piece by piece to get an idea of the tools and functions that Figma provides.

Exploring the toolbar

You'll start by exploring the top toolbar – this is where you'll find all of Figma's basic tools and settings. For the most commonly used basic tools, try to use right from the beginning as many shortcuts as possible because it will greatly improve your workflow.

Main tools

Figma divides its core tools into several sections, all of which you can see in the top bar. You will get an overview of all the sections in order, from left to right, and start by exploring the main set of features.

A – menu

The Figma logo in the upper left corner hides a significant drop-down menu that opens when you click on it:

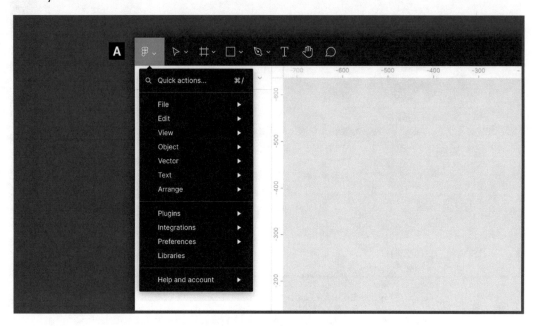

Figure 3.5 – Figma's main menu

This is the real main control center where you can find import, export, select, display, and many other functions. However, most of these features can be accessed in other ways. For example, anything on the **Text** menu is usually displayed in the context-sensitive panel (on the right) when any text is selected. It is not necessary to open each of the points contained here now, but you will try them in practice from time to time in the corresponding activities.

B – Move

This is the main tool that you will undoubtedly use the most. You can use it to select, move, resize, and rotate any element on the screen, including frames. By clicking and dragging, you can draw an area that will include and select all items inside it. The **Move** tool is quickly accessible with the *V* key on your keyboard, but you'll notice that Figma itself will automatically return you to this tool when you're done with any other tool:

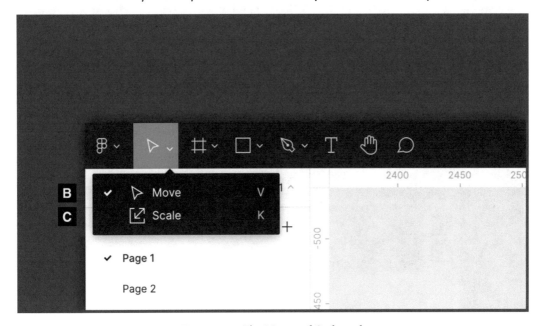

Figure 3.6 – The Move and Scale tools

C – Scale

Like the **Move** tool, the **Scale** tool (to quickly switch to this function, use the *K* shortcut) is used to resize any element in your working area. But the Scale tool works differently – it resizes any object in proportion to its original dimensions or the frame in which it is nested. To understand this better, type some text by pressing the *T* key, and then select and enlarge it with the Move tool. You can see that only the textbox will be larger and not the text itself. Instead, if you use the Scale tool, the font-size property will resize to fit the textbox.

D – Frame

As you know, with the **Frame** tool you can create a container by choosing from the available presets or by drawing a custom rectangle. Since this is one of Figma's core tools, you will be using it very often. You already have an understanding of frames in Figma, but you still have a lot more to learn about them, which you will do later in this book. For now, remember the useful keyboard shortcut for quickly adding a frame onto your canvas; there are two options – the *F* and *A* keys. Regardless of which one you choose, the result will be the same:

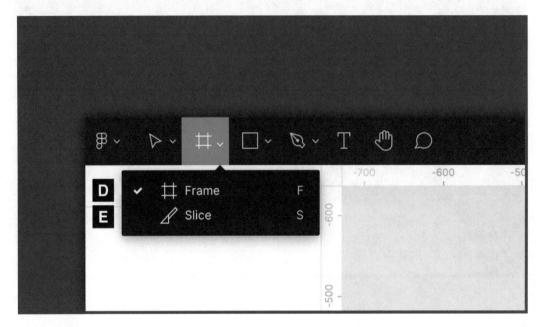

Figure 3.7 – The Frame and Slice tools

E – Slice

This is perhaps the least used of all tools, except in very special cases. The **Slice** tool allows you to select any areas in your workspace and export them with everything they visually contain. This tool comes from some old website design methods, so don't give it too much of your attention.

F, G, H, I, J, and K – shapes

This is a set of tools useful for creating all kinds of shapes, from simple lines to star shapes. Each of them has its own specific editing properties. For example, a line can become an arrow by changing the appropriate option in the context-sensitive right panel. Also, you should keep in mind that all shapes created this way are vectors, so you can easily modify them manually any way you want. You will explore shapes in detail in the next chapter:

Figure 3.8 – The shape tools

L – Place image...

If you need to quickly add an image to your workspace, click the **Place Image...** tool and a dialog box will appear, where you can select an image to import from your computer. Alternatively, you can directly drag and drop an image from a folder on your computer to your workspace.

M – Pen

This one is as easy as it is powerful. With the **Pen** tool, you can draw any shape using so-called Bézier curves, from a simple line to any abstract element. And all this will be strictly in the vector. While a traditional raster image is composed of a grid of pixels, a vector creates shapes using primitives and mathematical calculations. This allows you to draw simple or complex illustrations that can be scaled to any size without loss of resolution. The *P* keyboard shortcut for the **Pen** tool is undoubtedly worth remembering:

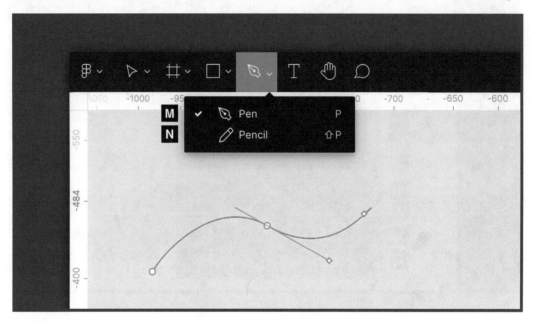

Figure 3.9 – The Pen tool with a Bézier curve example

N – Pencil

This is a vector tool like the **Pen** tool, but it doesn't have a curve system for drawing shapes. The **Pencil** tool is actually for freehand drawing but with the advantage that lines and curves are automatically enhanced and softened after you stop pressing the mouse button to end drawing. This can be useful, especially if you want to use Figma as a digital whiteboard or take quick freehand notes.

O – Text

The **Text** tool does exactly what you'd expect, allowing you to add text to your design. A shortcut for inserting any text is the *T* key on your keyboard, which you should definitely keep in mind. What's important to note about the **Text** tool is that there are two different methods for entering text. When you click anywhere on the canvas, the variable-width text is inserted into an external box that is sized based on the amount of text it contains. If you click and drag instead of a short click you will have a fixed-width textbox, and the entered text will not extend beyond the fixed space:

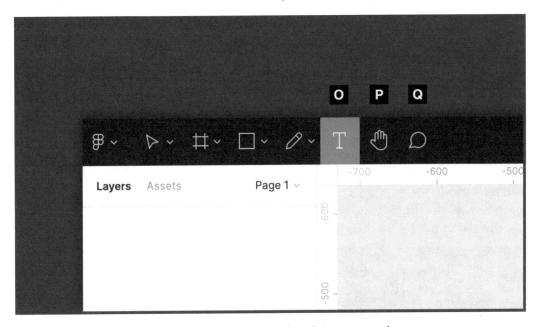

Figure 3.10 – The Text, Hand, and Comment tools

P – Hand

This tool allows you pan around the workspace using your mouse or trackpad, preventing accidental selection, repositioning, or any other impact on objects on the canvas. To activate the **Hand** tool, you can select it from the toolbar, but there is an easier and faster way to switch to it. To do this, you can press and hold the *spacebar* on your keyboard. This is a much more practical method that will definitely save you time. Imagine that you are currently using the **Move** tool, but from time to time you need to move around the board without affecting objects on the screen. In this case, you can simply hold down the *spacebar* to temporarily switch to the **Hand** tool. As soon as you release the key, you will automatically return to the **Move** tool. Also, if you are working on a trackpad, just swiping on it with two fingers will allow you to pan over your canvas.

Q – Comment

You should already know this one from working with FigJam. The **Comment** tool, which can be recalled with the *C* key, lets you click anywhere on the workspace and leave a text comment. All other users who have access to this project will receive a notification and therefore read what you have written at any time. All comments in the currently open file are visible only when the **Comment** tool is activated.

Settings and more

Now that you are familiar with all the basic tools, let's move on to looking at the rest of the functions located on the toolbar.

R – project title

"Untitled" is not the best name for a good organization of work, is it? To rename a file, just click on the current heading and enter a more appropriate and descriptive one. By clicking the drop-down arrow to the right of the title, you can access a number of additional actions, such as duplicating and deleting a file, or changing the path, which allows you to convert the file from a draft to a team project. Here you will also find version control – that is, the ability to access all saved files created in the current project and, if necessary, restore the old version. This feature saves up to 30 days of history when using the free starter plan, while there is no limit for the paid ones:

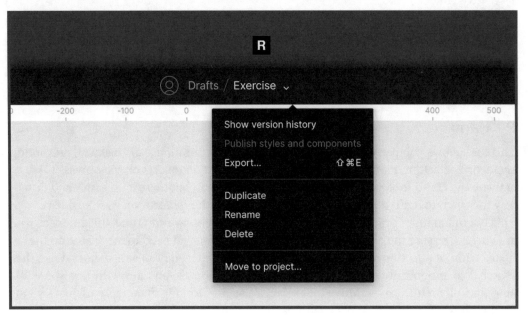

Figure 3.11 – A project's settings

S – active users

Here you will always have a real-time overview of the online users who are currently in this file. If you click the avatar of another active user, you activate observer mode for yourself, in which you can no longer independently move around the workspace, but you will see exactly what the selected user sees and does:

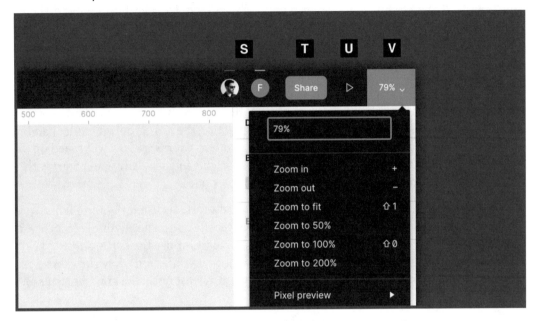

Figure 3.12 – The Collaboration, Testing, and View tools

T – share

This is a gateway to the many sharing opportunities that Figma offers. When you click on the **Share** button, a special dialog box will open where you can not only check the complete list of people who have access to this file and the permissions they have but also add new ones, or get a sharable link that allows you to invite anyone to the project. From here you can also make your project publicly available to the Figma Community. You will explore this opportunity in the last chapter of the book.

U – present

This is a function that will bring your design to life, allowing you to view both static previews of your chosen frames and complex interactive prototypes. The viewer opens in a separate tab and acts as a separate file, so you can share the preview with selected people or publicly while keeping the project source safe for yourself.

V – zoom/view

What you see here numerically is the current zoom value set in your workspace, and it changes in real time as you zoom in/out with your mouse wheel, pinching and zooming on a trackpad or with + and - keys on your keyboard. Clicking on it opens a drop-down menu dedicated to zooming and display settings, where you can not only use predefined functions to change zoom values but also manually set them by entering a number. There are also several toggles for options, such as the ability to activate or deactivate rulers.

Quick shortcuts

As you can see, Figma's top bar is the source of its core tools, some of which help you add elements to your design; others are for working with in your workspace. No doubt you can call this area very feature-rich. But the more you practice, the more you will understand how easy it is to find and switch from one tool to another. Your workflow will speed up even more if you implement the use of keyboard shortcuts in your daily work. Start with the easy ones and then little by little add more complex ones.

You can always check out all of the available keyboard shortcuts listed right in Figma, so you don't even need to consult the tutorials on the website or google anything. Just click **?** in the bottom right corner and select **Keyboard shortcuts**, or use the *Ctrl + Shift + ?* key combination, and you will see a hotkeys panel sorted by the functions they run. Those filled with blue mean that you have already used them at least once; the gray shortcuts are those that you have not yet tested out:

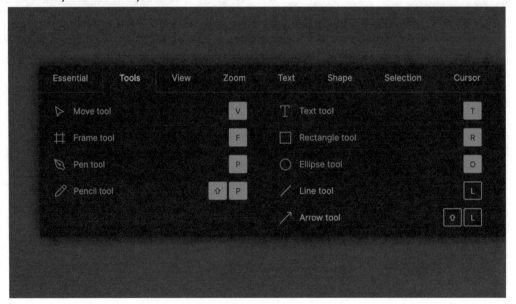

Figure 3.13 – The shortcut helper panel

So, now that you have a basic understanding of the general features of Figma and can add something to your workspace, it's time to see where you can access all the layers in your files.

Exploring the left panel

Learning Figma's tool sets can be challenging, but it is important to have at least a basic understanding of the features so you can quickly get started using them. Don't worry if you still feel insecure every time you launch Figma. You will soon learn the concept of each tool in a real workflow. However, tools are just one part of everything to learn in Figma. It is equally important to know how to work with layers and assets in your project. All of these will be displayed in the left sidebar, so let's take a deeper look at its interface.

Layers and pages

Every time you create a new text layer, shape, or any other element, its name is immediately displayed in the **Layers** panel. Likewise, when you delete an object from the work area (you can do this simply with the *Backspace* key on macOS or the *Delete* key on Windows), it will also be removed from the sidebar. So, think of the **Layers** panel as a container that collects everything in your project and helps you organize all the elements better:

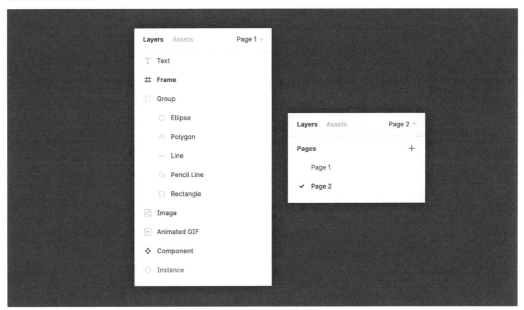

Figure 3.14 – The Layers and Pages panels

First of all, you should pay attention to the visual meaning of the icons in the panel and how they differ depending on the type of layer you are creating. A shape layer, for example, has a thumbnail of the shape itself. Don't worry if some of the layer types are not be familiar to you, you will soon be working with all of them, and as a result, you will remember every icon that appears in the panel.

The number of layers grows faster than you might imagine, so it's important to always keep them in order. It is very good practice to give each layer a suitable and meaningful name. However, be careful when moving the layers, because the hierarchy present in the **Layers** panel also reflects their order of depth on the canvas.

When there are too many layers to organize properly, pages come into play. Essentially, pages are separate workspaces, almost like independent files, but in fact, if they are placed in the same file, they belong to the same ecosystem, so you can freely use styles, resources, and more on all the pages. They are very useful for organizing, for example, different design stages in the same file. You will soon see how to build this kind of page structure in a file as efficiently as possible.

Assets

The **Assets** panel is an indispensable tab of the left panel that is used to organize all the elements of your design project for reuse. You haven't encountered components on your journey yet, which is one of the most important concepts in Figma, but this is not the place to get to know them. For now, you should just keep in mind that this is where you will soon be able to find them:

Figure 3.15 – The Assets panel

The more the **Assets** area begins to fill, the more difficult it becomes to visually search for the required components from the list. In this case, you should use the search bar at the top, which filters the results by the names assigned to the components. This is another good reason to choose the correct names for all of the elements – to make them easier to find.

Finally, in **Assets**, you can also find the team library (under the book-shaped icon), an incredible feature that lets you use styles and components from other files, personal or from the Figma Community.

So, now you know that on that left sidebar in Figma, you can see and organize your layers, add new pages, and find your assets quickly. This is still just a general overview of this panel, and you will inevitably get to know it deeper as you practice. Now, let's move on to the next section of the chapter, which will be devoted to the context-sensitive panel.

Exploring the right panel

Last but not least, you will explore the right panel, commonly referred to as the **Properties** panel. This area is context-sensitive, so it changes every time you click on something in your design file. Depending on the selected object, you can see different options, functions, and parameters. Therefore, it is better to learn and remember the functionality of the right panel in practice, and this section is just a short guide to it, which will simplify your further work. As you can see, the right sidebar is split into three tabs: **Design**, **Prototype**, and **Inspect**. Let's start and proceed in order.

Design

This is the panel tab that Figma opens by default, which makes sense, since you will no doubt use it the most. Whatever you're looking for about visual edits, you'll always find it in the **Design** panel. It sounds promising, but is it really so? If nothing is selected in your workspace, the panel may seem empty. But as soon as you click on any element on the canvas, you will see the required functions magically appearing there:

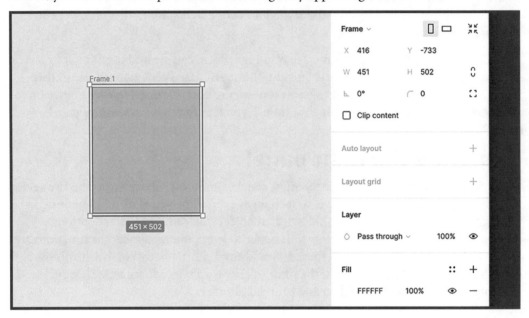

Figure 3.16 – The context-sensitive options of a frame

At first glance, this may seem tricky. So, to get a better understanding of the concept, ask yourself – would it be helpful to see the font size settings every time when working with a vector shape? Not at all. And therefore, in Figma, you will never see any function that is not needed or not usable at the moment.

Let's click on the frame you created earlier, which represents the screen size of the iPhone 11 Pro / X, and see what happens in the **Design** panel. Functions you've never seen before came out of nowhere. And if you look closely, you can see that all the options are absolutely consistent with the functionality of the frames. This way, you can change its size (manually or using the usual list of presets), the background color, corner rounding, and many other advanced features that you will discover later.

If you now try to deselect the frame by clicking anywhere outside the element, the **Design** panel will remove the display of all previous settings. You see that it is almost empty again and only offers you the option to change the background color of the workspace itself. You can do that if you ever need to increase the contrast between the design and the background.

It won't take you long to learn to appreciate the benefits of using context-sensitive functions, and soon you won't be able to imagine your workflow without them. But in case you're looking for a particular setting and can't find it, remember that most of the basic functionalities can also be accessed from the drop-down menu under the Figma icon in the upper left corner, or by right-clicking on any object in your workspace.

Prototype

The **Prototype** panel is fully consistent with the **Design** panel, allowing you to add interactions to your elements and presenting everything dynamically:

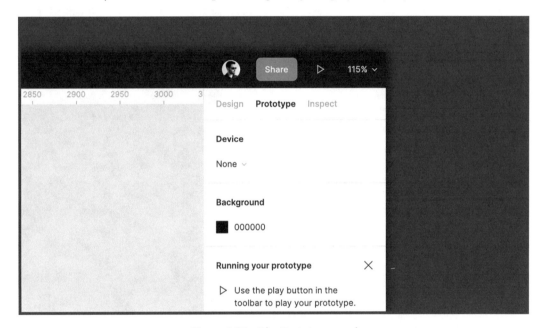

Figure 3.17 – The Prototype panel

This panel is also context-sensitive, so the settings you find here are related to the currently selected item and will be exclusively applicable to it. But in this case, however, not all elements really have functionality available upon selection. If you click on the text, for example, nothing will appear in the **Prototype** panel, just like clicking on a shape or image. This is because not all elements need to be made interactive.

Thus, the **Prototype** panel also has two states: inactive (after clicking anywhere outside of your elements in the workspace) and another state when frames or components are selected.

Inactive state

In the first state, as before, you are only allowed to change the background color of the canvas, plus you can see general project settings that are not specific to an individual element.

The first option presented in this panel is the **Device** section, which allows you to choose how the prototype will be displayed. If you open the drop-down list under the name of the section, you will see various presets for commonly used devices. You can choose any of the devices on the list, and for some models, there are even colors to choose from. As you remember, you previously selected the iPhone 11 Pro / X to set the size of your frame, but this does not mean that you will see this device in presentation mode. You can set this only by selecting the desired model in the **Device** section:

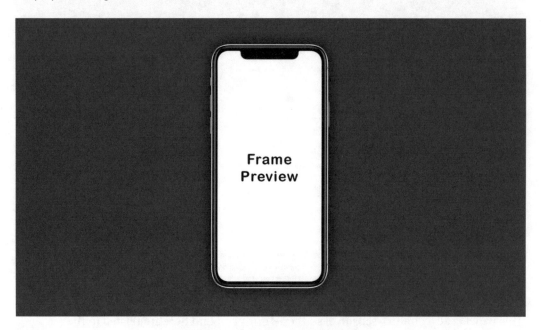

Figure 3.18 – The Frame Preview window

The next setting you'll notice is the background. Here you can set the background color for the prototyping screen if you want to change the color behind the selected device. You can also change the orientation of your device from portrait to landscape or vice versa.

When a frame or component is selected

Like the **Design** panel, **Prototype** is also context-sensitive. Thus, after selecting any frame or component on the canvas, instead of the device and background settings, the panel will display other more advanced features. In this case, Figma will not prompt you to make any changes to your objects but will offer functions for interacting with your elements on the screen, such as what follows a button press or the choice of scrolling direction:

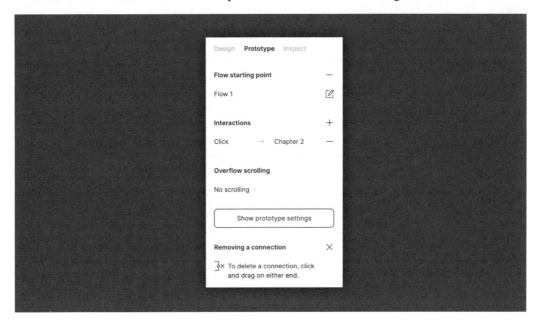

Figure 3.19 – The Prototype panel with an active selection

At first glance, the **Prototype** section might not seem as equipped with various settings as the **Design** panel. But its simplification is justified by the fact that everything here is done extremely intuitively. The entire interaction system plays on the mechanics of "if this, then that", allowing you to select an element, assign it an action type (touch, click, hover, and so on), and determine the result that this action will produce – for example, moving to another page, or opening or closing an overlay.

One of the most recent additions to the **Prototype** panel is the **Flows** section, which was a very significant upgrade. This feature allows you to create more than one flow in the same project file to compare or test different realizations of the same scenario.

Are you curious to know more about all this? Don't worry – in *Chapter 9, Prototyping with Transitions, Smart Animate and Interactive Components,* and *Chapter 10, Testing and Sharing your Prototype on Browsers and Real Devices,* you will have the opportunity to explore in depth the amazing power of prototyping in Figma.

Inspect

As mentioned earlier, the tabbing of the right sidebar is logical and consistent across the phases of the project, and the **Inspect** panel comes in useful mostly when your design is complete and the flow is approved:

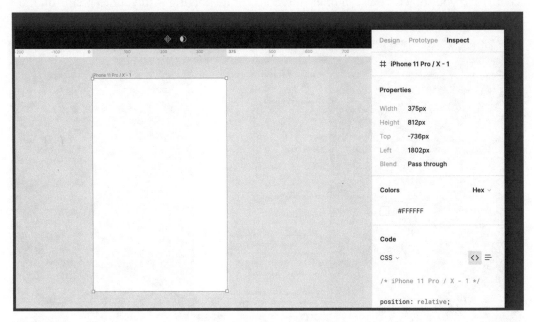

Figure 3.20 – The Inspect panel

The **Inspect** panel will be your bridge for effective communication with developers who are responsible for transforming your design into code. Here you can not only find the necessary raw data about element sizing, positioning, and so on but also see how to convert some of this data directly into code snippets.

Figma offers three available code transformations – CSS (web development), iOS (Swift), and Android (XML). But be careful in relying too much on this function, as it does not guarantee the exact implementation of your design in code. Think of it more as a tool to support developers, who will have quick access to an overview of information such as size, color, and position of any element, or even font size, font family, and font weight in the case of text layers. Instead of spending a lot of time to determine the correct attributes, they can check the **Inspect** panel and see everything displayed in code.

Help Center

As you can see, the right sidebar contains three tabs that represent the three phases of the user interface – design, prototyping, and exporting. It is in this order that you will get more and more practice, and as a result, you will learn how to use each function in the all panels in this area.

If you have any difficulty finding information about any Figma tool or want to refer to official resources, you can always do this in the **Help Center** by clicking the floating circle button with **?** in the lower right corner. Here you can find links to content from the official website, Figma YouTube videos, the support forum, and so on. So, all you need now is a bit of patience and a willingness to further explore Figma!

Summary

Well, if you feel like all the new information you've just received is too much to remember, you're probably right. When getting started in Figma especially, it takes time to get used to its interface and become fluent with its features. That's why it is highly recommended to return to this chapter from time to time to refresh your memory about the toolbar, and the left and right panels.

Now that you've successfully completed this chapter, you can see the true capacity of Figma and how powerful it can be in many ways. To help you create high-quality designs in the best possible way, Figma never stops working on introducing new features into its own interface. Stay tuned to the official Figma Twitter profile (@figmadesign) for new features and releases, and try testing them and incorporating them into your work routine so that Figma's tools will have nothing mysterious or unknown to you.

From now on, with each next chapter, you will get more and more practice with Figma! In the next chapter, you'll start working on your first wireframe, using shapes and other basic elements. Get ready for an exciting new challenge!

4
Wireframing a Mobile-First Experience Using Vector Shapes

You've reached the point where you have essential knowledge of the UX process and Figma's interface. Now it's time to put it all together and get started with the user interface of our streaming service application. As mentioned previously, it is best to always keep all the artifacts collected during the UX phase nearby – the mission statement, persona, user flow, and other data. In this chapter, you will take a significant step toward moving from theory and hypotheses to creating a real application structure using the wireframe method!

This is a very important part of product development, but there is nothing to worry about, since this chapter will guide you through the entire process of this phase. However, before moving on to wireframing, you will need to have a basic understanding of what it is and why it is so helpful for all UX/UI designers, no matter how much experience they have. You will also learn the tools you will need in this step and practice using them right on the canvas.

So, this time, the information will be quite varied, but by the end of the chapter, all the knowledge and skills that you have gained so far will magically turn into something directly related to your first prototype of a mobile application in Figma!

In this chapter, we are going to cover the following main topics:

- Evolving the idea to a wireframe
- Playing with shapes in Figma
- Advanced vectors with the Pen tool
- Developing the app structure

Evolving the idea to a wireframe

Since the analysis and research phase are completed and the idea is approved, you are ready to turn it into something real. This time, you'll learn how to create a skeleton for our previously introduced streaming service application, which is a wired structure for visualizing and experimenting with usability and product functionality. This is an important process called wireframing that takes place before you start designing the first prototype and allows you to choose the right product structure. There is some theoretical knowledge that you should know about this step, so in this section, you will learn some of the important concepts about the interface and the related navigation elements.

What is a wireframe?

If you are a beginner, you may not know what a wireframe is and what it is for. Perhaps you cannot wait to finally get to work on a real design, and this step may seem like one more obstacle. But wireframing is a crucial part of the process of creating a product that is really useful and practical. Over time, you will understand more deeply the incredible value of all the early design stages, and they will become a natural part of your workflow. The initial impulse to jump straight to style and color choices is common among those approaching design projects, but you should always remember that a designer's job is mostly about research, analysis, and problem-solving rather than creativity.

So, what is a wireframe? Basically, it is the first draft of a raw UI without any style, detail, or even color. The first iteration of the wireframe can also be done roughly with pen and paper (*Figure 4.1*), but this time you'll create it right in Figma so that you can practice what you've learned in the previous chapters. To start, you need to go back to the FigJam files with all your artifacts, most notably the user persona and the user flow, because at this stage, your decisions will be based on all the data that you have collected for product development:

Figure 4.1 – A paper wireframe example
(Photo by Halacious on Unsplash)

The wireframing itself does not take too long, and even a very raw draft can help identify problems during user testing. Thus, you can make any changes at an early stage and better work out the usability of a product based on the testers' feedback. If you skip the wireframe stage and jump straight to UI design, you run the risk of revealing all the problems in the near-final version of the product. As a result, you will inevitably spend a lot more time working because it will take a huge effort to make changes to an already polished prototype.

Don't worry if you still can't come up with a clear idea of a real wireframe that can be applied to our brief. You will soon learn how to structure it, and everything will become much clearer.

Why mobile-first?

Before proceeding directly with the creation of the wireframe, you have to select an initial product format. It is clear that this will depend on what is planned to be developed. For example, if you are creating a product that will be used primarily on a computer, the desktop screen will be the starting frame. And since the mobile version is secondary to this particular product, you can get started with it later.

However, in most cases, you will usually choose the smallest initial format, which is the format of mobile devices. Is this just a set rule? Not really. The reason for this choice is based on the analysis of statistical data. For several years now, people have been using smartphones instead of desktops to browse the web and use apps for basic internet operations. So, because of this significant change in the behavior of people in the digital space, except in special cases, the design of the interface has become primarily focused on mobile devices.

But even when choosing a mobile device as the primary format, a new dilemma arises as to which screen resolution to go for, since it can vary from device to device. Except in special cases where there is exact data on which smartphone model will be used by the majority of the users, it is better to stick to a medium-resolution mobile device format. Then, you can gradually increase the size of screens to higher resolutions for smartphones, then tablets, and finally desktops and TVs.

We will not design for every Android device and all iPhone models. It would be useless, since the main goal is not to release a real product but to design a product that can become a detailed blueprint for developers.

So, let's set up our application for release on a mobile device, a tablet, and a computer. And for the wireframe, the standard screen of the mobile device will be selected. At later stages of the work, an adaptive approach will be integrated to account for all intermediate resolutions and to ensure that the product works well on all available devices, without leaving anything to chance.

Now you know what is behind the creation of the skeleton of the future application interface and what the initial screen size should be for it. But before you start drawing in Figma, you'll learn and practice some of the tools you need to create your first wireframe.

Playing with shapes in Figma

You are already familiar with many of the basic tools in Figma, but so far, you have not tested them much. This is not a problem, as you will try out every useful feature actively, which you will start doing right now. And you don't have to worry about knowing any advanced tools to create a wireframe; all you need is simple geometric shapes.

Basic shapes

As you already know, the top toolbar has a **Shape** tool that allows you to add different geometric shapes that you can then edit on the canvas. Besides basic shapes such as ellipses and rectangles, you can use more complex ones. For example, the **Star** tool creates a classic five-pointed star by default, but the element can be edited after it is added to the canvas. You can change the number of the star points, increasing or decreasing them by clicking the **Count** handle (*Figure 4.2*) and dragging the cursor up or down:

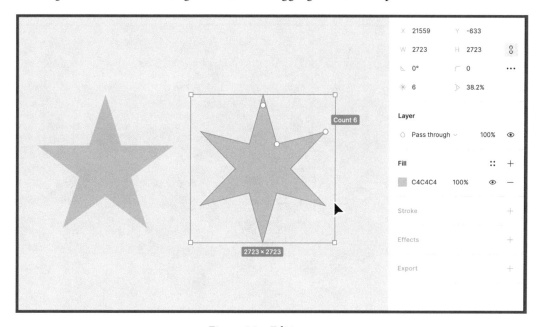

Figure 4.2 – Editing a star

Likewise, with the **Polygon** tool, you can create a default triangular shape and then increase the number of sides, thus creating more complex shapes, such as pentagons and hexagons. The other shape-editing handle, **Radius**, allows you to quickly adjust the roundness of each shape.

The **Ellipse** tool seems simple because you can obviously expect it to create circles or ellipses. But with the **Ellipse** tool, you can also create pie charts very easily. How? Draw a circle on the canvas, select it, and hover over it so that an **Arc** handle appears. Dragging this marker inside the circle creates a gap that allows you to create accurate pie charts. Moreover, this change will cause other markers to appear on your circle: **Sweep**, **Start**, and **Ratio**. The first one is the one we have already used earlier; the second allows you to rotate the starting point of the gap; and finally, the third transforms the circle into a ring, moving toward the center of the ellipse:

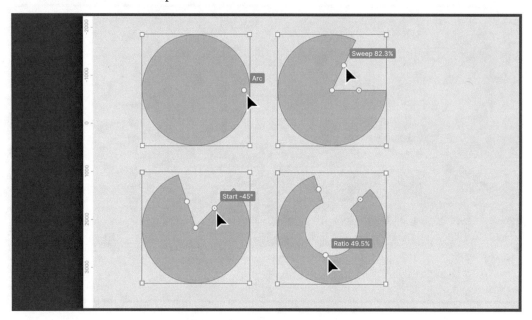

Figure 4.3 – A circle's edit handles

> **Note**
>
> By holding down the *Shift* key while resizing the shape, you can easily keep its proportions. If you instead press and hold the *Option* key (macOS) or *Alt* (Windows), the shape will be resized from its center. You can also use both keys together to resize the shape proportionally to its center. Feel free to experiment with these tricks on different shapes and elements!

You might have noticed that whatever shape you add to the canvas, Figma will automatically apply a default style to it, which is a gray background color and nothing else. This default style is sufficient to create your first wireframe, but you can make the flow more intuitive and functional with even minor additions to this style. For example, you can highlight elements that represent a suggested user path with a brighter color. This allows you to see immediately which actions will lead a user to the intended action.

Changing the style of a shape is easy. To do this, select any element in your working area, and you'll see that the right sidebar will show you the available style options. You can experiment with colors and other styles if you like, but you'll soon get to know each one in detail.

As mentioned earlier, any shape you add to the canvas is a vector, so you can edit it however you like. Just click a shape and press *Enter*, or double-click it, to activate edit mode:

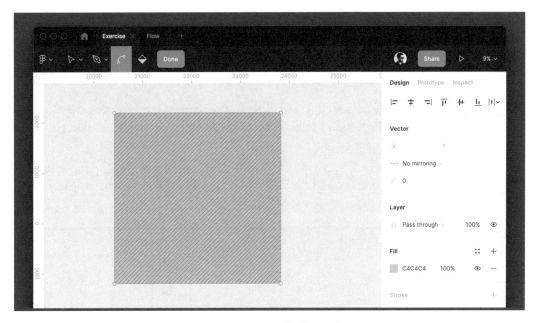

Figure 4.4 – Vector's edit mode

From now on, you can edit each point of the selected shape, or even add new points with the **Pen** tool. And that is not all. In edit mode, the regular Figma toolbar tools are replaced with some dedicated advanced vector editing tools. With the **Bend** tool, for example, you can click and drag any point on a shape and convert it to a curve. When you are finished editing the shape, click **Done** on the toolbar to exit edit mode, or press the *Enter* key again.

Edit mode is incredibly powerful, and you will need to take some time to learn how it works. Don't worry – in the next section of this chapter, you will find detailed information on the vector graphics capabilities and the functionality of the **Pen** tool in Figma, and this will be your starting point for practice on your own.

Combining shapes

You may have noticed that after you select any shape on the board, a new set of icons appears in the center of the top toolbar, where the filename is usually displayed. You can access even more features by selecting two or more items together. To do this, drag a selection on those elements by holding down the left mouse button, or simply click one of the shapes first, and then the rest while holding down the *Shift* key. Once selected, you will see three icons in the middle of the top toolbar, and the last of them, which is the Boolean groups, can only be applied to a group of objects, not a single element.

Using this newly discovered set of functions, you can perform many different operations on a group of objects. If you choose two shapes, you can, for example, combine them in a special way. To understand better, let's try to create a crescent using two circles:

1. Create the first circle by selecting an ellipse in the shapes or by pressing the *O* key on your keyboard. Remember to hold down the *Shift* key while drawing to get a perfectly round circle.

2. Change the default circle background color by selecting it and clicking the colored square below the **Fill** section in the right sidebar. A new window will appear with a color selector. Just pick any shade of yellow:

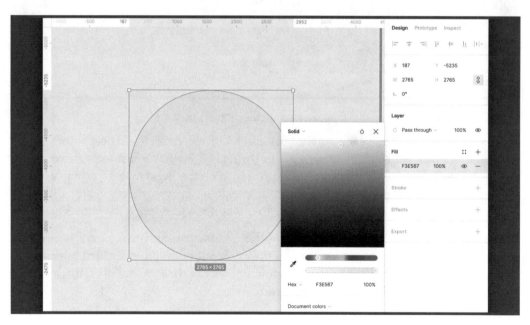

Figure 4.5 – Selecting a color

3. Duplicate the yellow circle by clicking and dragging it slightly to the right while holding down the *Option* key (macOS) or *Alt* (Windows), or alternatively, by using the *Command + D* (macOS) or *Ctrl + D* (Windows) keyboard shortcut. These shortcuts make it easy to duplicate any layer.

4. Select both shapes.

5. Click the drop-down arrow of the third icon in the center of the toolbar – the Boolean group – and choose **Subtract selection**. This will use the layer above to subtract from the layer below:

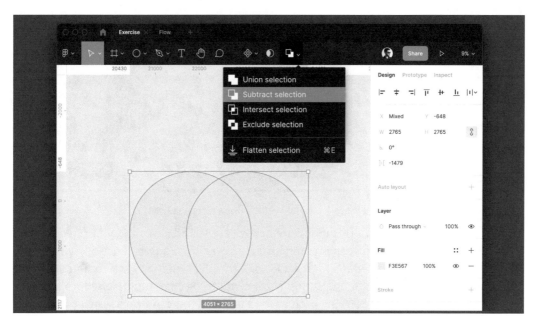

Figure 4.6 – Subtract selection

The end result will be our crescent.

Each of the functions in this drop-down menu allows you to get a different result, from combining individual shapes to excluding or intersecting selected shapes:

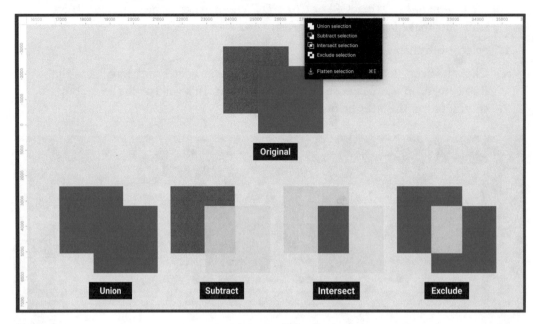

Figure 4.7 – The vector's Boolean groups

Almost all of the functions in this menu are pretty simple and clear, and you can test them by yourself on any two shapes you select. However, the **Flatten** function, which can also be run using the *Command + E* (macOS) or *Ctrl + E* (Windows) key combination, requires a detailed study. Flatten selection allows you to combine multiple shapes into a single vector while still preserving each shape's outline (you can find a visual example of this in *Figure 4.8* as follows, showing you the difference between shapes combined with **Union** and **Flatten**). This is possible due to Figma's incredible vector network feature, which we'll explore in the next section of this chapter:

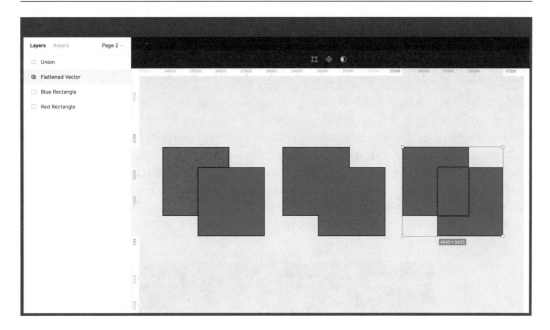

Figure 4.8 – The differences between Normal, Union, and Flatten

You've now learned a whole bunch of new tools that will make it really easy to get more complex shapes. The next topic in the chapter will be devoted to the more advanced features of Figma, and you will know how to effectively work with vectors.

Advanced vectors with the Pen tool

Before you get into practice with our brief, let's dive deeper into the principles of working with vectors. Vector graphics are one of the main concepts that need to be studied in detail, as you will definitely use them very often when working with Figma. The topic of this section of the chapter may seem more complex than what you learned earlier. This is why it is highly recommended not only to follow the instructions that you'll find here but also to practice on your own. Feel free to refer to the following information as many times as you need; try experimenting and getting creative with vectors to master this tool as quickly as possible!

What are vector graphics?

So, as you already know, the elements that you have created with the **Shape** tool so far are vectors; they are composed of lines, curves, and shapes, and are generated using mathematical formulas. Vector graphics are very helpful for several reasons. First of all, using them, you can freely scale anything without losing quality – from a simple shape to a complex illustration. This magic happens because when you resize a vector shape, Figma recalculates the data that it is composed of, so the result of the resized shape or image will not be grainy. In contrast, raster (or bitmap) images – for example, a .jpeg photo imported into Figma – are composed of a finite amount of data, which is a grid of pixels of specific sizes, where each pixel is associated with an exact color. If you double the size of this bitmap image, there is not enough chromatic information at its disposal to cover this mesh, and you end up with a grainy, low-quality image that should be absolutely avoided in production:

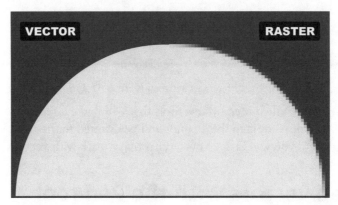

Figure 4.9 – Vector versus raster

Another advantage of a vector object is that it is very easy to edit and, more incredibly, it is very light in file size. But if vector graphics have so many advantages, why do you need bitmap at all? The point is that vector graphics are not suitable for all situations. For example, a photograph cannot be vectorized, unless you want to more or less accurately redraw it as a stylish illustration, since complex details, light, and shadows cannot be reproduced with lines, curves, primitives, and intersecting shapes.

When it comes to logos, icons, and illustrations, it's always best to create them in vector format. But how do you know that you have a vector and not a raster object? Everything that is created initially in Figma is already vector by default. But when you import an external element, you need to check the file extension – for example .JPEG or .PNG files can never be vectors. The most common format for vector content is **Scalable Vector Graphics** (**SVG**), which has increased in use in recent years thanks to its support in modern browsers and operating systems. Because of the simplicity of vector editing, SVG has also become incredibly efficient for animation.

> **Note**
>
> You can move vector shapes from Adobe Illustrator to Figma by simply copying and pasting them. Instead, if you want to do the opposite, right-click the shape in Figma and choose **Copy | Paste | Copy as SVG**. Go back to Illustrator and paste by pressing *Command + V* (macOS) or *Ctrl + V* (Windows).

There are also other vector file extensions such as `.AI` (**Adobe Illustrator**), `.EPS` (**Encapsulated PostScript**), and `.PDF` (**Portable Document Format**). These are proprietary formats, and you need to convert them to SVG before importing them into Figma. However, you should be aware that the extension is still not enough to be sure that you are using vectors because any of these file formats can contain some bitmap objects as well. You can check this by simply resizing the object. A vector element will always have smooth and sharp edges, no matter how large you make it. Also, you can recognize elements by their layer's icon, since raster images have the classic icon that represents a picture while a vector is represented with a custom shape icon.

Now that you understand some of the key concepts of the vector format, let's see how to create more complex vector elements with the incredibly powerful **Pen** tool.

Discovering the Pen tool

If you already have some experience with design applications, you probably know a form of the **Pen** tool – one that lets you create vector points, lines, and curves to create complex shapes. In fact, this is not a Figma-exclusive tool but a must in any design app.

This tool may seem very difficult to master at first, but once you understand its basic mechanics and then explore its powerful capabilities, it can become your favorite tool.

First, let's draw some simple lines and curves:

1. Select the **Pen** tool (*P*). You will see the cursor turning into a pen, ready to use.
2. Click anywhere on the canvas to place the first starting point. From now on, you will see the line following the cursor – consider this as a preview, showing you what your vector will look like if you click elsewhere again.

3. Let's create a straight horizontal line. Move the cursor slightly to the right of the first point, and when you are satisfied with the line shown in the preview, just click again. You will notice that it wasn't hard to be precise because Figma helps you draw straight lines with magnetic sensitive guides active by default:

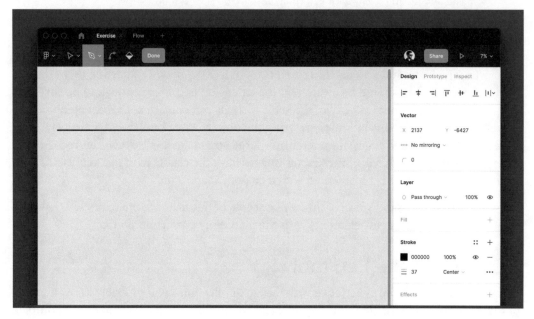

Figure 4.10 – A straight line made with the Pen tool

From now on, you can create as many points and lines as you want to achieve the desired shape. This was just one way to use the **Pen** tool; let's now move on to drawing your first curved line:

1. Select the **Pen** tool (*P*) again.

2. Click anywhere on the canvas to place the starting point. Make sure you are creating a new shape and not connecting your point to the shape from the previous example.

3. Move the cursor slightly to the right of the first point, and this time, click and drag. You will see that your line will now be curved, and the more you drag, the more pronounced the curve will be:

Figure 4.11 – The Pen tool with a Bézier curve example

Great! You've just created your first Bézier curve. Now, you can see that you have not only got two points and a line but also a few new handles to play with, positioned respectively before and after the curve point you have placed. The first handle changes the trend of the curve that you have already drawn, and the second allows you to anticipate and change, if needed, the direction, angle, and length of the next line or curve that you are going to draw.

If you connect the last point you created with the starting point, then this way, you get a closed shape, for which you can further customize the final result by adding, for example, a fill color in the **Design** panel. Try gradually to make more and more complex shapes with just a single line, like the one in the following screenshot:

Figure 4.12 – A complex vector example

All the lines and shapes that you create with the **Pen** tool are absolutely consistent with the original default shapes that you have already encountered. This means that you can combine, for example, a rectangle and a complex custom shape to get a whole new bunch of shapes.

Likewise, you can modify any line or shape created with the **Pen** tool at any time by switching to edit mode (by selecting the shape and pressing *Enter* or double-clicking on it). In this mode, you can not only move points and add new ones but also change corner points, smoothing them using the aforementioned **Bend** tool. You can also switch between a smooth and straight corner by holding *Command* (macOS) or *Ctrl* (Windows) and clicking the vector point you want to change.

Vector networks

In any other tool for vector graphics, the vector has very specific characteristics and is distinguished in open and closed paths. The path is defined as closed when the first point coincides with the last of a shape, thus generating a filled area. Figma, however, introduces a new concept – vector networks – a unique feature that allows you to push the boundaries of vectors even further.

While the standard vector is unidirectional, vector networks do not have a specific direction and can be closed by connecting any points, not necessarily the first and the last. This allows you to draw much more complex vector shapes in Figma without the need to merge many shapes and create multiple layers. One such example can be seen in the following screenshot:

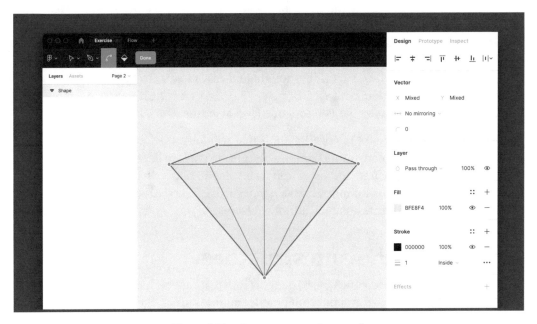

Figure 4.13 – A vector network example

If you've never worked with vectors before, this feature will come as behavior you would expect from the **Pen** tool, feeling like second nature. Otherwise, it will take some practice for those who are switching from other applications, but exploring the vector networks will open up unique opportunities for you.

However, with incredible opportunities, you can also face some difficulties. The complex shape that you create in one single vector path can be difficult to color, but there is still a way to do it in a simple and quick way. Activate edit mode by selecting the shape and pressing *Enter*, and now you can add more points and lines inside the shape to divide it into separate areas. To apply color to individual sections of your shape, you will need to use the new **Paint Bucket** tool on the top toolbar in **Pen** tool mode.

After selecting the **Paint Bucket** tool (*B*), and then hovering and moving your mouse over the shape, you will notice that various separate parts are highlighted. By clicking on the different sections, you can turn the fill color of that particular area on or off. In a recent update, Figma made it possible to use different colors for different sections of the same vector shape.

Before moving on, try creating different shapes yourself and then editing them. This practice is especially important if you are new to using these tools. The **Pen** tool and, in particular, Bézier curves may seem difficult to master at first, but with a lot of practice, you can draw all sorts of complex shapes. Keep in mind that a well-made vector shape has a minimal number of points, so it is lightweight and easy to edit. To better understand and practice these concepts, you can visit `https://bezier.method.ac` for a simple and fun game to help you master the **Pen** tool one level at a time.

Well, you've just learned a lot of essential tools that will form the foundation of your work in Figma. There will be many more complex features to explore later in the book, but knowing the basics is the first and most important step in mastering Figma. You could even say that this was the first milestone that you successfully passed! And now, let's finally see how to create an application wireframe.

Developing the app structure

Now that you have learned about the basic tools for creating graphical elements in Figma, you are ready to summarize and put into practice all this knowledge when creating a wireframe! However, if you need to practice more with shapes and vectors before continuing, it's best to allow yourself time to experiment a little with these tools until you feel more confident. When you're ready to move on, you can return to this section and continue practicing even more but, this time, with something directly related to our application. We will start by learning how to create a skeleton for our streaming service and end up with our first functional wireframe.

Flow to skeleton

Do you remember the flow you built earlier (see *Chapter 2, Structuring Moodboards, Personas, and User Flows within FigJam*) in FigJam? By creating it, you defined the potential future structure of the application. However, the flow is something quite abstract, and it was mainly useful for understanding the project, while the wireframe is a primitive version of the product with its navigation elements indicated. So, it's time to brush up on the flow and use it as the basis for building your wireframe.

Let's start with a new blank file and define the screen resolution as a starting point. Since our hypothetical stakeholders are interested in using the mobile version of the application, this will be the mobile interface. First, you need to transform the flow into frames, so let's add them to the canvas. Use the **Frame** tool from the top toolbar (or press the *A* or *F* key on your keyboard) and select a preset from the **Phone** category to set the container to the appropriate size. We'll use **iPhone 11 Pro / X**, but this doesn't mean that our interface won't fit an Android device, since, at this stage, we're just selecting a common screen size as a reference.

Obviously, this time, you will need more than one single frame in the working area. It's important to know that the more frames you have, the more difficult it is to recognize them and to work with layers if you don't give them unique and meaningful names. You can rename a frame by simply double-clicking the label at the top of the frame itself, or, which also works for any other element, double-clicking the name of the frame you want to rename in the **Layer** panel:

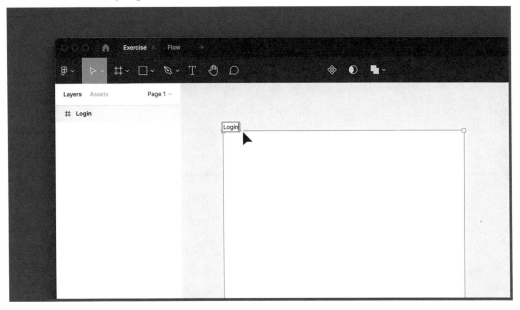

Figure 4.14 – Renaming a frame

According to the flow, after launching the application for the first time, the user sees the login page, so it makes sense to use Login as the name of the first frame. After this frame has been renamed, it's time to add the rest. You can do this again with the **Frame** tool, but it's much faster to just click and drag an existing frame while holding the *Option* key (macOS) or *Alt* (Windows). Then, you can add two more frames this way, or duplicate the last copy of the frame using the *Command + D* (macOS) or *Ctrl + D* (Windows) keyboard shortcut – this will automatically create a copy of the frame to the right of the duplicated one. Give each new frame an appropriate name, such as Sign Up, Home, and Detail page. Thus, you will prepare the basis for a complete wireframe.

Renaming layers can seem unnecessary, especially for drafts like this, but it's best to always keep the layers organized correctly. A convenient and well-thought-out naming system and layer hierarchy significantly increase the efficiency of teamwork, save your time, and in general, make your workflow much easier and more enjoyable. You can give the frames any names you see fit, or just copy them from the following screenshot:

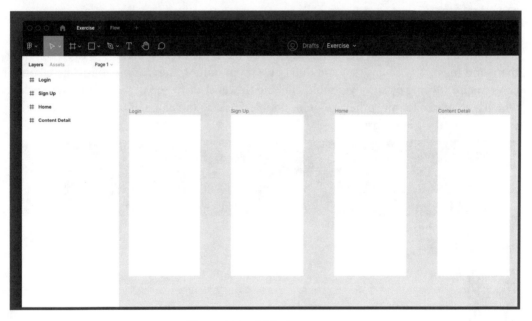

Figure 4.15 – A blank structure

Once you are done adding all the frames and renaming them, you will see that the flow is now fully displayed as the skeleton of our application. Now, you have a new challenge – to think about what elements to add to all the screens in order to set the individual view of each of them.

Shaping the interface

So, you have created a skeleton, which is a general display of all the screens of the mobile application. Now, it's time to work on each screen individually and determine what content structure they can display. There is no need to use Figma's advanced features such as constraints and auto layout to do this; you will learn about them later when working on the actual UI. For a simple wireframe, it is more than enough to use the tools you just learned about.

At this stage, as before, it's best to stick to the order of your flow, so let's start with the first view of the application, which is the **Login** page. At this point, you will need to do some research again. It's important to think through and define the elements that typically make up the page you create to make sure that nothing is overlooked. So, what elements must the **Login** page contain? No doubt, it must include username and password text fields, a confirmation button, a password recovery function, and a link to the **Sign Up** page if your user doesn't have an account yet.

Now that you have a list of all the screen elements you need, all you have to do is place each one in the **Login** frame, leaving enough room for text fields, buttons, and other elements. Let's get started:

1. Select the **Rectangle** tool (*R*) and draw a 315 x 50 rectangular shape (while drawing the shape, you can check its size in real time underneath it). It is important to know that if a shape or any other object is originally drawn in the frame, it will be placed directly inside it. Try creating another shape temporarily out of frame, and you'll see that the two shapes are positioned differently in the **Layers** panel.

2. If you select a rectangle within the frame, you can see its dimensions (**W** = width and **H** = height) and its position (**X** = horizontal and **Y** = vertical) in the **Design** panel on the right. Since this shape is placed inside the login frame, its positioning values will be relative to the outer container, starting at the top left corner. Place the rectangle at **30** on the **X** axis and **272** on the **Y** axis. You can modify these values visually by moving the rectangle with the mouse or directly by manually changing the numerical values in the right panel:

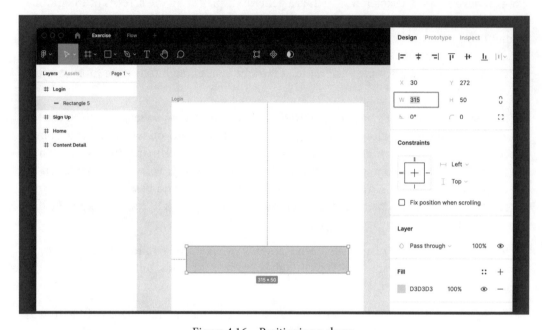

Figure 4.16 – Positioning a shape

3. In the **Fill** section of the **Design** panel, click the color code and write `lightgray` (no spaces) or, if you prefer, enter the hex code `D3D3D3`. You will learn more about colors in the next chapter.

4. Then, select the **Text** tool (*T*) and click just above the upper left corner of the rectangle. Enter Username. Make sure it is well aligned to the left. If you select the text and drag it, Figma will show you contextual guides to help you align that element with others nearby. Once this is done, your first text field with a corresponding indicative label is ready.

5. Next, select the label (text) and text field (rectangle) together and duplicate everything as you did before by clicking and dragging the elements while holding the *Option* key (macOS) or *Alt* (Windows), or using the *Command* + *C* (macOS) or *Ctrl* + *C* (Windows) classic keyboard shortcut to copy and *Command* + *C* (macOS) or *Ctrl* + *C* (Windows) to paste. In this case, you need to move the duplicated elements down by about 100 px:

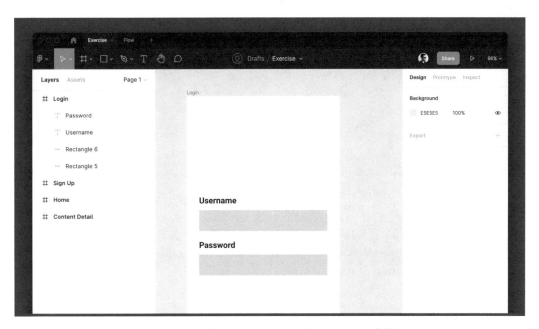

Figure 4.17 – The Username and Password text fields

6. The rectangle you just duplicated will be the **Password** field. Therefore, change the duplicated label text from Login to Password by double-clicking it to enter edit mode.

7. Now, select the **Rectangle** tool (*R*) again and draw a 315 x 75 shape below the two fields. This time, it will be a confirmation button to confirm the user's login, so let's place it about 200 px below the password field. To make the button more accented, since this is a key action, let's give it a `lightgreen` color:

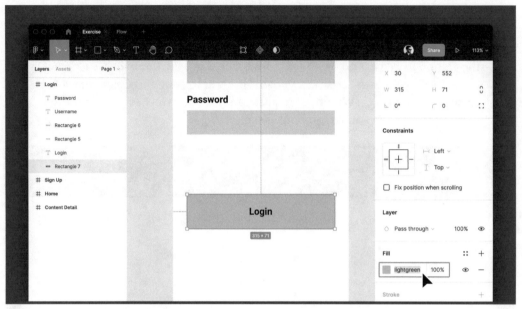

Figure 4.18 – Changing the background color

8. A button cannot be fully identified until it has a label on it. So, let's select the **Text** tool (*T*) again and click inside your button. Enter `Login` to mark the action for the element. Try to position the label exactly in the center of the button using the mouse and sensitive guides.

9. The last elements you need to add are the **Sign Up** button (it's a secondary button, so it will not be highlighted) and a link to restore the user's password right under the password text field. Before moving on, look at the **Layers** panel, and you will see that your layers are getting messy. It would be bad practice to leave it this way, so before you continue, dedicate 5 minutes to renaming each layer so that they can be easily identified:

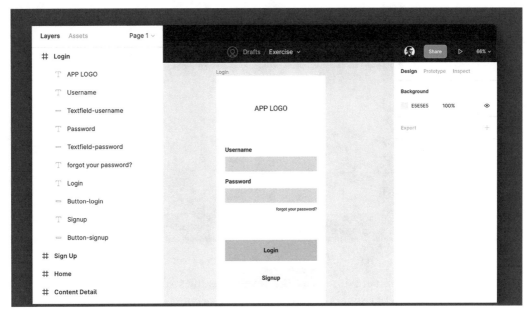

Figure 4.19 – The polished wireframe of the Login view

To organize your layers even better, you can group the username label with its text field by selecting them together and pressing *Command + G* (macOS) or *Ctrl + G* (Windows) on your keyboard. Try to group the password label and its text field in the same way and each button shape with its respective text label, and then give these new groups proper recognizable names in the **Layers** panel.

Great! You have completed your first screen view! Now, you need to fill the rest of the application screens with the necessary elements using the same methodology:

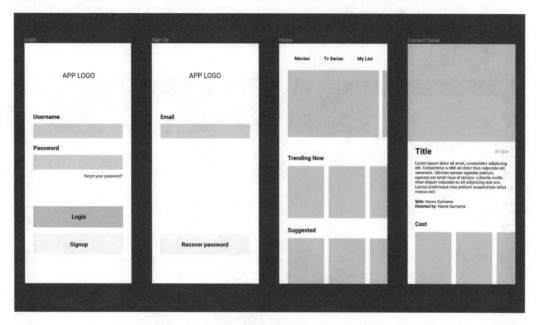

Figure 4.20 – The finished wireframe structure

You can see that once you are done with the wireframe, the structure of any application or website that you might be working on in the future becomes much clearer. After this step, the next one is to test the flow by sending your wireframe to users in your target audience. Remember that with a well-made, tested, and approved framework, further design steps will be much more deliberate and enjoyable.

What's next?

As you can see, this chapter was full of all sorts of new information for you, but if you have reached this point, you can be proud of yourself. Now, you've got an idea of what a wireframe is and why it's worth spending enough time on it. However, the real purpose of the wireframe isn't just filling the screen-sized frames with shapes that represent your future components. The essential meaning of this part is to make sure the flow you came up with during the UX design phase is the best one for your user. There is only one way to find out – to test this flow on a group of people belonging to the reference target. To do this, you have to make your wireframe live by prototyping it so that you can show and test the dynamic flow during user testing sessions.

The testing process is very important and must be taken very seriously; otherwise, you risk missing structural or usability issues. So, you should be prepared to review and modify your user flow and then the wireframe according to the test results, which will take more time, but it will still be much better than starting the implementation of the final product with uncertainty or doubt.

Since you are not yet familiar with Figma's prototyping function and the principles of user testing, we will keep our framework static. But when your journey of learning Figma is complete, you can come back to this chapter and build a prototype with this wireframe and then test it if you like. This would be great practice before you start doing it in your actual future design projects.

Summary

If you had any doubts about the importance of the UX part of your design workflow before, this chapter has hopefully cleared them up. Once you've identified the optimal user flow, it's pretty easy to build a wireframe based on it, although it may well happen that you need to spend more time researching which elements to use and how to place them on screens, especially if you don't have a lot of design experience. Of course, it takes time to learn about the different types of buttons, menus, bars, and other components, but with experience, you will have no problem figuring out which elements are suitable to include on a particular screen. You can also help yourself by paying more attention to the details of your favorite apps in daily use as well as discovering new ones.

So, this chapter was your first milestone in learning how to create a user interface in Figma. You learned and tried out many new tools, and then used them to create the first wireframe of our application, which was a great way to put your fresh knowledge into practice! It's twice as helpful if you haven't just followed the practical instructions in this chapter but have also worked on your own, as it will speed up your learning curve in Figma!

In the next chapter, you'll discover a whole new pack of amazing tools in Figma, specifically how to work with images, text, colors, grids, styles, and more!

Part 2: Exploring Components, Styles, and Variants

In this part, you will be introduced to all of the features of Figma, from the basics to the more advanced ones. By the end of this section, you will have designed a static user interface.

In this part, we cover the following chapters:

- *Chapter 5, Designing Consistently Using Grids, Colors, and Typography*
- *Chapter 6, Creating a Responsive Mobile Interface Using Auto Layout*
- *Chapter 7, Building Components and Variants in a Collaborative Workspace*
- *Chapter 8, User Interface Design on Tablet, Desktop, and the Web*

5
Designing Consistently Using Grids, Colors, and Typography

Well, you've done a great job learning the most basic Figma tools and even applying them to the wireframe of our application. In this chapter, you'll take a big step by getting started with the actual interface while discovering more advanced features. But before diving into the topic, you should know that when it comes to mastering any software or tool, it is important that your learning process is not just about memorizing all the functions but also trying to understand what is behind each feature, what benefits it gives you, and how best to use it. After all, your main goal is not to apply as many functions as possible but to make them work well and efficiently.

The set of tools that you are going to learn in this chapter is very important, and you need to not only be able to use them but also to use them correctly, since you will most likely need them in every future design project. In this chapter, you will also learn how to set up and apply these tools consistently across all your layouts. Excited? Let's get started!

In this chapter, we are going to cover the following main topics:

- Getting started with grids

- Working with typography, colors, and effects

- Introducing styles

Getting started with grids

At this stage, we understand that the design of any interface consists of technical and analytical solutions aimed at satisfying a user's needs. Remember that a good designer will never let personal taste affect a product. Therefore, the design of an interface, except for the initial stages of creating sketches and wireframes, must be done with precision for every detail. Figma has a whole bunch of dedicated tools to help you achieve this successfully.

Starting from this chapter, you will no longer have random frame sizes, colors, fonts, and other elements in your design files. From now on, you have to move forward only when you are confident in every step of creating the interface of your application. Therefore, you will need tools to help you minimize or eliminate possible errors. One of these is grids, and the first section of this chapter will be devoted to this amazing function.

Grids are everywhere

Grids are a very old design tool, dating back to the 13th century. At that time, all books were handwritten and therefore very expensive and valuable, and it took a lot of effort to create one book. Grids were invented to harmonize each page of a book by neatly positioning handwritten text on the paper and ensuring that content appeared evenly on each page. From then on, the grid system remained indispensable in publishing houses, as it was used to organize the layout of printed pages. Publishers, editors, and writers looked to grids for the perfect harmony of displaying content on pages. Grids are usually made up of columns and rows placed on a page, with a set spacing and padding from the page edges. Because the same grid was applied to all pages, text and images were consistent throughout the book or magazine. Thus, a reader was attracted to the visuals of the printed pages, but most importantly, it was easier to focus on the content. The following diagram shows an example of a layout grid:

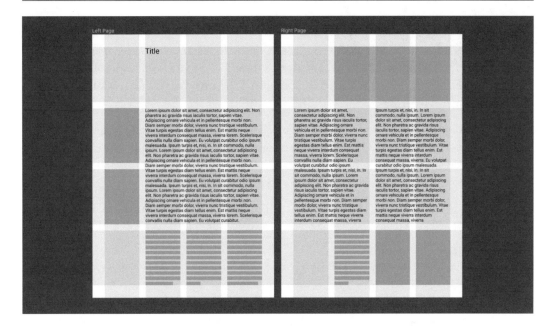

Figure 5.1 – An example of a book layout grid

The method of grids was then used in graphic design, and grids still form the basis of any simple or complex composition. If you look at any artwork for the first time, you may not notice right away that the elements are arranged according to some positioning rules, but there are certainly grids behind every self-respecting design project, from books to posters, and even photoshoots.

Because virtual pages have a lot in common with printed pages, grids are also widely used in creating websites, apps, and other digital products that we use on a daily basis. However, digital pages cannot be permanent, as they can be displayed differently and the screen sizes of devices can vary significantly. But the basic principle of grids still remains the same – all elements must be organized with harmony and consistency throughout all pages so that the user is not distracted from the content.

Since we previously established that our hypothetical audience will primarily use our application on smartphones, we will first determine the correct grid for the mobile screen, and then, based on the properties of this grid, move to higher resolutions. We'll come back to this later, but now let's learn about grids in Figma.

Guides and layout grids

Now that you know why designers use grids, it's time to learn how to create and operate a grid system in Figma. In addition to the grids function, Figma also has another tool for aligning elements nested within the same frame – **Guides**. Let's talk about them first before moving on to grids.

You will need guides when you need to relate elements and check their alignment, position, and size. Unlike grids with columns and rows, guides look like thin horizontal and vertical lines, which are quicker and easier to move and reposition than grids. To better understand how guides work, let's try them out on the canvas:

1. First, you need to activate the rulers in your file. To do this, simply use the *Shift + R* keyboard shortcut. You will see that two rulers appear at the top and left of your working area, as you can see in the following screenshot (*Figure 5.2*).

2. Create a frame of any size you like, which you'll delete right after using guides, on your canvas.

3. To add a horizontal guides, click and drag the horizontal ruler. You will see a red line that you can drag towards your work area. Likewise, to have a vertical guides, you need to click and drag a vertical ruler. Note that when a ruler is placed on a frame, it gets automatically cut to the frame's borders:

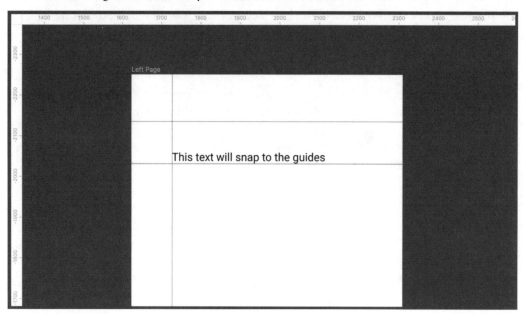

Figure 5.2 – Text snapping with guides

4. To remove the guides, drag it back to the ruler or simply use the *Delete* key after selecting it.

You can add as many guides as you like and move them manually anywhere on the canvas. This makes them a very versatile tool, but guides have their limitations, as it is difficult to create a flexible, efficient grid just using them. For this, Figma has layout grids.

> **Note**
>
> With a single *Shift + R* keyboard shortcut, you can toggle the ruler on and off in your working area.

As a more complex function than Guides, layout grids open up new possibilities for designers to create consistent product designs across multiple platforms. First of all, you need to know that layout grids can only be applied on frames – and therefore on components – both main and nested. To apply a layout grid to a frame, select one on your canvas, and, with selection active, click + next to **Layout grid** in the right sidebar. This action will enable this feature, and the default layout grid will be applied to the frame:

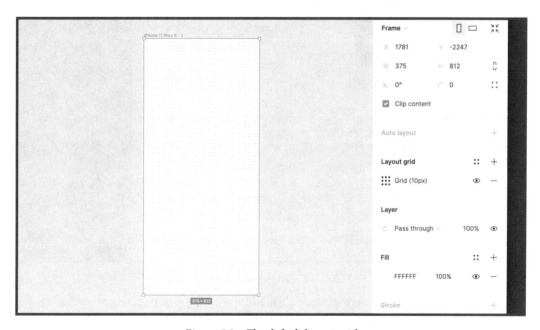

Figure 5.3 – The default layout grid

Before changing the grid settings, you need to understand what grid properties will fit the contents of this frame. The columns and rows of the grid must not be randomly arranged in the frame. You need to select the correct properties for them so that the grid becomes an effective design assistant when working on the interface for different screen sizes. Many web development frameworks such as Bootstrap, Tailwind, and Materialize use 12-column grids to better organize content within them, and what's more, this structure allows you to change the layout depending on the device and its resolution with a little effort. Therefore, at this stage, it is very important to find out, based on the needs of the project, which technologies will be used by the developers in your team. This can help in choosing a grid system that can then be efficiently converted to code without much difficulty.

To change the settings for the layout grid and update its properties, you should click the **Grid** icon under **Layout grid** in the right sidebar when frame selection is active. Here, in the drop-down menu at the top, you can see three options of layout grids – uniform square **Grid**, **Columns**, and **Rows**:

Figure 5.4 – The layout grid types

While the settings for a uniform grid are limited only by the size in pixels of each resulting cell and the grid color, columns and rows allow you to select, respectively, the column or row **Count** value you want to apply, as well as set **Margin**, **Gutter** (the distance between each row or column) and **Type**. With the grid type feature, you can align the grid **Right**, **Left**, or **Center**. But if you want the grid to adapt to the size of the frame, there is a **Stretch** option that automatically sets the column/row widths and makes your grid responsive.

It is important to know that the layout grid can be applied not only to the outer frame but also to the nested ones; thus, you can create inner grids that can be very useful – for example, when designing a small icon in your interface. Alternatively, you can add more than one layout grid for a frame, meaning you can apply a column-based layout grid and then add a row-based grid on top of it, having an even more customizable structure.

From the moment you apply the grid to any frame, it will always be visible on top of all other elements. While working, you will certainly need to turn off the grid visibility sometimes to reduce visual noise on your interface. You can do this with one click by selecting the frame to which the grid is applied and clicking the **Eye** icon in the layout grid section in the right panel, or alternatively, by pressing *Ctrl + G* (macOS) / *Ctrl + Shift + 4* (Windows).

As with any tool, you will have a better understanding of its use in practice. So, feel free to try guides and grids by setting different properties for them. For your personal practice exercises, you can create a separate file in the draft area. And when you're ready, you can move on to the next section, where we will learn about typography, colors, and effects.

Working with typography, colors, and effects

This section of the chapter will be dedicated to the fonts, colors, and effects in Figma. At first glance, these functions may seem more creative than what you have done before – and they certainly are – but you should never forget that every choice, including elements of style, should always be based on analytical conclusions. Therefore, you will need to refer to your artifacts to make the right choice, but for now, let's take a closer look at each tool.

Typography matters

Typography is one of the most important aspects of design and one of the most overlooked by newbies. However, the wrong typography choices instantly render a product non-functional and aesthetically unpleasant. This is because choosing the right font is not easy, and only experience, study, and practice can help you master this aspect. To learn more about typography, it is recommended that you read *Just My Type: A Book About Fonts* by *Simon Garfield*, which will help you better understand the uniqueness of each font and therefore determine when it is appropriate to use them.

Typographic choice can be dictated by several factors. If, for example, if you want to build an app exclusively for iOS, it might be a good choice to use a system font such as San Francisco (sans-serif) or New York (serif) in order for the product to comply with Apple's visual guidelines (which you can consult here: `https://developer.apple.com/design/human-interface-guidelines`). Likewise, when building an Android app, the Roboto font might be a safe choice. In the following figure, you can see a visual comparison of these famous fonts:

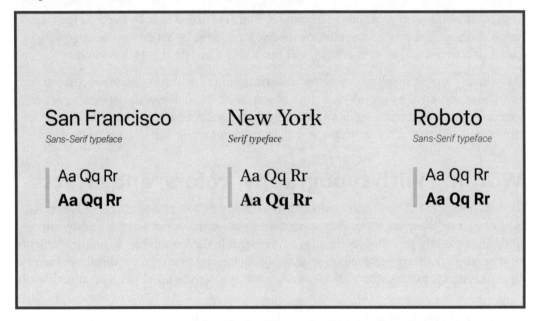

Figure 5.5 – The differences between serif and sans-serif typefaces

Another important factor is, of course, context. A font may be more appropriate for one use and less appropriate for another. In general, with sans-serif fonts being more readable by the human eye, they are suitable for menus, buttons, and so on. And if you need to display very long text content, a serif font may be more appropriate. It may also be that the brand you are working for already has its own brand book with particular recommended fonts for digital use.

There are times when it is possible, or even necessary, to use more than one font in an interface. In this case, you should first check whether there are any technical limitations on the development side – each integrated font has weight and can consequently slow down the loading of an application. After that, you need to make sure that the selected fonts match well.

> **Note**
>
> If you need useful suggestions, you can find some functional font pairing here: `https://www.figma.com/google-fonts`.

Typically, software that has a text-editing function has a list of fonts installed on the computer and ready to use. But in Figma, things are a little different. Firstly, Figma provides a huge selection of Google fonts (be sure that **Show Google Fonts** is enabled in **Preferences**), ready to operate in design files. Google fonts are also well designed (which is an important aspect when choosing a font) and complete in terms of the weight available for each font family. In addition, they are web fonts, which means they load quickly and are easy to implement during product development.

Therefore, because of the simplicity and flexibility of Google Fonts, it is highly recommended to use them. However, it may be that you have to use fonts that are not listed inside Figma. In this case, you should use the desktop version of Figma, where in addition to Google fonts, you will have at your disposal all the fonts installed on your computer. Optionally, you can also access local fonts through the Figma web app, but this requires an extra step, namely installing the font service (available here at `https://www.figma.com/downloads` for both macOS and Windows).

Now that you know what fonts you have at your disposal, let's take a look at the **Text** tool. You have already used it before, but now you will find out all the possibilities that it offers. The first thing you need to know is that the **Text** tool lets you insert two different types. If you select the **Text** tool (*T*), and then just click somewhere on the canvas and start typing, you will get text with an automatic width that will isn't limited. This means that the width of the text container will be growing indefinitely as you type until you start a new paragraph with the *Enter* key. The width of this container can then be reduced by clicking outside of it and manually using the cursor to adjust its size, both horizontally and vertically, within which the text will be contained. There is another way to place text on the canvas. Instead of just typing, you can draw a text container right after selecting the **Text** tool (*T*). This way, your container will keep the width you set earlier, and the text will not go beyond it and only change the height as you type. You can then modify the width of the container manually.

Regardless of which method you prefer, both will have the same result, namely creating a new text layer in the **Layers** panel. If you select any text layer, the **Design** panel automatically adjusts to your selection and displays functionality exclusively for texts and paragraphs in the **Text** section.

In the following screenshot (*Figure. 5.6*), you can see all the available options for working with text layers. Let's take a closer look at each of them:

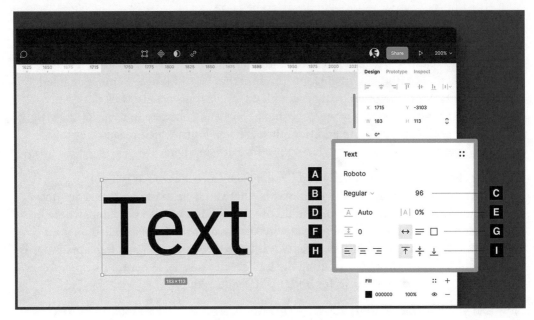

Figure 5.6 – The text options

The first parameter (**A**) is the already mentioned list of all available fonts. You can click the drop-down menu and see a great variety of different fonts for any occasion. To quickly check for a specific font that you might need, instead of scrolling through this long list, you can start typing the name of the font, and the autocomplete system will suggest the best search results for you.

> **Note**
>
> If you use local fonts, make sure that the other people working on the same file also have these fonts installed on their computers; otherwise, Figma will show them a yellow alert with an **A?** symbol next to the missing font name.

In addition to a font family, you can choose a specific **Weight** (**B**) for it – for example, **Light**, **Regular**, **Bold**, and **Extra bold** – and styles (for example, **Italic**) of the same font. Not all fonts have the same number of options for adjusting weight and styles, so it's best to consider this when choosing the main font for your project. It is recommended to use the one that has enough options to play with in order to be able to create a visual hierarchy of interface elements, highlight important text information, and so on. For similar purposes, different **Sizes** (**C**) of the selected font are also used.

The following options for working with a text layer can be better understood by having a multi-line block of text on the canvas. **Line height (D)**, also called leading, is the spacing between each line of text in a paragraph. In the default mode of any selected font, the lines will not overlap, but you can manually change this value to improve the readability of the text. Here, you can enter a value in pixels or a percentage, and in both cases, it is closely related to the font size. A standard paragraph with font size 18 has a line height of 21 (or 115%). **Paragraph spacing (F)** works in much the same way as line height, with the difference that only complete paragraphs are separated, not individual lines of text.

Letter spacing (E), or kerning, is used to separate individual characters in text from each other to make small optical adjustments. You can add or decrease the spacing between all letters in your block of text by simply selecting the entire layer and changing its letter-spacing value. But what's more, you can also separate any two single characters in a paragraph from each other by placing the text cursor between them and changing the spacing in the panel.

As you can see, Figma provides many options for working with the text layers. However, if you are a beginner, you should not overuse these functions, as the most famous fonts, made by experienced designers, are already worked out to the millimeter, and any careless modification can break this harmony. With time and experience, you will train your eyes, and you will know when it is worth making any such modifications to the selected font.

Finally, there are three sets of toggle parameters, each of which only has one option. The first group of functions (**G**), mentioned earlier, allows you to change the behavior of the text layer itself. If you are creating auto width text (with a simple click after selecting the **Text** tool), for example, the first option will be active, then you can easily switch to fixed size, and then the text area will have the specified size. The last option, automatic height, is a combination of the two. If you select it, the width of your text container will remain fixed and defined by you, but its height will automatically adapt based on the amount of text you enter. The second group (**H**) concerns the alignment of the text relative to the area in which it is contained. Here, you can choose one of the following text alignment options – left, center, or right. The third group (**I**) is also for aligning the text relative to its area but this time vertically, and you can choose between top, middle, and bottom alignment.

So, the changes you can make to the text are very numerous, but if that's not enough, you have a **More (...)** button. If you click on it, you will see many additional features, such as underling and strikethrough, numbered or bulleted lists, or converting an entire text box to uppercase, lowercase, and so on. This expanded panel also has a practical preview window, the contents of which change, depending on which of the available options you hover over. The preview is shown to help you better understand all the features in this panel. In the following screenshot, you can see this panel with the preview and some additional functions:

Figure 5.7 – Advanced text options

So far, we have explored all the specific and exclusive features of text layers. But don't overlook the fact that other common features we've already applied to shape layers are also available here for text. Therefore, you can change the position and size of the text box by editing the corresponding values at the top of the **Design** panel, apply any color to the text using the **Fill** options, or even add a stroke to it using the **Stroke** options.

As you can see, all the settings for working with text layers in Figma are pretty simple. But the real difficulty lies in choosing one or more fonts for your projects. But don't worry – there are tons of resources to help you learn this skill. Later in this chapter, we will choose a font that suits the content and functionality of our application, but first, we will learn about colors in Figma.

Choosing a palette

Like typography, color is an important design aspect of any project that should never be overlooked. You can have a great user experience in your application, but the perception of this can be spoiled by the wrong choice of color palette, and all your efforts will be wasted. Each color has its own message and has a particular impact on people, so you need to make sure that your product interacts properly with the user. Before starting the actual UI design, you should have a clear idea of which direction to go in terms of colors, or at least enough data to easily figure it out. We'll make color choices together later, but first, let's figure out how to work with colors in Figma.

The most important tool for working with colors, as you can imagine, is the color picker, which we already tried out in *Chapter 4, Wireframing a Mobile-First Experience Using Vector Shapes*, while learning about shapes. Whether it's a background color, fill color, stroke color, or anything else, the **Design** panel will always display a preview of that color, so you can simply click on it to open a dedicated window:

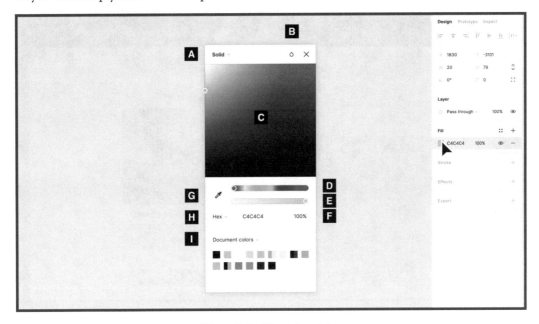

Figure 5.8 – The color picker

To learn more about each color picker option, either select any element with a color on the canvas, create any shape, or add a fill or stroke to the created element. Then, just open the expanded window in the **Design** panel by clicking the square with the element's color.

A – color modes

From this drop-down menu, you can choose from several color modes. All of these modes are quite different, but they can be grouped into three categories, each of which partially or completely affects the contents of the color picker. The first category includes the default option, **Solid**, that allows you to simply select a solid color using the appropriate visual selector. The second category includes **Linear**, **Radial**, **Angular**, and **Diamond**, which are gradient options, each with a different diffusion. If you choose any of those gradient options, you will be prompted to choose not one but two or more colors, the combination of which will smoothly transition from one color to another. To change one of the colors, simply click on it in the gradient bar and then use the classic color picker. To apply any additional color to your gradient, click on any empty spot in the gradient bar, and a new colored square will appear. You can move the markers of individual colors to determine how smooth the color transition will be, as you can see in the following screenshot:

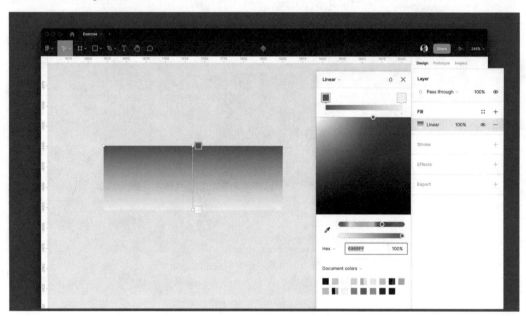

Figure 5.9 – The Linear gradient

You can also change a specific gradient trend by moving the start and end points of the gradient strip that appears directly on the selected element on the workspace. Take time to experiment with gradients to see how any changes you make produce different results.

Finally, the last **Image** option falls into the last category and allows you to import static or dynamic images in `.GIF` format from your computer and use them as an element's fill property. To import an image, click the **Select Image** button while hovering over the preview field, or drag any image into this space:

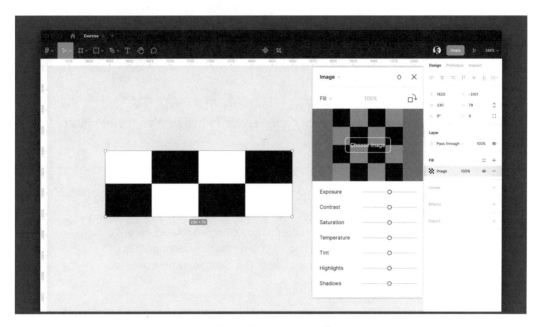

Figure 5.10 – Image Fill

This mode completely changes the color picker window, turning it into a small but functional image-editing center with the ability to retouch **Exposure**, **Contrast**, and so on. Keep in mind that the imported image is the fill of your element. This means that if you select a star shape and set an **Image** fill, it will be inserted into the shape, and above all, the layer will continue to be a shape type. Thus, importing an image on the canvas and inserting an image fill are completely different operations. For this reason, with the **Image** fill option, you will find various settings in the color picker – you can fill the space, adapt to it, crop the image, or repeat it in tiles.

B – blend modes

With this tool, you can blend the two layers in different ways. All the options are listed in the drop-down menu. Depending on the selected mode, the blending is calculated for each individual pixel of this layer and the layer below it.

C – the color palette

In this area, you can visually pick whatever color you want. Moving the lower hue slider (**D**) changes the displayed color tones. The opacity slider (**E**) adjusts the opacity of the color, or you can manually enter the opacity's percentage value (**F**). A circle with a white outline represents the currently selected color.

G – the eyedropper tool

This is a standard tool found in every design software. The eyedropper tool allows you to sample a color from any element on the screen, whether it's a vector object or a raster image.

> **Note**
>
> By pressing the *I* key on your keyboard, you can activate the eyedropper tool at any time. If you click on any object with a fill or stroke color – that is, activate its selection – and then use the eyedropper tool, the original element's color will be replaced with the sampled one. With no active selections, it is still a valid tool for displaying the color code of the color you hover over on the screen.

H – color models

By default, the reference color model will be the **Hex** code, which is the hexadecimal alphanumeric representation of the color. This mode is most popular in digital design and is equally convenient for web developers. But if needed, you can switch modes in the dropdown and choose **RGB** or **CSS** (which is also RGB but formatted in a web-friendly way). RGB, which stands for red, green, and blue, allows you to assign a value from 0 to 255 to individual channels. Finally, there are **HSB** (**hue saturation brightness**) and **HSL** (**hue saturation luminance**), which are very similar to each other, as they generate color by changing their respective parameters.

I – color styles

In **Document colors**, you can quickly access the entire color palette ever used in your current file. You can also access color from shared libraries using the drop-down menu. We will learn more about how libraries work later.

We have explored all the tools that can help you work effectively with the colors. There is one more thing to clarify before moving on to the next tool. As you already know, the **Design** panel, being contextual, displays settings according to the selected element, and the color tools work the same way. But what if you select more than one object at a time? Well, if the fill or stroke of the selected elements matches in color, you will not notice anything unusual, as the unique value will be displayed in the panel as before. However, if the colors of the elements were different, a new section called **Selection Colors** will appear in the panel. In this section, you can see all the colors present on the selected objects, and you can change every property individually:

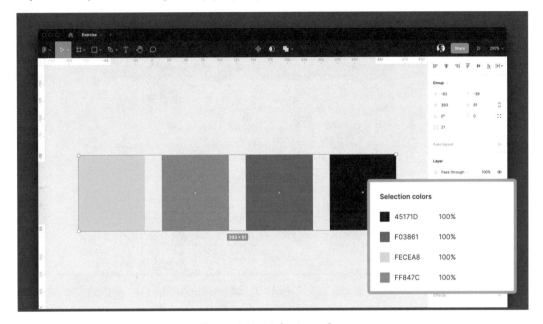

Figure 5.11 – Selection colors

Colors are a big topic to learn, but Figma makes them easy to, giving you a set of tools that are easy to master. Always remember that before adding any color to your design, you must make sure that your choice is correct. We'll pick a color palette for our app a little later in this chapter, but now, feel free to play with colors in your drafts if you like.

Creating effects

In the **Design** panel, you may have noticed a section not yet mentioned, namely **Effects**. This is definitely a tool that deserves an in-depth study, as you can apply various effects with it to elements, such as **Inner shadow**, **Drop shadow**, **Layer shadow**, **Layer blur**, and **Background blur**.

Each of these effects has its own characteristic behavior. **Drop shadow**, for example, replicates the depth of Material Design (which is the official design system made by Google for its apps and services; you can check it out here: `https://material.io/design`) or cards in general, and **Background blur** simulates the iOS opaque glass effect. To change the effect's settings, simply click the sun icon, and you will see all the properties that can be modified, such as positioning, **Spread** for outer/inner shadows, or **Blur** levels for blur effects:

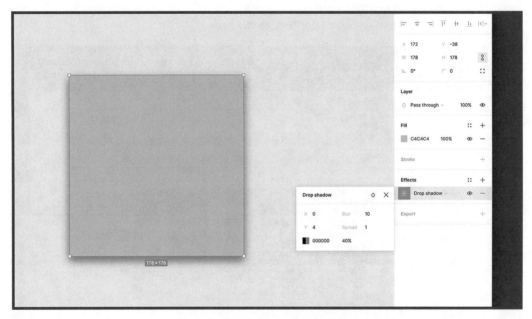

Figure 5.12 – The Drop shadow effect

As you can imagine, **Effects** has many properties, and describing each of them would take too many pages of this book, which is rather irrational, given that our main goal is to learn how to design a fully fledged interface in Figma. So, try exploring the effects in more detail in your draft file, setting different effect properties and watching the results. But you should know that it is better not to overuse effects when working on real projects. The main purpose of this feature is to highlight elements to make them more visible to the user. Especially in your first steps in design, it's best to stick to the well-known guidelines for effect recommendations. As your experience grows, you can experiment and create your own effects.

In this section, we have enriched our knowledge of Figma with three main functions, without which it would be difficult to imagine design. If you are concerned that you have not used any of these functions in our interface so far, don't worry, as in the next topic, we will learn how to do it in the simplest and smartest way.

Introducing styles

Well, we've successfully mastered the basics of grids, typography, colors, and effects, but now it's time to learn how to effectively manipulate these tools. And that is what we will practice in this section. As you can imagine, it would be incredibly irrational to apply our chosen font to every text layer in our design. In this hypothetical situation, you risk changing the fonts of every text on all screens in your application if you ever decide to replace the selected font with a different one. To prevent this from happening, Figma provides you with a simple and flexible feature called styles.

Styles in Figma is an incredibly powerful feature that allows you to save and reuse color palettes, fonts, and effect attributes in your design project. This means that you can apply the approved style properties to any element with a single click. And if you ever need to change any property, you can do it just as quickly in all layers of your file, or even across multiple files!

Preparing your file

So, let's see how to style our application in practice. This step is very important because it is the transition from a **Low-Fidelity (Lo-Fi)** wireframe to a **High-Fidelity (Hi-Fi)** final design, so you need to prepare your file in the best possible way:

1. In the upper-right corner of the **Layers** panel, there is a drop-down label that shows and hides all the pages in your file. At this point, you only have one page in your design file that contains the wireframe, which Figma has automatically named Page 1. Let's rename it Lo-Fi by double-clicking the page name.

2. Duplicate the page by right-clicking its name and choosing **Duplicate Page** from the drop-down menu. A second one with the same name will appear right under the first page.

3. Rename the duplicate page to `Hi-Fi` – this is where we will be working on the actual UI of our application. Remember, a Starter plan can contain up to three pages in one team file. As a result, you should have a similar structure:

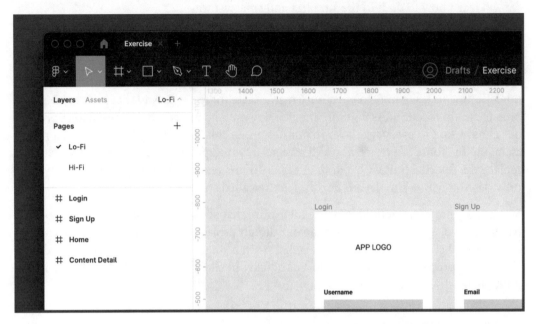

Figure 5.13 – Lo-Fi and Hi-Fi pages

As you have probably figured out, the first page of your file will only contain the wireframe you have already created, and the second will be dedicated to the actual design of our application.

Creating and managing grid styles

As you probably already figured out, duplicating any page means copying all of its content, so can you see all the same wireframes created earlier on the Hi-Fi page. Let's not change the elements inside the frames for now but start by setting layout grids as a first style property. To do that, follow these steps:

1. Select the **Login** frame.

2. Add **Layout grid** from the right sidebar by clicking on the + icon.

3. By default, the uniform grid will be applied. Click on the grid icon and select **Columns** from the dropdown.

4. From the grid settings, we set the column **Count** value to **12**, the **Type** value to **Stretch**, the **Margin** value to **16**, and **Gutter** to **8**:

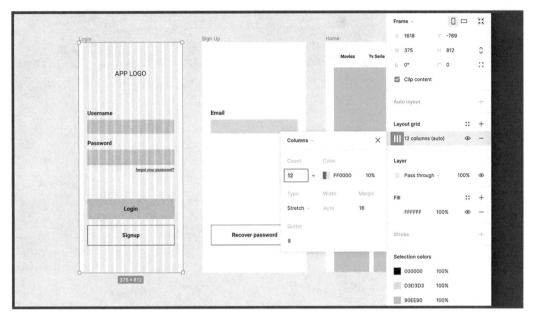

Figure 5.14 – The grid settings

Obviously, the values that you have just entered for your grid cannot be random. In our case, as mentioned earlier, the 12-column structure is one of the most commonly used in well-known development frameworks. The **Gutter** value is set for a design with an 8-point system, in which everything will be a multiple of 8, starting with a **Margin** of 16px. This system of multiples makes it much easier to keep spacing consistent. This grid system is very simple and effective, but it is not the only one, right? So, feel free to experiment with new options as soon as you feel more confident.

Since you applied the grid to the **Login** frame only, you need to do the same for all other screens for consistency. But doing it manually for each frame is clearly an inconvenient operation, especially if you have many more views than in our work area. To simplify, speed up, and optimize this process, let's save this grid as our first style:

1. Select the **Login** view with the layout grid you've just created.

2. Click the **Style** icon (see the following screenshot).

3. Create a new style by clicking on the + icon of the **Grid Styles** dialog.

4.   Give a proper name to this grid style, such as `12-column-fluid`, which quickly makes it recognizable as a stretchy 12-column grid:

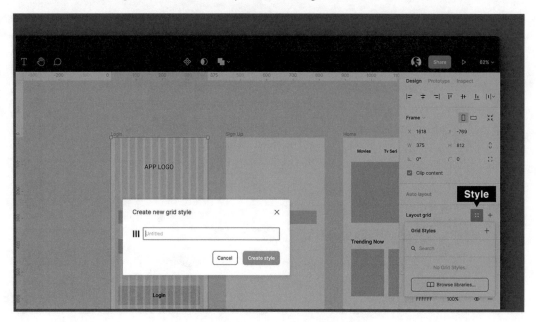

Figure 5.15 – A new grid style

Done! The layout grid you created has just been converted to a style, and you can see it in the right sidebar. Now, all that remains is to apply this grid style to all the other frames:

1.   Select all the frames with no grids (**Sign Up**, **Home**, and **Content Detail**).

2.   This time, instead of pressing +, click the **Styles** button, and you will see the grid style that you just created.

3.   Select your grid style to apply it to all the views in your file with one click.

Now, you can see how easy it is to complete this operation with minimal effort. However, you should always remember that after applying the same style to multiple frames, you will no longer be able to change the layout grids of individual views, as they all relate to the same source of truth. If you want to change your grid style, you can do so in the **Styles** dialog box by selecting the style you want to edit and clicking the **Edit Style** icon:

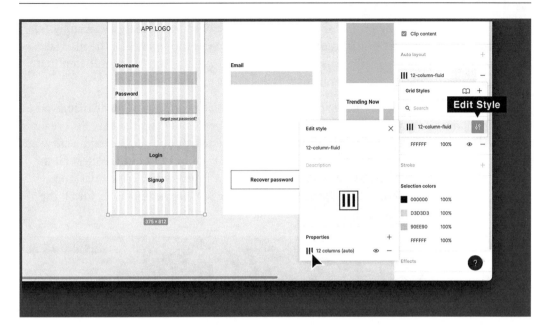

Figure 5.16 – Editing a grid style

After you have saved your changes, all the views to which the style was applied will undergo the same modification. See how easy it is, and again in a few clicks!

> **Note**
> You can still change an individual grid. To do this, select the frame you need and click **Detach Style**, the broken chain icon next to the applied style. It will unlink the selected frame's grid from the grid style.

So, you've just created your first style, which will be one of many – great work! Now, let's select a font for our project and convert it to a style as well.

Creating and managing text styles

In creating a grid style, we saw all the advantages and possibilities that the style function can provide. Our application will contain quite a lot of text on each page, so we need to have text styles as well. As before, the first thing you do is create a foundation for the text styles that you will apply to the text layers in our interface. If you're feeling overwhelmed right now, remember that you don't need to create all the text styles at once. It is normal practice to integrate new styles later if the original core of the style is well organized.

The choice of fonts for any project should, of course, be based on research and analysis. You may want to consider one or more fonts (try not to use too many) for the interface. For the current project, we will be using *Source Sans Pro*, a modern yet simple font that suits interfaces very well and remains incredibly legible even at small sizes.

When working with styles, it is best to have all of the style properties visually displayed somewhere outside of the interface layouts. We can allocate one page for this. So, create the third (and final) page in the file. This time, the page will not be duplicated but new and empty. Rename this new page `Styles / Components` – here, you will collect all the reusable parts of the UI. On this new page, create a new frame with a preset desktop size (1440 x 1024) and rename it `Typography`. This frame will be the container for all the text styles you will add soon:

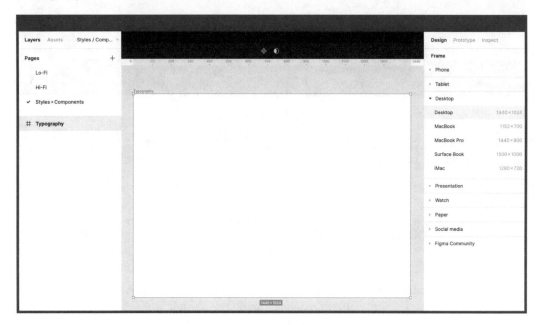

Figure 5.17 – The Typography page

You don't need to add a lot of styles for this project, only the ones that you really need for the app layouts. As for the text style, we'll use multiples of eight and start with the body text (the one used for standard paragraphs). We'll then move on to other text styles in terms of their importance. Follow the next few steps to get it done easily:

1. On the **Styles + Components** page, create five new text layers. It is best to use a pangram as a sample text. A pangram is a sentence that contains all the letters of the alphabet. This way, you will always have a visual display of all the characters of the selected font. One of the most famous pangrams is **The quick brown fox jumps over the lazy dog**.

2. Place these text layers vertically one after the other.

3. Starting with the top text layer, assign the following parameters to each text layer:

   • **Source Sans Pro | 32px | Bold**

   • **Source Sans Pro | 24px | Bold**

   • **Source Sans Pro | 16px | Bold**

   • **Source Sans Pro | 16px | Regular**

   • **Source Sans Pro | 16px | Light**

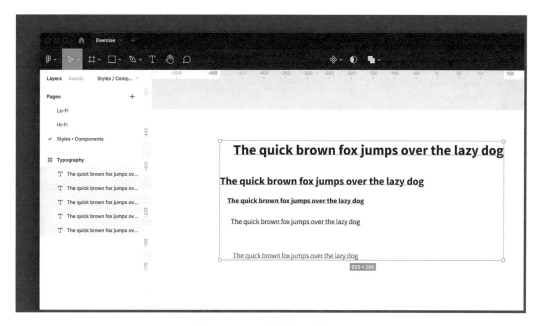

Figure 5.18 – Styled text layers

After you've finished formatting all the text layers, you can align them if the result looks messy. You can easily do this in the alignment section of the **Design** panel. Just select all the text layers, click the **Align left** button, and then in the right drop-down list with a few more options, click **Distribute vertical spacing**. After these two clicks, the contents of the frame should be arranged perfectly.

> **Note**
>
> If you want to select multiple elements from the **Layer** panel, you can do so by holding the *Command* (macOS) or *Ctrl* (Windows) key.

To finish tidying up your text style container, you can add a label next to each sentence, which is a simple overview of the rules applied to each text layer. It's even better if you combine labels and related texts into groups:

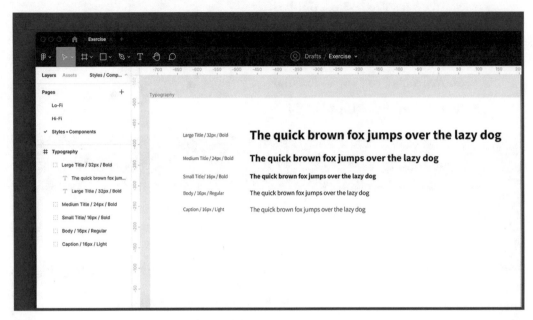

Figure 5.19 – Styled and ordered text layers with labels

It's time to finally create text styles based on this structure, and it won't be much different from how you did it earlier with grids:

1. Select the top text layer.
2. Click on the **Style** button next to the **Text** section label in the right sidebar.
3. In the **Text Styles** dialog, click the + button.
4. Give this first text style a name. It can be the same as the label (such as `Large Title/ 32px / Bold`).
5. Repeat the process for every successive text layer.

So, the text styles are set up and ready to be used in our app design. It is important to know that each text style can contain a set of rules regarding font family, font weight and size, line height, letter spacing, text decoration, text transformation, and so on. But unlike other design tools, text styles do NOT include alignment and color. This feature makes text styles incredibly flexible to use, eliminating the need to create text styles for each alignment or color. In the following screenshot, you can see the display of text styles in the right panel of Figma:

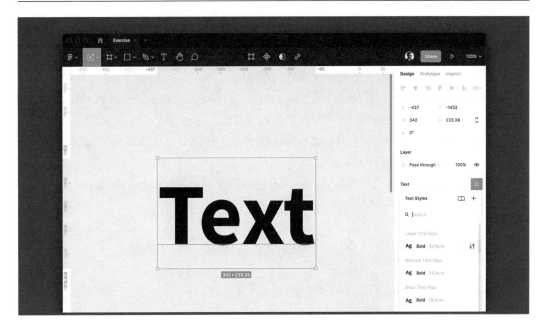

Figure 5.20 – Text Styles

When you feel more confident about your design, you can experiment with creating a complete UI kit that includes styles for any need and can be reused as a basis for your future projects. The rhythm of the font scale is actually a much more complex subject than it might seem. To get the most harmonious scales, you can use ratios, but since not every creative is in love with math, here is a convenient site that can help you with that and take care of all the mathematical aspects: `type-scale.com`.

Creating and managing color and effect styles

At the moment, our project has styles that consist of a layout grid and typography, so it's time to add the third essential property – colors. Again, in order to make the right choice of color palette of any application or site that you develop, it is important to refer to the artifacts that you collected in the process of research and analysis, namely the mood board in this case. You will see which colors are suitable for our video streaming app project in a moment. But first, let's add a new **Desktop** frame to the **Styles + Components** page, next to the **Typography** frame, and rename the new frame `Colors`. Then, follow a few simple steps to create color styles:

1. In the new **Colors** frame, add five rectangle shapes of 130 x130 px.

2. Place them vertically, at a short distance from each other. To arrange them neatly and make the vertical spacing between elements equal, select them all and use Figma's auto-alignment feature.

3. Starting with the top shape layer, assign the following parameters to each rectangle:

    •   FF5959 as the fill: This will be our accent color, which we will use for calls to action and other important operations.

    •   272B45 as the fill: This will be our secondary color, which we'll eventually use on a secondary user's actions.

    •   0F1022 as the fill: This will be our background color, which we'll apply to the interface background.

    •   8A8C99 as the fill: This will be our inactive color, applied to elements that are disabled for some reason.

    •   FFFFFF as the fill: This is pure white. This one will be our text color, since the background will be dark, and it will be needed if we want to change all the text colors in one click.

As with the text, take some time to add labels to the side of each square, containing brief descriptions of the color use cases. In addition, you can add a 1px-thin black stroke to all the colored squares to make the light colors stand out from the background easily:

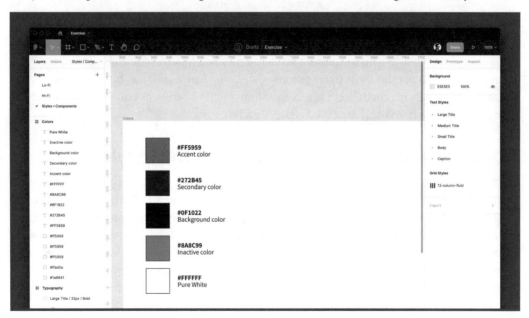

Figure 5.21 – The color palette

Now, as you have probably guessed, all the colors need to be converted to styles. Therefore, you need to select colored squares one by one and create a corresponding style for each of them. You can name each color style the same as its label (such as Accent color). Note that creating a style from the **Fill** section does not mean that this color can only be used for fill. If you ever want to apply it to a trace or shadow, it can be done without a problem. As with fonts, you may need more colors than you chose at the beginning, so you can include new color styles later. You can add new color styles at any time, if necessary, but it is very important that all colors that are used in your file are always linked to styles, except for a few special cases.

Choosing the right color palette is a skill that comes with experience. Once you have mastered the basics, you can learn more about colors. There are many resources that can explain the psychological meaning of colors, as well as their relationship to different cultures. It is also very important to study the subject of accessibility in depth, which also includes the use of sufficiently contrasting colors to a set of rules so that legibility is adequate, especially for people with visual impairments.

Last but not least, you need to style the effects, following the same pattern. Follow these steps:

1. Select the white square in the **Colors** frame.
2. Add an effect from the right sidebar by clicking the + button near the **Effects** label.
3. Click the sun icon to the left of the **Drop shadow** dropdown.
4. Set **X** to **0**, **Blur** to **15**, **Y** to **4**, **Spread** to **5**, color to **82B2DE**, and opacity to **22%**:

Figure 5.22 – The Drop shadow settings

5. Save this effect as a style and name it `Light Drop Shadow`.

6. Now, you can apply this effect style to each of the colored squares, removing the black stroke for a nicer look:

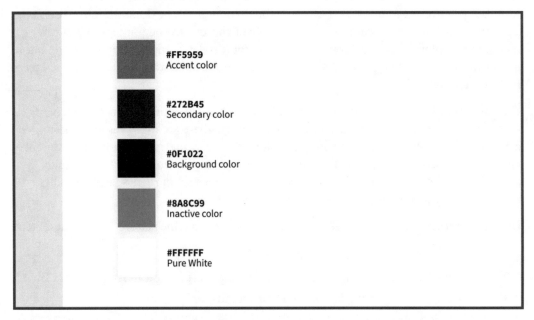

Figure 5.23 – The color palette with drop shadow

This effect can be applied to any layer you want.

Well, you have finally created all the sources of truth needed for our project. In the next chapter, you will learn how to make the best use of styles. Let's take a look at everything you've created so far. To do this, simply click on any empty space on the canvas of the page. When nothing is selected, you can see the list of styles in the **Design** panel, and from here, you can quickly edit any of them. After making changes to a style, all elements to which it was applied undergo the same change:

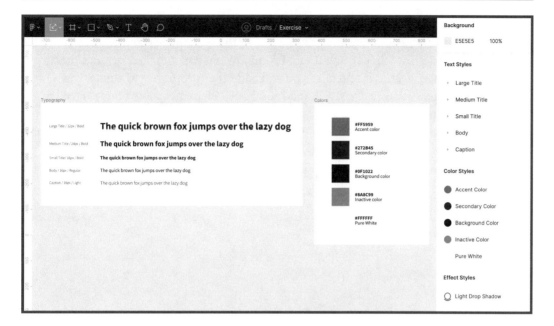

Figure 5.24 – grid, color, text, and effect styles

So, your design file now contains three pages, one of which is completely dedicated to styles. Later, you will add other elements, such as reusable components, and after working on the design of our application, you can even reuse this library of styles and components in other projects. You will learn about this and everything else as you travel along this exciting journey!

Summary

As stated earlier, the main goal of a UX/UI designer is not to be creative but to provide an interface in which every user will feel confident, and nothing will distract them from the functionality of any digital product. Thus, you need to make sure your design is intuitive and inclusive. This means you have to be well aware of your user's needs and pains, and anticipate specific cases where your app or website might be used to keep your design consistent and accessible. As you learned in this chapter, even when choosing typography, colors, and effects, you must follow these principles.

Aside from practicing these tools, we now have an idea of how to make the best use of them by converting them to styles. Styles are one of the most important features in Figma, and you've done a great job learning them. From now on, you will discover and practice even more advanced features, and later you will add other properties to your Styles + Components page, such as extra styles and reusable UI elements. Now that you feel more confident using Figma, you are ready to explore its unique and incredibly powerful features. One of them will be auto layout, which you will learn about right away – in the next chapter!

6

Creating a Responsive Mobile Interface Using Auto Layout

In the previous chapter, you already started the transition from lo-fi to hi-fi, which is the actual design of our video streaming app. It is important to know that this is the stage of the project where you need to be focused, precise, and clear, since your hi-fi files will be used by the developers. It may take you a while to achieve this, which is perfectly fine, but thanks to Figma's awesome tools, you can avoid inaccuracy as much as possible. In this chapter, you will discover one of those tools, namely auto layout.

The topic you are about to explore in this chapter can be defined as advanced. So, you will first start with theory, and then smoothly move on to practicing on our project file. But this does not mean that you cannot complement the process of learning new principles in this chapter with your own practice in your draft files. It would be even better if you include in this practice some of the tools that you have already learned, especially those that you may not feel very confident with yet. The more you experiment, the faster you learn. So, open up your Figma, and let's get started!

In this chapter, we are going to cover the following main topics:

- Introducing auto layout
- Resizing and constraints
- Applying auto layout to our interface

By the end of this chapter, you will have a good understanding of the auto layout, resizing, and constraint features in Figma and will be able to create responsive views using them.

Introducing auto layout

In this section, you'll start by discovering the powerful Figma auto layout feature. Its use covers many aspects of a designer's work, from improving your interface to speeding up your workflow. At first, auto layout may seem similar to the **grids** you explored in *Chapter 5, Designing Consistently Using Grids, Colors, and Typography*, as they are both used for precisely aligning elements in your designs. As you know, grids are incredibly useful for ensuring that all elements follow the same harmony and layout logic. However, in many cases, relying only on them is a very risky decision, which cannot be said about auto layout. The word "auto" gives you a hint that once you set properties, you don't need to worry about checking whether everything is positioned correctly. With this feature, you can save yourself from mistakes that are sometimes difficult to track down. But auto layout goes beyond that and does a lot more, and you'll soon find out about all of its amazing capabilities.

Before diving into the massive topic of auto layout, let's take a look at where you are in your journey right now. At this point, you've already seen that the process of creating a good interface is not as easy as expected. It is not enough to have an idea and then implement it by simply placing elements on the screen and coloring them. So, after the research phase, you started working on the wireframe interface in *Chapter 4, Wireframing a Mobile-First Experience Using Vector Shapes*. Wireframes are made up of simple shapes and lines where you don't have to pay too much attention to detail and be too precise. Now that you have successfully completed that task and have already started preparing the base with styles and grids for your layouts in the previous chapter, it's time to create a real design. So, let's finally take a look at what auto layout is and how it will help you in your future work on the interface.

What is auto layout?

Auto layout is one of the most significant features in Figma. Once you apply this function to any frame, it will become dynamic – that is, it will shrink or grow according to the size of the element (or elements) that it contains. This means, for example, that if you have an auto layout frame containing a text layer and then add another layer to it, that frame automatically resizes itself to easily fit both elements. Moreover, **auto layout** is great for creating lists and menus, as any new element triggers a responsive frame adaptation, as you can see in the following figure:

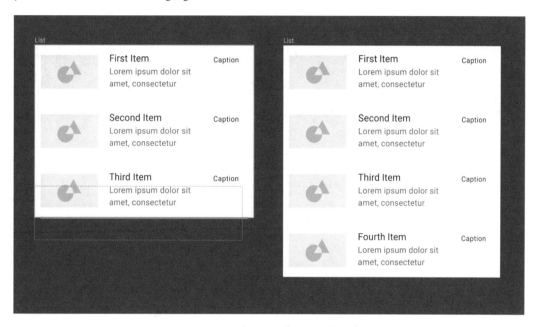

Figure 6.1 – Auto layout affecting a list of items

Auto layout is a huge and difficult topic to explore, but once you learn how it works, it can greatly simplify your workflow and improve the quality of your design. You will discover more about this in the next section of this chapter, but for now, let's start with a general overview of this tool. All the auto layout settings are presented in the contextual right sidebar. But as you have already seen in other typical cases, it will only be shown and activated after the element with auto layout is selected. You can add auto layout to frames (whether empty or full), to components (which you will explore in the next chapter), groups, and multiple layer selections.

> **Note**
>
> Auto layout can only be applied to frames (or components), which means that if you select a group and activate auto layout, the group will be automatically converted to a frame with auto layout properties.

From the moment auto layout is activated – by clicking the + buttons next to the **Auto layout** label on the right sidebar, or simply using the *Shift + A* keyboard shortcut – the frame automatically resizes to fit the content inside it. If it has no elements inside it, it will be adjusted as soon as you add anything to this frame. Activating auto layout opens up a whole range of new options in a dedicated section, as shown in the following figure:

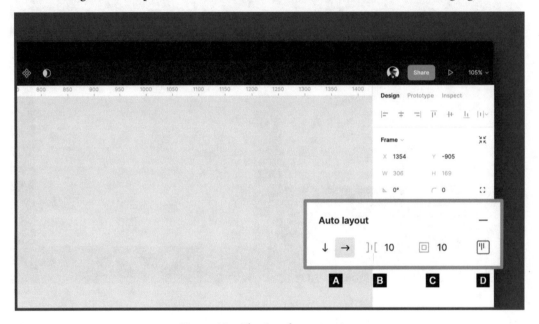

Figure 6.2 – The Auto layout section

Let's take a closer look at each of these settings in the **Auto layout** section.

A – Direction

With this option, you can set the direction of your layout, namely horizontal or vertical. Depending on the option selected, the layout will automatically align to a row or column, readapting all the elements contained in the frame.

B – Spacing

When a frame with an active auto layout contains more than one element, whether horizontally or vertically, there will be equal spacing between them. You can change this property if necessary, as you can see here:

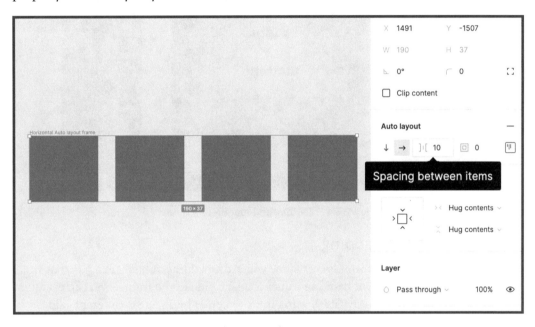

Figure 6.3 – The Spacing between items option

C – Padding

Padding is a common design concept. If you already know what it is, this parameter should be quite clear to you, since it simply applies a numeric padding value to each side of the frame (not to an individual element but the entire content of the frame). If you don't know what it is, the following figure explains the subtle difference between padding (inner spacing before the stroke) and a margin (outer spacing after the stroke):

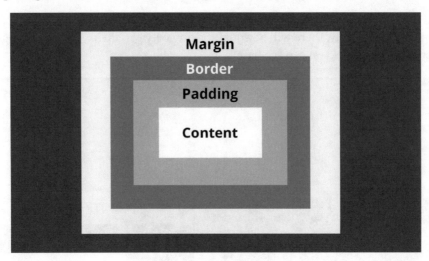

Figure 6.4 – Padding and margin differences

D – Alignment and padding

This parameter may seem unnecessary, since you see a padding value here again, but in this case, you can set different padding values for each side of the frame. You can easily navigate through each of these values using the *Tab* key. When you set different values, the previous universal padding parameter will change its value to **Mixed** because it is no longer uniform.

But that's not all. In addition to the numerical values, you can interact with the visual grid by clicking on each of its points, including the diagonal points. This way, you can align and arrange all the elements contained in the frame. From the moment the auto layout is activated, you can no longer change the position and alignment of an individual element, only in relation to the whole group of all elements, positioning it in relation to the outer frame. To understand this function better, take a look at the following figure:

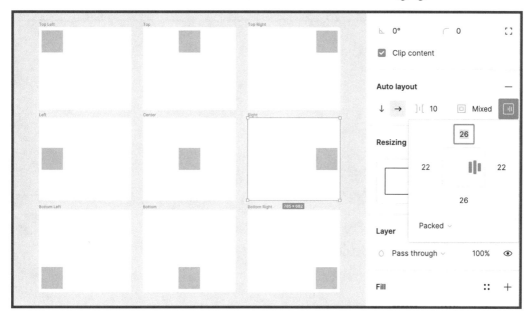

Figure 6.5 – The different alignments on a fixed size frame

Under the interactive grid are the distribution options. By default, you have the **Packed** option, which means that all objects in the frame are grouped together with a specified precise spacing between them. If you click the dropdown and select **Space between**, the items will move apart from each other, filling the entire space of the parent frame and maintaining an equal spacing, the value of which will be calculated automatically. You can see an example in the following figure:

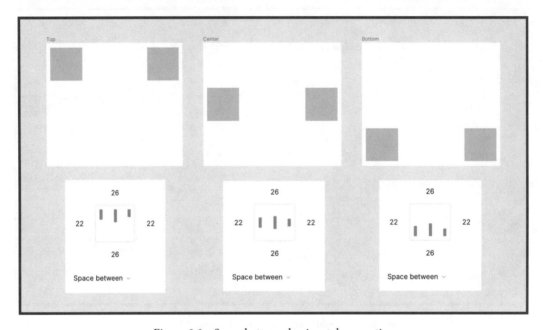

Figure 6.6 – Space between horizontal properties

Moving from the **Packed** option to the **Space between** option significantly reduces the number of alignments available in the interactive grid, as elements are now positioned differently. The options also differ depending on the direction of the auto layout. Also, note that distribution and alignment have a visible effect on the frame only if it is not adapted to the elements it contains and is larger. You may be confused at this point, but you will learn more about these cases in the *Resizing and constraints* section.

Adding, removing, and rearranging elements

Once auto layout is applied to a frame, you can no longer freely position the inner elements, as they will all follow the set auto layout rules. On the other hand, from this point on, the frame becomes more flexible and stable, which allows you to quickly create complex but very accurate layouts, so you can be sure that everything is consistent with the logic.

If, at any point, you need to add a new element to the horizontal or vertical stack, all you have to do is simply drag that element into the auto layout frame. What's more, you can choose exactly where to insert the new element. As you drag your element and move it over the existing ones, a blue indicator appears to help you place the object where you want it to be:

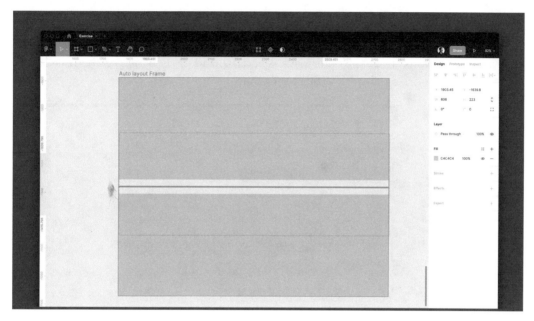

Figure 6.7 – A blue indicator showing where the new item will be added

Note

You can also duplicate any element in the auto layout frame by selecting it and pressing *Command + D* (macOS) or *Ctrl + D* (Windows). The new element will be placed right next to the original one.

Deleting elements is also very easy. Just select one and press *Backspace* on your keyboard. If you want to just remove it from the current frame without deleting it, you can simply drag it out of the container. Your stack will change accordingly.

It's just as easy to reorder elements in an auto layout frame. For example, to swap the positions of the second and third elements of the stack, simply drag the second element onto the third. You can also do this by selecting the element and using the *Arrow* keys on your keyboard. Without auto layout, moving elements and keeping the correct spacing between them would be much more time-consuming and risky.

Nesting auto layout

Since a set of elements combined with auto layout is actually a frame, it acts exactly the same way. This means that you can nest an auto layout frame within another auto layout frame as much as you like. With this in mind, you can create incredibly complex layouts using auto layout from top to bottom. This is what makes auto layout an incredibly powerful feature.

Let's take a classic card layout as an example. It can be composed vertically from an image, text, and two buttons. Thus, the outer stack is vertical, and the two buttons themselves are combined into a horizontal stack with auto layout:

Figure 6.8 – A vertical auto layout frame containing a horizontal one

This design mode makes it easy to change the layout at any time and really makes Figma a high-end design tool.

Of course, you can get the same result by creating a frame each time and then inserting the merged elements inside each time, but as you've already seen, it is much easier to just select the elements you want and add an auto layout from the right sidebar. Alternatively, you can use the *Shift + A* shortcut, which activates the auto layout function for the current selection (with one or more elements).

Using and mastering auto layout is certainly not an easy task for both beginners and more experienced designers who are used to other tools without this feature, but the more you use it, the more you'll understand how this tool can make your workflow easy and enjoyable. Later in this chapter, you will practice more with auto layout, and your understanding of this function will become much clearer for you. But first, you need to explore other important features directly related to auto layout, namely resizing and constraints.

Resizing and constraints

In this section, you will learn about the resizing and constraint features, which, like auto layout, are used to create responsive designs. If there was only one screen resolution in the world, everything would be incredibly simple, and there would be no need to implement anything further. However, in the real digital world, things are different, and you should consider all resolutions, if possible, as well as the cases of switching from portrait to landscape mode with devices, or even from a mobile phone to a tablet or a desktop. Fortunately, modern design tools aim to help designers with this problem by providing incredible features for creating responsive interfaces that can automatically adjust based on resolution and screen size. Later in this book, you will dive deeper into the process of converting mobile interfaces to tablets and desktops, but it's important to start with a foundation and structure to get your design ready for future adaptation.

Resizing elements

As you already know, using auto layout allows the outer frame to automatically adjust based on the size of its inner content. But this is only part of the possible behavior of this function, and it can be changed in the **Resizing** section. You can see this just below the **Auto layout** function:

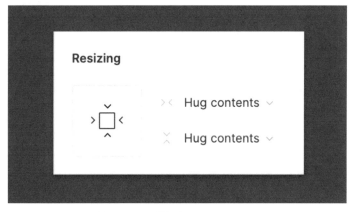

Figure 6.9 – The Resizing section

By default, you have the **Hug contents** behavior, which means that the outer frame resizes in real time, depending on what it contains. This feature is set in two drop-down lists and also appears in the interactive grid on the left, which has the same editing capabilities. This way, you can choose different behavior for the width and height of the selected frame. For example, it can hug contents in width but have a fixed height in pixels.

> **Note**
> In an auto layout frame, padding is counted as part of the nested elements, which means that if the frame adjusts based on the size of these elements, it will also take the padding into account.

Setting the **Hug contents** parameter for your frame means that its width and height will be automatically determined by the content inside it. But if you manually change the width or height of this frame in your workspace, the properties will change to the **Fixed width** or the **Fixed height** values respectively. This may seem confusing to you at this point, and you might be wondering when you need to use a fixed-size auto layout instead of hug contents, so let's take a look at a few examples in the following figure to get a better understanding of this:

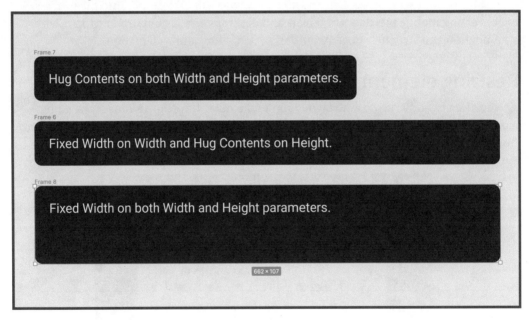

Figure 6.10 – Hug contents and fixed sizes

Depending on the case, fixed width and variable height can be useful, or vice versa. What's especially surprising about the resizing function is the possibility to assign the **Fill container** property not only to the outer frame but to one of its inner elements (or their group/inner frame). This allows the nested element to be flexible and stretch to the width and/or height of the parent frame. In the following figure, you can see the behavior of the **Fill container** property compared to **Hug contents** in both the horizontal and vertical axes:

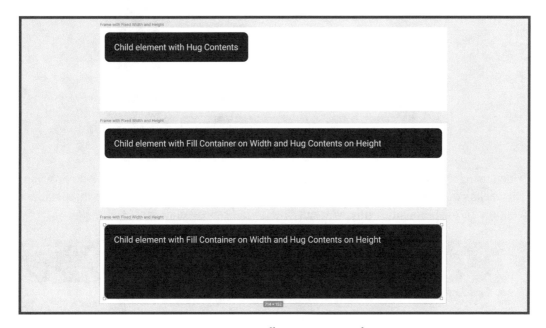

Figure 6.11 – A Fill container example

Among the many Figma features you've seen so far, auto layout is the most complex one, and there is only one way to fully master it – a lot of practice. It will be even more effective if you can combine what you have already learned to find out how different tools can work together and impact one another. For example, try nesting multiple auto layout frames and applying a specific behavior to each one, or set different **Resizing** properties for the elements in the group – one can be flexible in size and the other fixed. Remember that experimenting with the tools is extremely important because it is the only way to get the most out of them.

Differences with constraints

You've seen how auto layout allows you to change the outer frame based on the elements it contains, but is there a reverse way? Is it possible to resize the inner content by increasing or decreasing the size of the outer frame? You can get the answer with **Constraints**.

To better understand what constraints are, let's create a frame, this time without auto layout, and insert any type of element inside it. After you select the inserted element, the **Constraints** section appears in the right sidebar instead of **Resizing**:

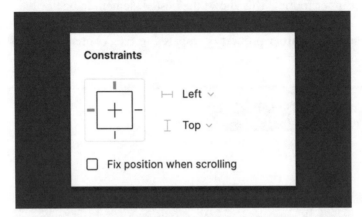

Figure 6.12 – The Constraints section

When using a constraint, you are essentially locking the inner object at a specific position. This means that when the outer frame is resized, the element inside will keep its absolute position. In the following figure, you can see a visual representation:

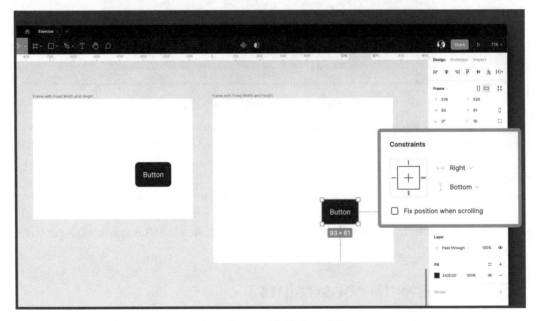

Figure 6.13 – Resizing a frame with Right and Bottom constraints

This way, you can choose whether to block the element vertically or horizontally, on one side only, on both sides, or in the center. If you deactivate all the constraints instead, the default behavior will be **Scale**, which means that the inner element will be scaled the same way as the outer frame.

Last but not least, in the **Constraints** section on the right sidebar, you can activate the **Fix position when scrolling** checkbox. You may need it if the frame cannot completely fit the device screen, but you want this element to always be visible. Therefore, when you scroll this frame in the prototyping window, your element remains fixed.

Now we know enough about auto layout, resizing, and constraints to get started on the interface of our application and structure the elements in the best possible way. You'll do this in the next section, but you will also have the opportunity to practice these functions more in *Chapter 8, User Interface Design on Tablet, Desktop, and the Web.*

Applying auto layout to our interface

In this section, you will apply the functions you have learned in this chapter to a couple of screens in our interface. As always, you will be guided by step-by-step instructions, but try not only to follow them but also to understand and analyze what actions each of your operations cause. In this part of the chapter, you will work with the **Hi-Fi** page and learn the best practices for auto layout. Without further ado, let's get straight to it and apply auto layout to your interface!

Shaping a button

For now, all you can see on the **Hi-Fi** page in your project file are four wireframed views. As you might have guessed, this page will contain the actual layouts, and this is the one that will be delivered for further development. So, here you have to be very focused and make the best of what you have learned, and also organize your layers well for yourself and developers. But don't worry – you will start working on your layout by creating the simplest elements that will allow you to summarize what you have learned so far. Basically, you will replace placeholder elements with ones that you will be final. Usually, the order of building an interface is from top to bottom, but this time, you will start with the smallest parts so that you can create an incredibly modular layout, especially when using the components that you will explore in the next chapter.

Let's start with the **Login** page first and create a **Login** button. To do this, follow these simple steps:

1. Make sure you are on the **Hi-Fi** file page. Since you are going to fill the frame with new elements and want to keep a visual reference of them, select all the elements of the **Login** frame and move them aside to the left:

Figure 6.14 – Preparing a blank frame on the Hi-Fi page

Note

To make the illustrations more readable, the layout grids will be hidden on them. However, for real work, it's a good practice to always keep them active in your layouts, especially in the initial stages when you have to be very accurate. You can turn off grids from time to time to see your progress better.

---

2. Select the **Login** frame and apply your first color style to it. To do that, go to the **Fill** section, click the **Style** icon, and select the previously created **Background color** option. Remember that you can quickly check the color names by hovering them over the panel for a few seconds. You can also change the view mode by clicking the **Show as list** icon next to the **Color Styles** dialog header so that the color appears in the list along with their names.

3. Create a new text layer by clicking anywhere inside the **Login** frame and enter Login.

4. This text has default properties, so you need to apply the style you created earlier for the texts. To do this, select this text layer, click the **Style** icon next to the **Text** section, and select **Medium Title / 24 Px / Bold**. Then, apply a color style to it of **Pure White**. The result should look like this:

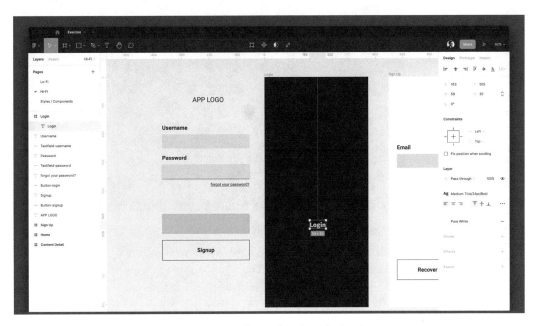

Figure 6.15 – A text layer placed on the Login page

It's time to create a real button. To do this, you can hypothetically draw a rectangle under the text, as you did in the wireframe, but there is a much better and simpler way – create a new frame and nest the text inside it, as explained in the following steps:

1. Right-click the text layer and choose **Frame selection** to quickly wrap the text in a new frame. Rename this frame layer `Button / Primary / Default` (you will learn more about this naming convention in the next chapter):

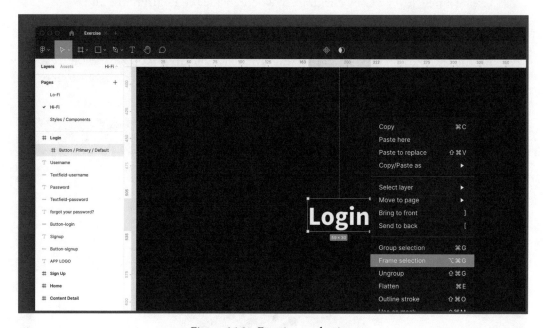

Figure 6.16 – Framing a selection

2. Select this new button frame and add the auto layout to it by clicking the + button next to the auto layout section heading. Then, add some padding so that the text stays exactly in the middle of the frame. To do this, click the **Padding around items** value (the universal one) and enter `16` (remember that we are working with a grid in multiples of 8). Lastly, click on the **Alignment and padding** interactive area and set the alignment to **Center**.

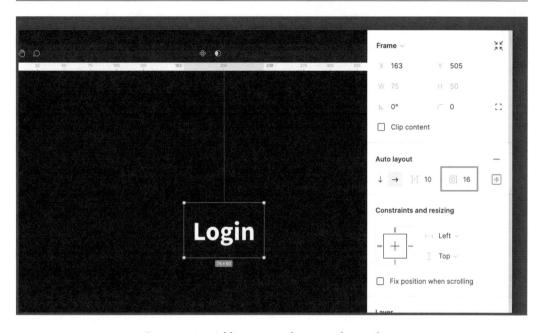

Figure 6.17 – Adding an auto layout to the text layer

3. Now, apply a **Fill** style to the button to make it visible. Since this will be the primary user action in this view, let's use an **Accent** color.

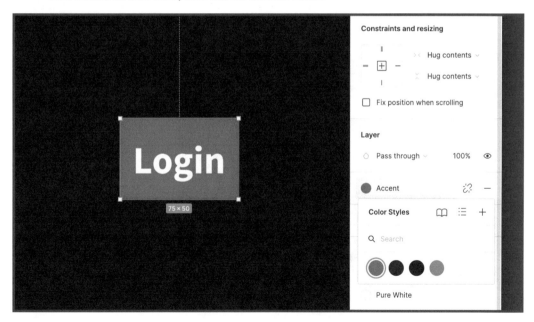

Figure 6.18 – Applying a previously created color style

> **Note**
>
> There is also a faster way to create your button! Select the element, then press *Shift + A*, and a new auto layout frame will automatically be created around it. By default, it will also have a 10px padding all around. This is a great way to save time when working on complex projects with multiple elements, and we'll use this a lot from now on.

What you have been doing so far has not been difficult, has it? And with time and practice, it will become even easier for you! You now have the perfect **Login** button, so let's go a little further and work on a secondary action button, which is **Sign Up**. This time, you won't just repeat all the previous steps to create it; there is another quick and easy way:

1. Select the **Login** button frame you just created.

2. Press *Shift + A* on your keyboard to quickly wrap the button in another auto layout frame.

3. Rename this new outer frame `Button Group` in the **Layers** panel.

4. Make sure the direction in the new auto layout frame is **Vertical** and set the **Spacing between items** value within the **Auto layout** properties to **16**.

5. Now comes the fun part. Select the **Button / Primary / Default** layer and press *Command + D* (macOS) or *Ctrl + D* (Win).

The result should look like this:

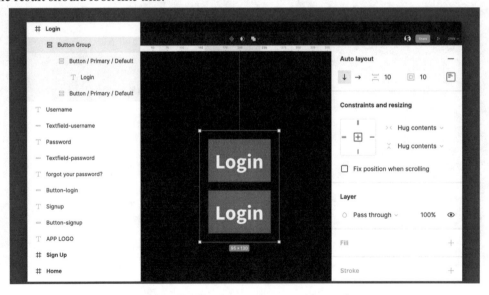

Figure 6.19 – Duplicating an element with auto layout

As you can see, auto layout helps you get the job done so quickly with minimal effort! There are just a few more steps left to do before the button is finally ready:

1. Select the bottom button and rename it `Button / Secondary / Default` in the **Layers** panel.

2. Now, change the text in the new button – by double-clicking it – to `Sign Up`. Note how the wrapper frame automatically adapts based on what you type. This happens because of the default **Hug contents** option, and it is the real magic of auto layout.

3. With the **Sign Up** button selected, open the list of the color styles in the **Fill** section. Since this is a secondary action, choose the **Secondary** color style:

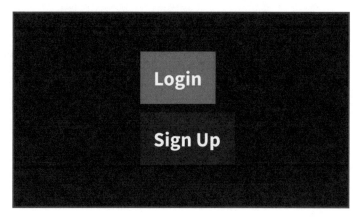

Figure 6.20 – The Sign Up button styled as a secondary button

Looks good enough already, doesn't it? You will take a few additional steps to make your layout even better:

1. Increase the size of the **Button Group** layer so that it is the same width as your outer frame:

Figure 6.21 – Resizing Button Group to fill the parent frame

2. You may notice that your design doesn't fit the layout grid. Let's solve this problem by changing the general padding of **Button Group** to **16px**.

3. Now, click on the **Alignment and padding** interactive area and set the alignment to **Center**. This way, the buttons are perfectly aligned to the center of the view:

Figure 6.22 – Aligning elements to the center

4. Select both **Button / Primary / Default** and **Button / Secondary / Default** and change their horizontal resizing options to **Fill container**. You should get this:

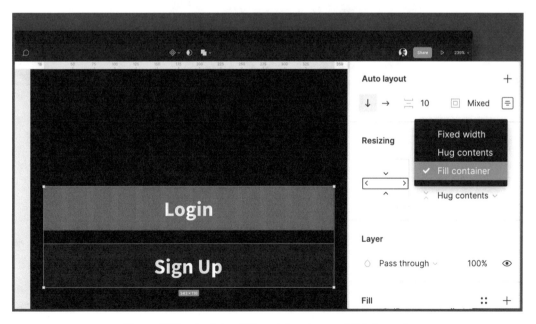

Figure 6.23 – Applying Fill container to our child elements

Great! The buttons look much better now! With the functions you have tried out so far, you we have created a piece of the interface with the ultimate precision in a short time. Moreover, what you have just created is a real modular block of elements, in which you can add, delete, and invert objects at any time without worrying about losing spacing, alignment, and size.

However, you have not yet practiced constraints. To understand the best use case for them, first, select a **Login** screen frame and try to manually enlarge it in width. Here's what you will see:

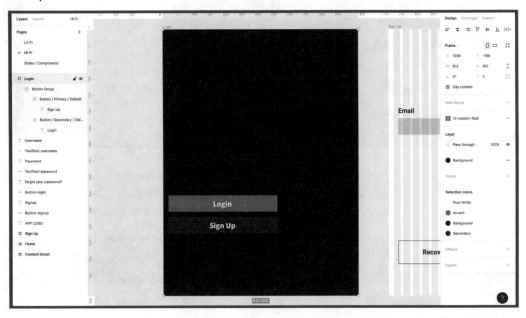

Figure 6.24 – Resizing the outer frame to reveal unexpected behavior

This is not what you expected, or at least not exactly what you want your layouts to be. This is about responsive design, and as mentioned earlier, you will explore this topic in more detail later in the book. Anyway, to fix the problem at this point, we can use the constraints feature:

1. Select the **Button Group** frame.

2. In the **Constraints and resizing** section on the right sidebar, change the horizontal behavior from **Left** to **Left and right**. Basically, this is how you tell Figma to anchor the elements on both sides and scale them proportionally. The result should now be more solid:

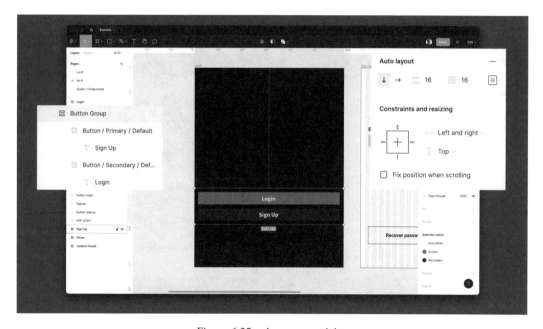

Figure 6.25 – A proper resizing

Now your design not only scales proportionally horizontally and looks nicer but also fits perfectly into the basic layout grid structure you created earlier. Be aware that you still don't need to resize your frame's width – we'll do that in a later chapter – so before proceeding to the next section, bring back the previous **375px** width to your **Login** frame.

Completing the view

The first view of our application is starting to take on a finished look, but there are still some fundamental elements missing. In this section, you will replace the lo-fi text fields and labels with the elements of the actual design. The next steps will not be very difficult for you as they are more or less similar. So, let's move on to the final part of working on the interface of the first screen:

1. Create a new **Rectangular** shape vertically in the center of the interface. Make sure its height is **50px** (the width value is not important for now). Rename this layer `Text Field`.

2. Apply **Pure White** as the **Fill** style of the new element:

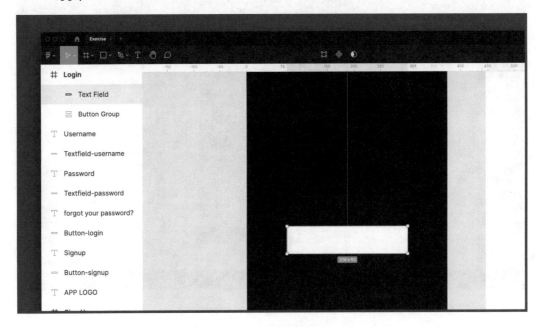

Figure 6.26 – Creating a text field

3. Create a new **Text** layer just above the text field and enter `Username`. Apply a **Pure White** color and a **Medium Heading/24px/Bold** text style to it.

4. Select both the text label and the text field, and then add an auto layout to this selection by clicking the + icon next to the **Auto layout** label on the right sidebar, or, more simply, using the *Shift + A* keyboard shortcut.

5. As a result, you should have a new frame containing both elements, which should be left-aligned by default. Rename this new frame `Form Element`.

6. Set **Spacing between items** with the corresponding auto layout property to **8**:

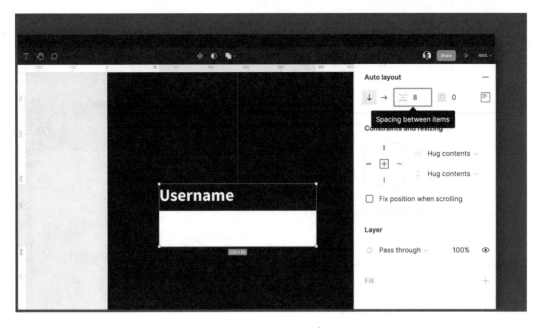

Figure 6.27 – Adding a text label

7. Now, wrap the **Form Element** layer in another auto layout frame. This will again create a new frame around the selection, and you will soon see why this is relevant.

8. Rename this new frame Form (since this will be our parent form container) and change its global padding to **16** to fit your layout grid:

Figure 6.28 – Structuring our form element

9. Select the **Form Element** layer, set its width to **375px** and change its horizontal resizing property to **Fill container** instead of **Hug contents**.

10. Now, select the **Text Field** layer and change its horizontal resizing property to **Fill container** instead of **Fixed width**:

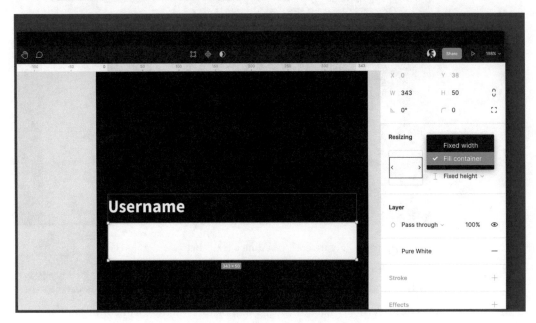

Figure 6.29 – Applying Fill container to the child elements

The first of your text fields is ready, and now it's time to create the second. Since you've used auto layout correctly, the following step will be incredibly simple:

1. Select the **Form Element** layer and duplicate it by pressing *Command + D* (macOS) or *Ctrl + D* (Windows).

2. Double-click the **Username** label in the lower field and replace it with Password.

3. Select the **Form** layer and change its **Spacing between items** property to **32** to create a proper spacing between all the form fields.

4. Move the **Form** layer up a bit so that it does not overlap **Button Group**. To do this, you can change the **Y** value on the right sidebar, setting it to about **180px**. The following figure shows the end result of these operations:

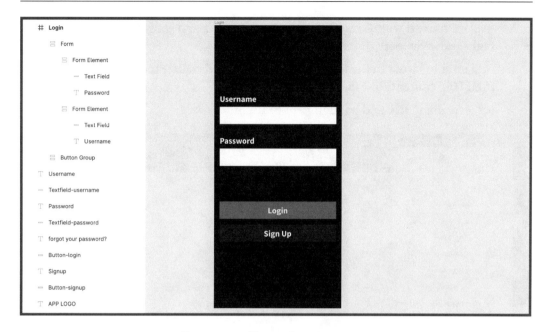

Figure 6.30 – The resulting Login view

5.   Don't forget to add the **Left and right** constraint to the **Form** layer so that it will quickly adapt to any resizing of the outer frame.

So, how easy was that? Of course, this is not the limit of all the capabilities of Figma, but you can already see how advanced features can speed up your design process. Using auto layout is, of course, optional but still highly recommended, as the result will be easily editable and scalable. It is also handy for code because all the auto layout frames in your files will automatically be converted to flexbox items for web development.

Adding the **Forgot your password?** label will be the last task for now to complete the **Login** page. It seems very simple at first, but it's actually more complicated than you expect. Anyway, this is a great occasion for you to discover new auto layout properties, as this element will be right-aligned text in the left-aligned auto layout container. To create this interface element, follow these steps:

1.   Select the **Password** text layer in **Form Element** and duplicate it.

2.   Click the duplicated text layer and move it below using the *Down* key, or drag with your mouse.

3. Replace the text with `Forgot your password?` and apply the **Caption / 16px / Light** text style to it.

4. Add an auto layout frame to this new text layer and change the horizontal resizing from **Hug contents** to **Fill container**.

5. Set its padding to **0** and its alignment to **Right**:

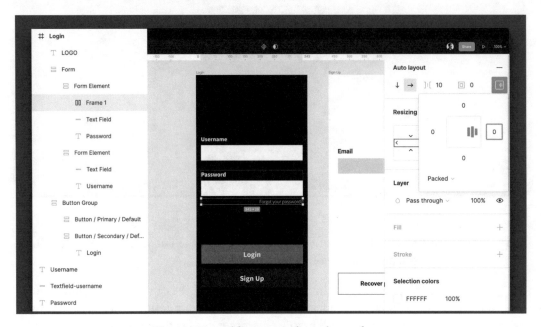

Figure 6.31 – Adding a nested auto layout frame

Nesting auto layout frames may seem tricky at first, but it can help you create complex interfaces in a very short time with exceptional precision.

The view is almost done, and all you need to do now is just polish it up a bit to achieve a more convincing visual result. So, what can you do to accomplish this? Well, it might be a good idea to add a logo at the top of the page and tweak the vertical spacing of the elements. Also, if the text labels seem too large, you can create a new text style on the **Styles / Components** page, just as you did in the previous chapter. For example, you can go with **Bold Label / 20px / Bold**, as shown here:

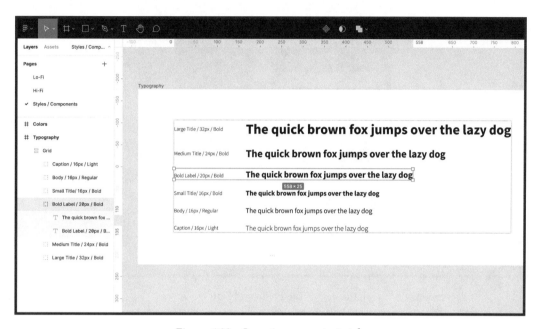

Figure 6.32 – Inserting a new text style

Feel free to experiment with your first interface to practice your skills better. Before moving on to the next chapter, try converting the **Sign Up** page from lo-fi to hi-fi, which shouldn't be much different from what you just achieved. Your final result should be something like this:

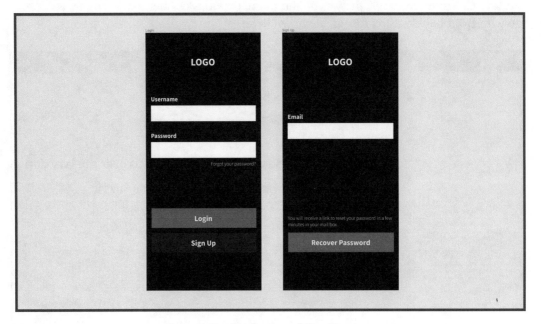

Figure 6.33 – The Login and Sign Up views

Summary

As stated earlier, the topic of this chapter is quite complex, and the Figma features presented here can be considered advanced. But you've successfully overcome this challenge, and now you know what auto layout is and how it can take your design to a whole new level. You have also learned about two more incredible features – resizing and constraints. Proper use of all three of these makes any layout flexible, responsive, and highly structured. And that's exactly what you did in the hands-on part of this chapter by creating two views for our application – great job!

Obviously, all the other views will also be created using auto layout, so you will practice this function many more times throughout the book to discover even more incredible design options. The learning process will become even more effective if you experiment from time to time with different automatic layout properties and elements in drafts.

So, using auto layout, resizing, and constraints in your design makes it a lot easier and faster to create an interface. But what if there was another feature that could further improve our workflow? There is – Components (which has already been mentioned several times in this book)! Soon, this feature will no longer be a mystery to you, as you will learn all about it in the next chapter!

7

Building Components and Variants in a Collaborative Workspace

You are now right in the middle of your Figma journey, where you are facing the most difficult but exciting challenges. You've already used advanced features such as styles and auto layout, and even successfully applied them to your project's design. Remember that mastering Figma, as with any other design tool, means not only knowing its functions but also having a deep understanding of the purpose of its use. So, it's better to think first, analyze the created wireframe, and then move on to building the interface elements.

In this chapter, we'll discover components – a fairly common feature for modern design tools, but Figma has gone to a really big effort to deliver them elegantly and smartly. Components are great, but when combined with the other features you've learned, they make it possible to create something extremely powerful. From now on, you will be practicing a lot, and you will create components in the best possible way by using auto layout and styles together! Plus, you'll learn about the collaboration, sharing, and auto-save features in Figma. Get ready – this chapter is as interesting as it is intense!

In this chapter, we are going to cover the following main topics:

- Creating and organizing components

- Extending components with variants

- Multiplayer mode, libraries, and version control

Creating and organizing components

Your journey started with basic shapes and tools, and then moved on to more advanced features such as **Layout grids**, **Styles**, and **Auto layout** that you need to know, as they all make your design much better. At the same level, there are **Components**, a quite common feature for design tools (the name of this function can be different – for example, in Sketch, it's called Symbols), as it is truly indispensable.

In this first section of this chapter, components in Figma will no longer be a mystery to you and you will learn mostly by using them directly in your project! So, open up Figma, and let's get started!

What are components?

Understanding components will be easy for us, since we already know the principles of styles from *Chapter 5, Designing Consistently Using Grids, Colors, and Typography*. Using styles, you set uniform property rules for the elements of our design, namely colors, text styles, and effects, that then you could easily implement anywhere in your interface. From here on in, editing a style will change every instance of it in the product you create.

Components are based on the same concept, but instead of object properties, as with styles, they include the object itself. This means that you can transform any element – from a simple shape or button to a complex layout – and reuse it in your designs as many times as you need.

To convert an element to a component, simply select it and use the *Command + Option + K* (macOS) or *Ctrl + Alt + K* (Windows) keyboard shortcut, or, alternatively, click on the **Create component** icon in the top bar of the interface:

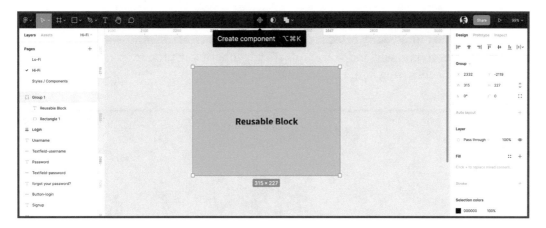

Figure 7.1 – Creating a component

Once you do this, your element becomes what is called the main component – the source of truth, or key element, that will dictate instructions to all of its instances. The main component can be identified by the **Component** icon (the four-diamond-shaped icon) that appears next to the object name, both on the canvas and in the **Layers** panel. Moreover, if you switch from **Layers** to **Assets** in the left-hand side panel, you will see the component that you just created in the library:

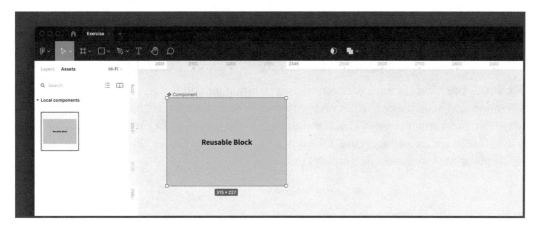

Figure 7.2 – The Assets panel

> **Note**
>
> Unlike Sketch, Figma doesn't automatically move a component to a separate dedicated page but instead leaves it where it was created, and from now on, it's up to you to decide where it should be stored.

You can reuse your component as many times as you like by dragging and dropping it from the library into your workspace. All the elements created in this way will be instances of the component and will automatically inherit any properties of the main component. The following figure shows an example of a main component and its three instances:

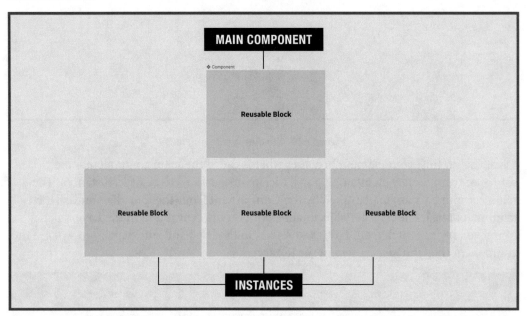

Figure 7.3 – The main component and its instances

So, what's the big difference between a main component and instances? It's very simple. A component acts as a parent for all the instances created from it. Thus, if you change something in a main component, these changes will be applied in the same way to all its instances. In the following figure, the color of the main component has been changed, so all instances inherited this property automatically:

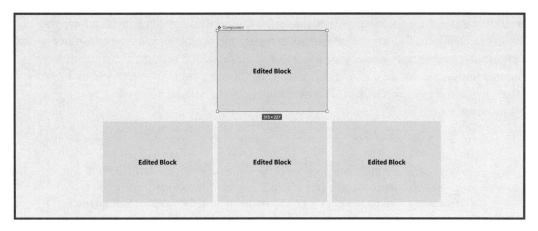

Figure 7.4 – Editing the main component

As you can see in this example, all objects are now blue. However, if you do the opposite and change any property of an individual instance, those changes will be applied exclusively to that instance, without affecting the others and the main component itself:

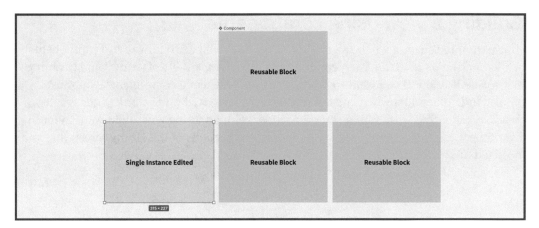

Figure 7.5 – Editing a single instance

And this is precisely the great potential and flexibility of components, which have the ability to change each instance of an element with one click. Note that after you overwrite an instance property, that specific property will no longer be modified through the main component. For example, if you change a color, the color property will no longer change based on the parent, but all other properties will still be controlled by the main component.

> **Note**
>
> You can create multiple components at the same time; just select all the items you want to convert to components and select the **Create multiple components** option after clicking the dropdown near the **Create component** icon on the top bar.

Now that you know the basics of components and instances and how they relate to each other, it's time to try it all out and see how you can optimize and improve your workflow using this powerful feature!

Building a view using components

This part of the chapter will be all about practice; you will learn how to use components while working on the **Home** screen **Hi-Fi** layout – the main interface of your streaming service application. If you want to create your interface using components, you must think a little differently when creating individual views. It's best to think of the whole process as building blocks and create components for anything you might want to reuse over time. Let's take a quick look at the highlighted sections of the **Home** screen that you need to build:

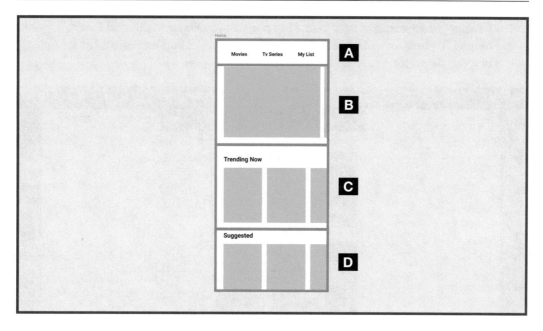

Figure 7.6 – Our Home view structure

Before you start, it is very important to deeply think about how best to optimize our work before creating elements, styles, and components. Here, it is better not to rush and to make an extra effort to analyze so that you will not regret making hasty decisions.

The first thing to do is to remove all elements from the **Home** view. It is up to you whether to delete everything, and refer to the corresponding **Lo-Fi** page from time to time when necessary, or duplicate the view and keep it nearby to have a permanent visual reference. Then, follow these steps:

1. Select the outer frame of the **Home** view and enable **Auto layout**. Make sure it has a vertical direction.

2. From the **Color Styles** library, set the frame **Fill** color to **Background**.

3. In the **Alignment and Padding** options, set the horizontal values to **16** and the vertical values to **0** to match your layout grid.

4. Change the **Resizing** option from **Hug contents** to **Fixed width** and **Fixed height**. This ensures that the frame size never changes and represents the screen of a real device:

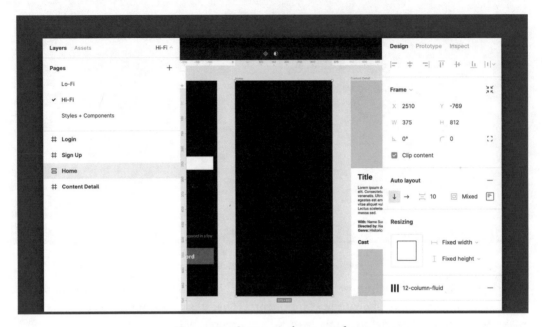

Figure 7.7 – Setting up the parent frame

> **Note**
>
> You can also duplicate any element in the auto layout frame by selecting it and pressing *Command + D* (macOS) or *Ctrl + D* (Windows). The new element will be placed right next to its original one.

Great! Now that the parent frame is ready to go, you are ready to create the first section!

A – the top navigation menu

Now, you might think that the easiest way is to just paste in your text, apply styles, and voilà! However, you always need to look one step further, and since these elements will be made dynamic, certain rules will have to apply to each of them. For example, one tab on the navigation bar will be active, while others will remain off, and so on. Wouldn't it be more convenient if all these rules and future interactions were applied only once? There are components for that, so let's implement our very first ones in our interface design! To do so, follow these steps:

1. Go to the **Styles + Components** page and create a new frame that will contain all the components of the navigation elements. Rename it `Navigation`.

2. Since the interface of your app is mostly dark in color, you can set the **Navigation** frame's fill to the **Background** color style to represent the background of the views. This will make it easier to create and preview the elements that you will be using.

3. Create a new text layer in the **Navigation** frame and enter `Item` (this will be your text placeholder). Apply **Small Title/16px/Bold** as the text style and **Pure White** as the fill style:

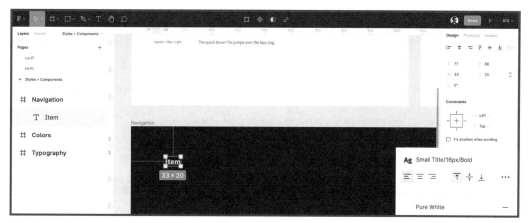

Figure 7.8 – Creating your first menu item

4. Wrap this text layer in an **Auto layout** frame using the *Shift + A* keyboard shortcut. Set its **Padding around items** value to **16** and rename it `Menu Item`. The padding is critical here as it will also be the interactive element area.

5. Now, select **Menu Item** and click the **Create component** icon in the top bar, or use the *Command + Option + K* (macOS) / *Ctrl + Alt + K* (Windows) keyboard shortcut.

Great! Your first component is done, and you can check it yourself by going to the **Assets** tab:

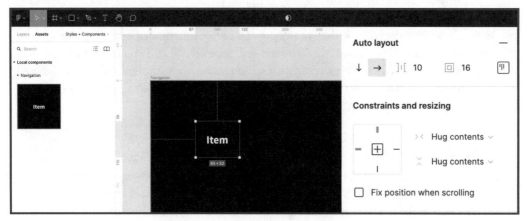

Figure 7.9 – Your menu item component

Now is the time to try this component in a real interface. Go back to the **Hi-Fi** page, and then simply drag yourmenu item from the **Assets** panel three times into the **Home** page frame. You can also drag it just once and then duplicate it the way you learned, and the result will be exactly the same.

> **Note**
>
> An easier way to access your **Components** library is with the *Shift + I* keyboard shortcut. This will immediately open up a dialog window containing all of your components, so you can quickly add them to the canvas.

At this point, your **Home** page should look like the following figure:

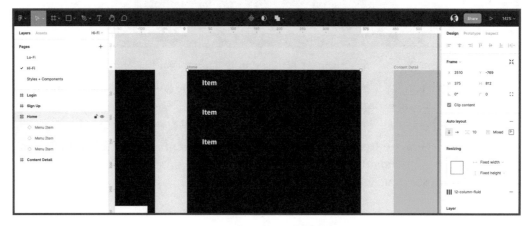

Figure 7.10 – Inserting multiple instances

To complete the design of the top navigation menu, follow these steps:

1. Select all three **Menu Item** layers you just added and combine them into an **Auto layout** frame with *Shift + A*. Rename it `Top Navigation`.

2. Set the frame direction to horizontal.

3. In the **Alignment and padding** section, set the **Top** padding to **32** and the **Bottom** padding to **0**, **Left** and **Right** to **0**, and **Alignment** to **Center** by clicking on it in the visual grid.

4. Set the **Resizing** horizontal option to **Fill container**.

5. Finally, change the text in the text layers of each component instance to `Movies`, `TV Series`, and `My List` in order from left to right:

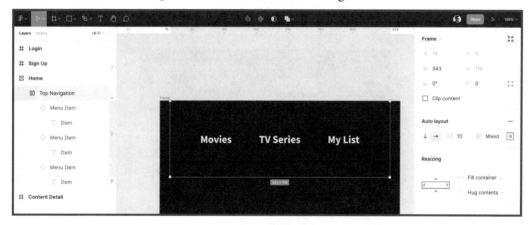

Figure 7.11 – The top navigation menu

The top navigation menu is complete and looks great. Take a moment to think about what you have just achieved and how clean, editable, and scalable your complex layer is thanks to the combination of components and auto layout. Without these tools and features, you would have spent a lot more time and effort to achieve the same result.

B – the main carousel

The second block will be the main content carousel that shows featured videos in your application. Go back to the **Styles + Components** page and create a new frame; this time, rename it `Cards` and fill it with the **Background** color style as you did earlier. This frame will store all of the card elements of your layout. When you're done, follow these steps:

1. In the created **Cards** frame, insert another frame (*F*) with a size of **300 px** (width) x **200 px** (height).

2. Enable **Auto layout** to it and change its **Padding around items** value to **16**.

3. Enable **Fill** to this frame and change the type from **Solid** to **Image**:

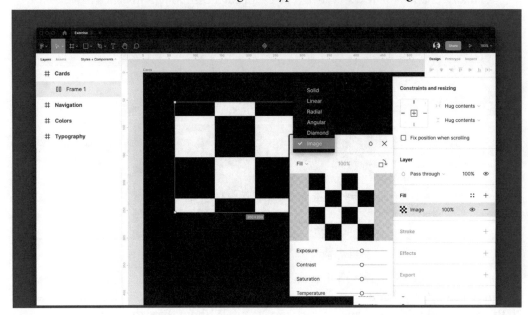

Figure 7.12 – Inserting an image for a card element

4. Drag and drop an image into the preview area in the **Image** panel. You can choose any image that resembles a movie poster. You can easily find something like this on the `unsplash.com` website, which has many free images for both personal and commercial use.

5. Make sure you give the newly created frame a clear name, such as `Carousel item`.

6. Set the **Corner radius** value of your carousel item to **8** px. The frame should now look like the following figure:

Figure 7.13 – Adding the corner radius to the element
(photo by Michael Oeser on Unsplash)

It is clear that the images can be different and the video titles will be placed on the bottom of them, so it may happen that the text is difficult to read on a light background. To prevent this, you need to add a second **Fill** layer at the bottom of the image, with an opaque black gradient. If you set the fill correctly, it will have sufficient contrast with the text so that the title will always be visible. You can apply as many fills, strokes, and effects as you like to the same layer. Here's how to do it:

1. Click on the + icon next to the **Fill** label. This will create a second **Fill** overlay, with a default opacity of **20%**. Change it to **60%**.

2. Click on the fill you've just added and change the type from **Solid** to **Linear**. Then, edit the gradient points, as shown in the following figure:

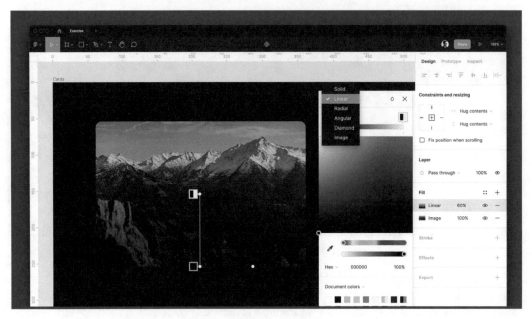

Figure 7.14 – Adding a Linear gradient for text readability

This way, the bottom half of any image will be slightly darker. Let's add a title to the card and see how it looks on your image.

3. Change the carousel item **Resizing** option to **Fixed** both vertically and horizontally. This will ensure that its size will be not automatically adapted to the text you are about to add.

4. Add a **Text** layer in the carousel item frame, enter Movie Title as a placeholder, and then apply a **Small Title/16px/Bold** text style and **Pure White** as a fill to it.

5. In the **Alignment and Padding** panel, change the **Padding** value to **16** px on every side and set the **Alignment** to the bottom-left, as shown in the following figure:

Figure 7.15 – Alignment and Padding options

6. Select the carousel item and click the **Create component** icon to add it to yourlibrary and make it reusable.

Just like earlier, your component now appears in **Assets** (note that it takes the layer name and automatically adds a parent folder with the name from the canvas that contains it). It's now ready to be inserted into the **Home** screen, so head back to the **Hi-Fi** page and follow these steps:

1. Select the **Home** frame so that the component will be already inserted into the right spot, as the lower item of the stack.

2. Through the **Assets** tab, drag the carousel item into the stack, or add it from the **Library** dialog using the *Shift + I* keyboard shortcut.

3. Change the horizontal **Resizing** option to **Fill container**.

4. Wrap your carousel item in an auto layout frame by selecting it and pressing *Shift + A*; then rename it `Carousel`.

5. Change the **Carousel** direction to horizontal, set the **Spacing between items** value to **16** and **Padding** to **0** at the top, left, and bottom, and to **16** on the **Right**. This way, your stack will have some distance from the edge of the screen, which will remain even when scrolling.

6. Select the inner carousel item and duplicate it twice with the *Command + D* (macOS) or *Ctrl + D* (Windows) keyboard shortcut:

Figure 7.16 – Inserting multiple carousel item instances

7. Fill them with different images and set each title accordingly.

The duplicate elements in your carousel are now out of view, but don't worry – it is absolutely normal. These cards will only be visible to you in prototyping mode when you simulate a real horizontal scrolling carousel. If you are having trouble editing these hidden elements, simply select the appropriate one in the **Layers** panel and change the images and text directly from there. Later in the chapter, you will learn about the **Clip content** function, which makes it easier to edit elements that are placed outside of their parent frames.

C – content cards

As you can see, it is incredibly easy to structure your content cards, as until now, there has been nothing very different from what you have done before. According to the application wireframe, the top stack of cards is dedicated to featured videos, so their previews should be larger. Now, let's go ahead and work on another type of card that will be smaller and contain elements within that will be structured differently. This means that you need to create a new component for this card, but it will still be placed in your **Cards** frame. So, let's now go back to the **Styles + Components** page and follow these steps:

1. Create a **120** px (width) x **140** px (height) rectangle and rename the layer Poster Image.

2. Set the **Fill** type to **Image**. You can leave the default black and white checkerboard background for it, since you will customize it in each instance of the component individually.

3. Use the *Shift + A* keyboard shortcut to wrap the shape in an **Auto layout** frame. Name it Content Card and change the **Padding around items** value to **0**:

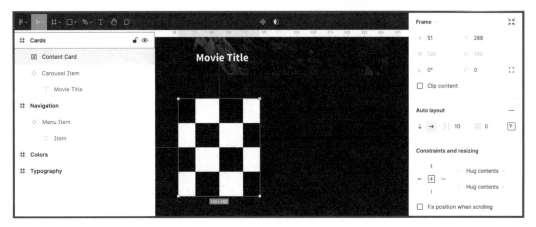

Figure 7.17 – The Content Card element

4. Change the **Auto layout** direction to vertical, since the title and subtitle will be placed below the image.

5. Add a first **Text** layer in the **Content Card** frame below the image and enter Content Title. Apply **Small Title/16px/Bold** as a text style and **Pure White** as a fill style.

6. In the **Content Card** frame, add a second **Text** layer below the content title and enter Content Subtitle. Apply **Body/16px/Regular** as a text style and an **Inactive** color as a fill style.

At this point, it would be great to use the auto layout **Spacing between items** option to set the appropriate hierarchical spacing between your elements. But this option will simply allow you to set the spacing between EVERY item, and this is not the best option when you want to visually group some elements and separate them from the others. In the following figure, you can see how the card will look if you use the **Spacing between items** option for the entire auto layout frame:

Figure 7.18 – Spacing between items

The space between the image and the title looks good, but the title and the subtitle are now placed too far from each other. To fix this, all you have to do is merge the title and subtitle in an inner auto layout frame by selecting both of them and pressing *Shift + A*, and then rename it `Title + Subtitle`. From now on, you can still change the spacing in the outer frame, but it will not affect the inner frame, which will have its own spacing parameters. With the right hierarchy, it looks better, doesn't it? To achieve this result, set the **Spacing between items** value to **16** for the outer auto layout frame and **8** for the inner one. The card is almost done; there are only a few steps left to complete it:

1. Set the internal **Title + Subtitle** frame horizontal **Resizing** option to **Fill container**.

2. Select all the inner elements of the card – the image, the title, and the subtitle – and then set the horizontal **Resizing** option to **Fill container**.

Setting the **Fill Container** option ensures that the card will still look nice when resized. What's more, if the actual title and subtitle text are longer than the placeholder, the card layout won't fall apart, as you can see in the following figure:

Figure 7.19 – Testing out the structure with a longer placeholder text

Great! The **Card** layer is ready, and it's time to convert it to a new component by selecting it and clicking the **Create component** icon at the top center. If done correctly, all the layers inside this component will turn purple, and a **Component** icon will appear right next to the **Content Card** frame on the canvas, as well as in the **Layers** panel. Again, you can see the new component in our **Assets** library, in the Cards folder.

Since the content cards will be presented as a sliding row, you can simply drag multiple instances of the new component into one frame and place them horizontally in your **Home** view. However, this wouldn't be a good practice, since the entire sliding navigation block can be used multiple times to create different media sections, and it would take too long to create it from scratch every time. Moreover, it would be difficult to change all the carousels if something needed to be changed in the design. Don't worry – there is a way to prevent these risks and minimize overload – a nested component!

D – repeated rows

Let's take a look at how you can optimize your work even better by taking full advantage of the component's capabilities. For now, stay in the **Cards** frame on the **Styles + Components** page and do the following:

1. Drag a **Content Card** instance from **Assets** and drop it somewhere inside the **Cards** frame:

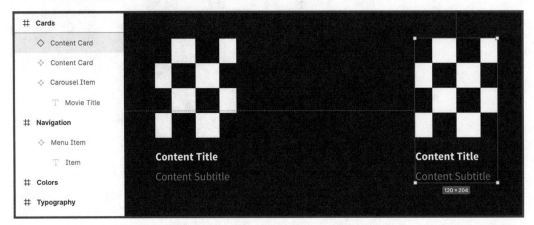

Figure 7.20 – Duplicating our component to create an instance

Note that the main components and their instances have different icons next to the layer names in the **Layers** panel. You are now going to work on the instances only without touching the original **Content Card** component.

2. Select an instance and wrap it in an auto layout frame using the *Shift + A* keyboard shortcut.

3. Rename this new frame `Cards Row`, and set **Padding around items** to **0** and **Spacing between items** to **16**. Make sure that the auto layout frame direction is horizontal.

4. Select the **Content Card** instance within the frame again and duplicate it by pressing *Command + D* (macOS) or *Ctrl + D* (Windows). Repeat this action three times. You should now have the same result as shown in the following figure:

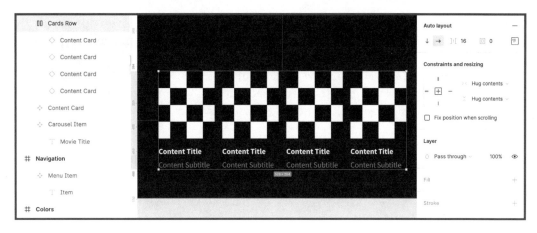

Figure 7.21 – Cards Row

5. Select **Cards Row** and press *Shift + A* again to place it in the auto layout frame. Rename this new outer frame `Cards Section`.

6. Set its **Padding around items** value to **0**, direction to vertical, and **Spacing between items** to **32**.

7. Add a **Text** layer on top of **Cards Section** and enter `Section Title`. Apply medium **Title/24px/Bold** properties as the text style and **Pure White** as the fill style:

Figure 7.22 – Structuring the section

Great job! Now, you are going to create your first nested component. To do this, simply select the **Cards Section** frame and click on the **Create Component** icon button. Done! From now on, you can modify the single **Content Card** component, which will affect all the instances in the **Cards Section** row as well, but you can also easily edit the structure of the complete section by editing the **Cards Section** component. To implement this new element into your design, go back to the **Hi-Fi** page and follow these steps:

1. Drag and drop from **Assets** (or use the *Shift + I* shortcut to quickly open the **Library** window) your **Cards Section** component instance right below the carousel in the **Home** view.

2. Repeat the first step (or just duplicate the first element) to create a second row of cards under the first one.

3. Select the outer **Home** screen frame and change **Spacing between items** to **32** to evenly space each element in your view.

4. Customize each title, subtitle, and image. We can follow the example in the following figure:

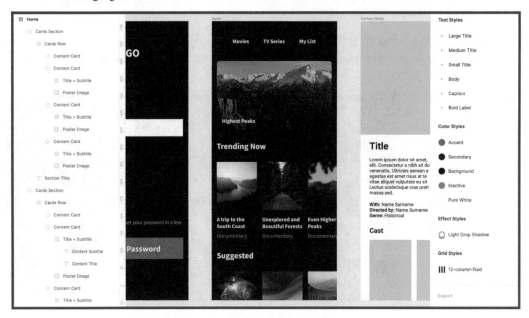

Figure 7.23 – Our finished Home view
(Photos by Kristaps Ungurs, Zachary Delorenzo, Perry Kibler, Daniel J. Schwarz, Tasos Mansour, and Daniel Sessler on Unsplash)

The **Home** view now looks complete. Moreover, this view is modular and flexible, so if you need to change something on this screen, it will be very easy to do so through the main components, even if they are crucial changes. Also, if you select any component's instance in the frame, you will discover many new features, as you can see in the following figure:

Figure 7.24 – The component's options

Let's take a closer look at the actions in the right panel that you can now do with any instance in your design:

- First, if you click on the instance name in the panel, a dropdown will appear with all the components in your library, allowing you to swap that selected instance with any other component.

- To the right of the instance name, you can see the **Component** icon, and after clicking on it, you will be taken directly to the page where the main component is located (for example, our **Styles + Components** page).

- The three-dot (**…**) **More** icon contains all the other manipulations you can do with your instances. **Detach instance** is a critical action that disconnects the selected instance from the main component, and from then on, this instance becomes a regular frame. The **Push overrides to main component** action allows you to quickly update the main component with the changes made to the selected instance. The last option, **Reset all overrides**, return the instance to its original state, resembling its main component parent. This function can be useful if, for example, your instance behaves in an odd or undesirable way after editing and you cannot determine the exact reason. Note that if you change the width and/or height of any instance, a new option will appear, **Reset size**, which allows you to reset the size of the instance as its source of truth but not any other edit you may have done.

This section of the chapter was your first and very important step in mastering components. You learned what components are, why and when to use them, and how the main component and its instances affect each other. You have created several components for the **Top Navigation**, **Main Carousel**, **Content Cards**, and **Repeated Rows** blocks of the application's **Home** view. Finally, you've explored the additional functionalities that Figma allows you to apply to instances. This is a really big step! And of course, it's completely okay if you're feeling overwhelmed by all this new information, so don't rush to the next section – try playing a little bit more with the components in your drafts. You can create some of them from scratch, from simple to nested ones, and then experiment with their instances as you want.

In the next section, you will learn even more about components and, of course, immediately try out this feature to improve your design.

Extending components with variants

As you've seen, components are incredibly powerful, especially when they are nested or combined with other features such as styles. However, they can do even more to improve your design and make your workflow more efficient. At this point, you have created a few components, and they were quite easy to implement in your layouts. But when you are working on a more complex project or creating an entire design system, the number of components immediately begins to grow very fast. This means that your **Assets** library will be full of similar components, and it will be very difficult for you to navigate them. To solve this problem, Figma has another great feature called **Variants**. In this section, you will learn everything about this amazing function by implementing it in our app design!

Why use variants?

You can think of variants as a set of components that share similar properties and are used for the same purpose. Usually, all the components in this set differ from each other only in small details, and grouping them reduces the complexity of our **Assets** library and makes it flexible and easy to navigate. However, it is important to know that not all components need to have their own variants, because in some cases, it is right to avoid combining things that simply do not work together.

To better understand the concept of variants, let's look at a case when it is appropriate to use them. A common practice for using variants is a button component, as it is a design element that has many types and states, all of which need to be presented in your design. So, since this is such a convenient case, you will learn about variants by creating them for the button component, but first, you need to build a **Content Detail** page, using a few new tricks.

Setting up our Content Detail view

Before getting to know variants, let's set up a new view to take advantage of our new feature. As with all the other views you have built on your Hi-Fi page, the first thing you need to do is empty the **Content Detail** frame by moving all the wireframe elements to the side, or deleting them. Next, you are going to customize the view by following these steps:

1. Select the **Content Detail** frame and enable **Auto layout**.

2. Set **Direction** to vertical.

3. Set **Spacing between items** to **0**.

4. Set **Padding around items** to **0**.

5. Set the horizontal and vertical **Resizing** options to **Fixed width** and **Fixed height** respectively.

Great! Now the parent frame is ready to position the inner elements in a better and more flexible way. Make sure your settings match those shown in the following figure:

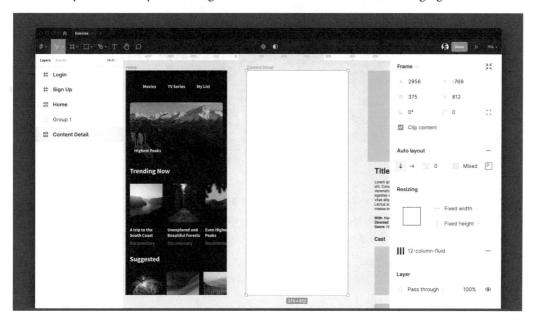

Figure 7.25 – Preparing our Content Detail parent frame

> **Note**
>
> If you prefer to leave the wireframe elements aside, it's best to group them all using the *Command + G* (macOS) or *Ctrl + G* (Windows) keyboard shortcut to keep your **Layers** panel as clean as possible.

The top elements of the **Content Detail** view are very similar in design to what you have done for the **Home** view, so this stage should be pretty clear to you. However, the points that differ will be explained in detail. Now, let's get the job done by following these steps:

1. Select the **Content Detail** frame and set its fill style to **Background**.

2. Create a **Rectangle** shape of **375** px (width) x **360** px (height) and rename it `Poster Image`. Set its horizontal **Resizing** property to **Fill Container**.

3. Change the **Poster Image Fill** style to **Image**. You can choose any image you like, but since there will be detailed information about one of the videos from the **Home** page, picking the same image that you previously used for the **Home** view will be more consistent. Your frame should now look something like the one shown in the following figure:

Figure 7.26 – Poster Image

You may have noticed that, in this particular case, you did not set the padding from the right and left edges of the parent frame, unlike what you did earlier to respect your layout grid. This is because the **Poster Image** element does not have side spacing but will fill the screen from edge to edge.

4. Now, let's create a new container for the elements that should fit the layout grid. Add a frame of any size right below the **Poster Image** element. Rename this layer `Container`.

5. Enable **Auto layout** on the **Container** frame. Set **Direction** to vertical, **Spacing between items** to **16**, **Padding around item** to **0** (top), **16** (right), **0** (bottom), and **16** (left), and the horizontal **Resizing** property to **Fill container**, as shown in the following figure:

Figure 7.27 – Preparing a container

At this point, you are going to try to complete the view in the same way as when working on the **Home** screen. Take this opportunity to practice what you have already learned, and for any difficulties, refer to *Chapter 6, Creating a Responsive Mobile Interface Using Auto Layout*, where you can find everything about the auto layout feature. The final **Content Detail** view should look like the following figure:

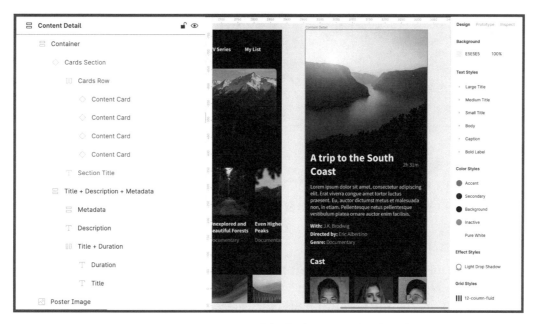

Figure 7.28 – An overview of the final Content Detail results

When exploring the figure, you can take a look at the layer structure to make sure you did everything right. Note that **Cards Section** was used as the basis for the **Cast** section. It is possible that getting the right result will be a challenging task, but with a lot of practice, attempts, and even mistakes, you will definitely succeed! In any case, you can always make your own small design changes or simplify the whole structure a little if you run into problems.

The content in your interface grows noticeably, and you will reach a point where the vertical space of the frame is almost filled, making it extremely difficult to add new elements to the view. It happens because the canvas automatically masks anything outside the parent frame, which is great for prototyping, but while you're working on a design, you might find it very convenient to see elements outside of the vertical scroll. Don't worry – you can fix this problem simply by selecting the **Content Detail** frame and unchecking the **Clip content** option on the right sidebar, as shown in the following figure:

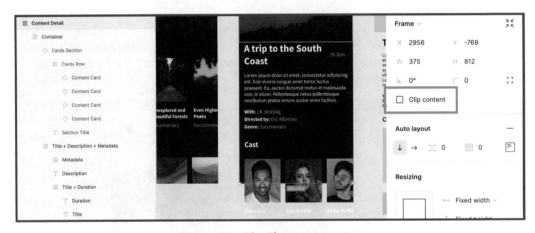

Figure 7.29 – The Clip content option

(Photos by Joseph Gonzales, Raffaella Mendes Diniz, and Ivana Cajina on Unsplash)

When the basic interface of our application is complete, you are ready to create and implement variants in the most useful way by adding action keys to your layout.

Implementing variants

According to the wireframe, the **Content Detail** view has two action buttons at the bottom of the screen, one of which allows the user to perform the main action – that is, watch multimedia content; the other leads to the video download for offline use, which is a minor action of less importance. Remember that you already experienced button creation when working on the **Login** and **Sign Up** views, but weren't using components at the time, and so now is a good time to fix that.

As stated earlier, button elements required in any interface design need to have different styles, types and states, and this is a typical case when it makes sense to use variants. To better understand the importance of this feature, let's think about the buttons in our app. You know that you need to create at least two buttons, primary and secondary, but each can have a set of different sizes – for example, small, medium, and large – which triples the number of components. Also, each button certainly has different states that you need to show when prototyping, such as **Hover** (when the mouse pointer hovers over an element), **Focus** (when an element is selected) or **Disabled/Inactive** (when an element is disabled and not clickable). Each of these states must also be explicitly applied to each style and size of your buttons. Now, you may have lost the number of components for a button element that you need to create, and this is where variants come into play to help you organize and set all the components that have similar characteristics.

To start creating your variants, let's move to the **Styles + Components** page and follow these steps:

1. Create a new frame that will contain all the button components and rename it `Buttons`. Set the fill style to **Background**.

2. On the **Hi-Fi** page, copy the **Login** and **Sign Up** buttons from the **Login** frame and paste them directly into the new **Buttons** frame.

3. Change their text labels to a more general `Button`, as shown in the following figure:

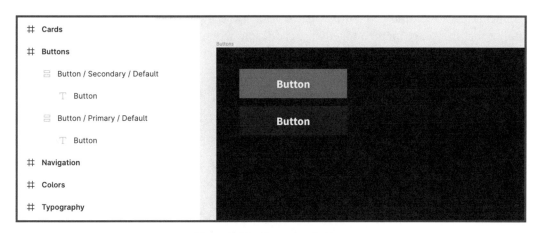

Figure 7.30 – Preparing buttons

The layer names that were previously assigned to your buttons are very important because it tells Figma that these elements are part of the same button class, allowing us to create a variants set. Basically, from now on, you can structure your button element with two different styles but in the same state, which is **Default**. Instead of creating components from each of the buttons individually, select both, and now a new **Create component set** option will magically appear on the top panel, as shown in the following figure:

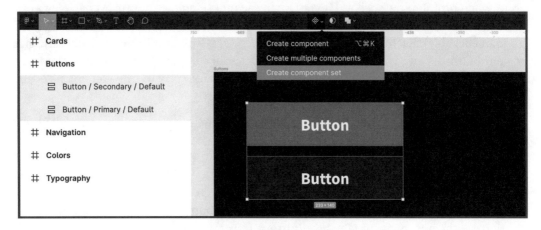

Figure 7.31 – Creating a component set

After this action, a lot happened in the **Buttons** frame that you had not seen before. The elements are now combined with a dashed stroke, and if you look at the layers, you will notice that they have merged together. In addition, when this area is selected, the right sidebar now shows many new options, as you can see here:

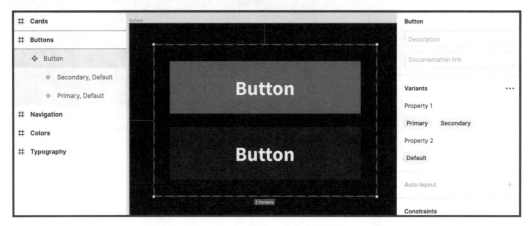

Figure 7.32 – An overview of the component set

> **Note**
>
> Don't worry if you already have button components created separately. You can still combine them into variants and you will get the same result. Just select multiple components and click the new **Combine as variants** option on the right sidebar.

Now, if you open your **Assets** library, you will again find an unusual situation there – instead of two button components, there will only be one. So the question is, where is the other one? Don't worry – go back to the **Hi-Fi** page and just drag the button component from the library and drop it right below the **Cast** section in the **Content Detail** frame. The primary button will appear, which is quite predictable, but select it and look at the right sidebar. You can see a lot of new options, as in the following figure:

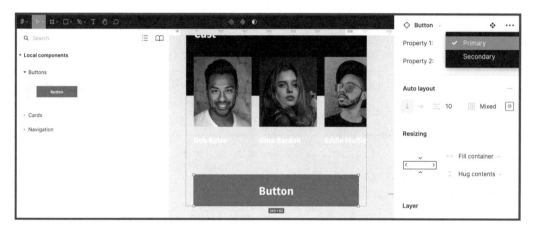

Figure 7.33 – Switching between two button's properties

As you can see, you can now easily swap your button in the drop-down selector for **Property 1**. Let's see how this works! Drag another instance of your new **Button** component, place it below the **Primary** one, and swap it with the **Secondary** one in the right panel. Remember to set the horizontal **Resizing** property to **Fill container** for each button. It's also better to wrap the two buttons in an **Auto layout** frame and set their distancing to **16**. Change the button labels to Watch Now and Download, and you're done with the **Content Detail** view! The final result should look like the following figure:

Figure 7.34 – Details of the final results

When you're done, select the main **Content Detail** frame and re-enable the **Clip content** option to temporarily mask all the elements outside of the view.

Variants are incredible, and you can already easily implement them into your designs, but there is still more you can do to organize them even better. Go back to the **Styles + Components** page and select your **Button** set. In the right-side panel, change the names of **Property 1** to Style and **Property 2** to State. This will make your button component even more accessible and easier to use. The renaming result is shown in the following figure:

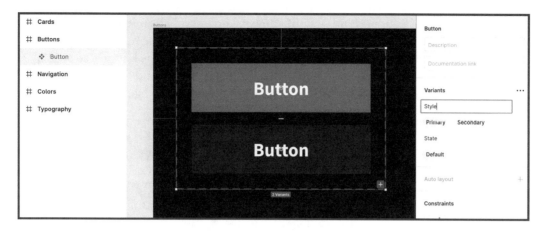

Figure 7.35 – Renaming our variants

Let's go back to the button components and think about states. Besides **Default**, you need to create the **Hover** (which will only be available on the web/desktop, since touchscreens have no cursor), **Focus**, and **Disabled** states. The easiest way is to manually expand the width of the set's external dashed stroke and duplicate both buttons as many times as needed for all states (or alternatively you can also use auto layout to better manage the set structure). Figma will warn you that some conflicts are occurring, which is perfectly normal, since you have elements with the same names and properties at the moment. Select each button individually, and in the **State** drop-down list, create a new value for each state. You can see how to do that in the following figure:

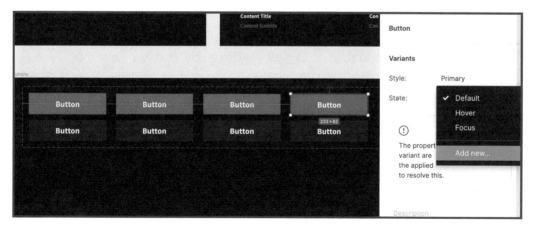

Figure 7.36 – Creating new properties with the drop-down menu

Once all the states of each button (**Default, Hover, Focus,** and **Disabled**, in that order) have been assigned to both button rows, you can customize each element as needed. The color you currently have in your library won't be enough to style the buttons, so start by creating a few new ones for the new states (that is, lighter **Accent** and **Secondary** colors for **Hover**). You can use the **Color Styles** example in the following figure:

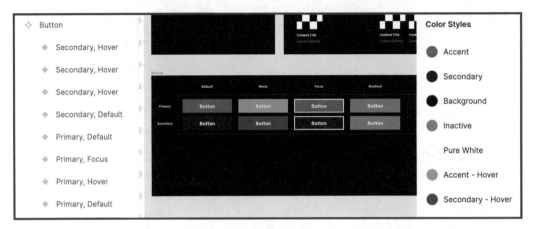

Figure 7.37 – An overview of the results with new color styles

No matter how many button component variants you add, the **Assets** panel will still show only one. But, after you add it to the canvas, you will have not only the option to choose a style but also a state that you might not use for now but will definitely need at the prototyping stage. If you want to go further, you can create a new type of button – for example, with an icon on the side of the label, which can also be very useful in some design cases. To do this, duplicate the two rows of buttons that you have and click the **...** icon next to **Variants**, and then select **Add new property**. You can name this new property `Icon`, which should have two options – `True` to show the icon on the button, or `False` to hide it. Before trying it yourself, make sure that you have enough knowledge and practice of using variants. In the end, your result may look like the following figure:

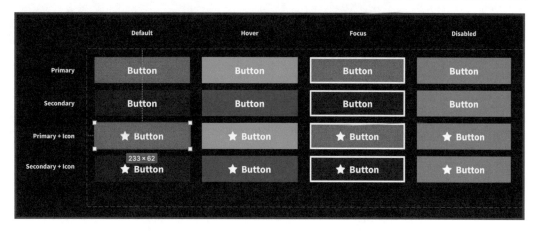

Figure 7.38 – Pushing variants and properties even further

> **Note**
>
> Once you set **True** and **False** as values, this property will appear as a cool toggle button in the right sidebar, not a dropdown. You can literally turn the **Icon** element on and off in the button!

What you now have in the **Buttons** frame can be created simply by using **Components**, but the end result in this case will be a library filled with tons of different button components to accomplish every single combination of properties. The benefits of variants will become more apparent to you as you advance to complex interfaces or, more significantly, design systems.

Well, now you have covered everything you need to know to start using components efficiently by implementing variants to your design. For sure, using these functions requires a lot of practice, but eventually, you will find your own system to decide what elements need to be converted into components, which of them can have variants, and how to organize all of it in a library.

In the next section, you will learn about some other amazing features that Figma has, namely collaboration, sharing, and version history. This way, you'll take a little break from our project and explore new Figma functionalities.

Multiplayer mode, libraries, and version control

It was a lot to manage, wasn't it? And yet this project is a simple one. It is likely that your future projects will be more complex, and you will not be working on them alone. Collaborating with other people is always a fun but challenging process, and it is also an important part of your design journey. In this section, you will discover what solutions Figma offers for effective teamwork and real-time collaboration.

Working with multiplayer features

From the very beginning, Figma tried to outperform other tools by building its entire software architecture on modern web technologies. This, on the one hand, turned into significant limitations, such as the need for a constant internet connection, a condition that no other design tool requires. But, on the other hand, it presented an incredible number of advantages, such as immediate synchronization of files and projects, the ability to work directly from the browser without downloading anything, and above all, multiplayer features.

In Figma, as well as in FigJam, you can invite up to 500 collaborators in one file, which is too much to handle for other design tools. Moreover, 100 of those 500 can be editors (and can make active changes to the file), and the rest will be viewers.

You can see another editor or viewer working in the same file as you by their avatars appearing in the top bar, as well as their cursors moving in real time on the canvas, as shown in the following example:

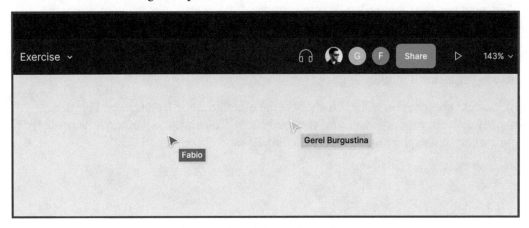

Figure 7.39 – Multiplayer mode and the top bar with active editors/viewers

Looks cool, doesn't it? So, in this section, you will learn how to share a file with friends and colleagues, as well as what other collaboration opportunities Figma can offer you. It's easy to invite someone to a file; all you have to do is click the **Share** button in the upper-right corner. Then, a pop-up window similar to the one you see in the following figure will appear:

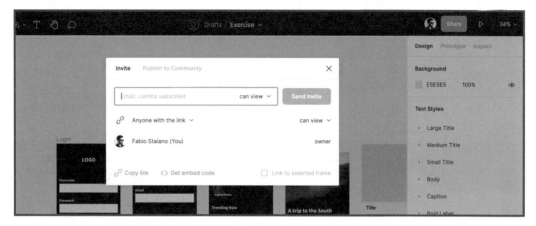

Figure 7.40 – Adding new editors/viewers to the file

There are two ways to invite people to your file through this dialog. You can do this by typing in your teammates' emails, specifying their roles in the drop-down menu right in the textbox (editor or viewer), and clicking **Send invite**. Alternatively, we can choose the **Copy link** option and then send direct links to the people you want to share the file with. Do not forget to specify the role before copying the link in the drop-down list on the right side of the window, as shown in the following figure:

Figure 7.41 – Choosing a default rule for people joining via a link

Sending the same link to others is undoubtedly a quick and easy way but also very risky, as you may end up unwillingly giving unwanted people access to our file.

Also, at any time, you can change the roles for each individual participant in the file, from editor to viewer or vice versa, close access, or even transfer ownership of our file to third parties, simply by selecting the option you need from the corresponding drop-down list.

What has been said so far in this section is about your personal separate files, but sharing and collaboration are even easier when you're working in a team! In fact, if you create a new team on the Figma welcome screen (refer to *Chapter 1, Exploring Figma and Transitioning from Other Tools,* to brush up on this), you can add your colleagues directly to the team, after which they will have access to every project and file already existing and added afterward. The team owner can always manage team members and all permissions. You can see an example of a team management page in the following figure:

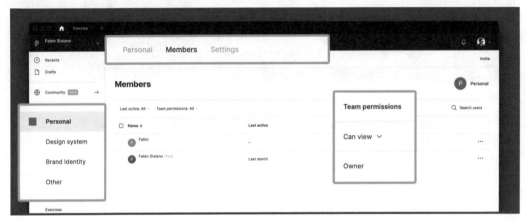

Figure 7.42 – Team members and permissions

That's pretty much everything you need to know about multiplayer mode at the moment, since Figma has everything very clearly organized in its interface. However, sharing in Figma is a big topic, and it doesn't end there, so the next thing you need to learn is how to publish and manage libraries.

Managing libraries

Through practice, you have seen that components as a function have limitless potential – they behave like building blocks, allowing you to create reusable elements. Styles are also a very powerful feature, although they are nothing more than a set of properties that can be applied to elements. After creating your components and styles, you can easily use them in the file in which they were placed. But what if you can go beyond and extend this behavior by sharing them across other files and projects? All this is possible thanks to libraries in Figma!

Let's see how this works in action. On the **Styles + Components** page, you have saved all your components and styles, and those are always accessible locally in this specific file. Now, you will create a library that will contain all of those elements. First, open the **Assets** panel, and then click the **Team Library** icon (the book-shaped one). You should see a popup, as shown in the following figure:

Figure 7.43 – A team library

In this dialog box, you will see the name of your file with a **Publish...** button next to it. Publishing the entire library is only possible if your file is in a team and not in **Drafts** (in this case, you will be asked to move your file to a team). If you don't want to move it from **Drafts**, you will be prompted to choose to publish styles only, which is always possible. To check out all the features of the library, move your file to any team.

Okay, great, you're ready to go! So, the next thing you will find is a long list of all your previously created styles and components that you are about to publish to this new library. There is a helpful description textbox at the top of the dialog, which should always be used for a quick comment on what you intend to publish or update in the library. As you can see, the entire list is presented as checkboxes, so in the end, you can only select the ones that you really want to publish. In the following figure, you can see what this step should look like:

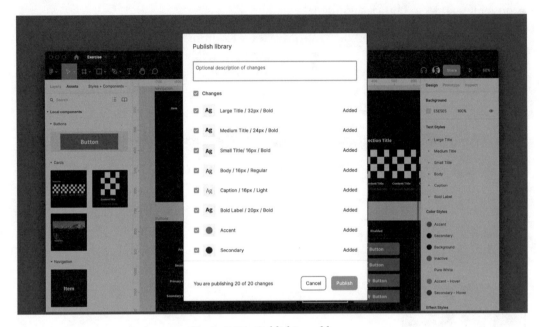

Figure 7.44 – Publishing a library

> **Note**
> If you have made any mistakes – especially by incorrectly creating variants or properties – this will lead to a conflict when trying to publish. You will see a notification next to the conflicting element that asks you to resolve everything before moving on. Alternatively, everything but the reported items will be posted.

If you make any changes to any component or style after the library is published, you will see a notification on the **Team Library** icon. By clicking on it, you can easily submit all your updates – and describe them in the text field – to the shared library. You can try it yourself or refer to the following figure:

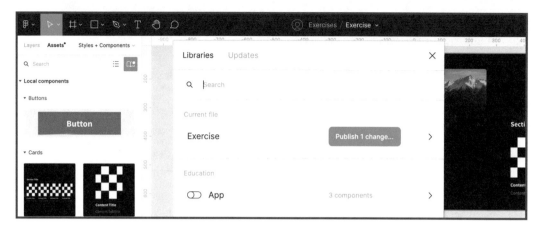

Figure 7.45 – The team library's notification and Publish 1 change… button

The published team library is now ready to be used anywhere in team files and projects in your Figma. You can test this by opening – or ultimately creating – a new file in the same team. Then, go to **Assets** and click on the **Team Library** icon. In the popup that appears after that, you will see the name of your library and the toggle button next to it, so once you enable it, you and your Team members can instantly use all the styles and components that you previously created in the new file. In the following figure, you can see an example of this popup:

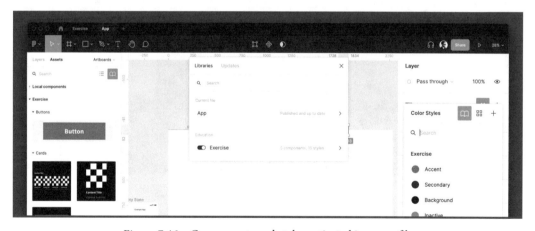

Figure 7.46 – Components and styles activated in a new file

> **Note**
> You can edit main components and styles only in the source files in which they were originally created, except when they're moved or detached.

Now you finally know the full potential of styles and components and how to create shared libraries. This last feature helps a lot when working on, for example, different projects but for the same client. Therefore, you can create a base of styles and components only once and then reuse it over time. If, one day, a client decides to change something, such as the main brand color, all you have to do is change its style in the source file and publish the update to the team library. This way, you can be sure that the color will change in every project in which it is used.

You will discover even more about libraries in *Chapter 12, Discovering Plugins and Resources in the Figma Community*, which is dedicated to the Figma community!

Preserving your work with version history

When you worked on the project in your file, you may have noticed that you never had to save your work in progress. This is one of the incredible benefits of a web tool that removes once and for all the worry of saving and you don't lose your last changes. But Figma doesn't only do that; it also keeps your **version history** as well. To see it, open the drop-down menu next to the filename in the top bar and click **Show version history**, as shown in the following figure:

Figure 7.47 – The Show version history option

Once clicked, the version history will be shown as a new right panel, where you can see and navigate past versions of your file. You can see an example of this panel in the following figure:

Figure 7.48 – The Version history panel

As you can see, **Current version** is now selected, which means that you are using the most recent version of the file. Also, you can see the save point that Figma created automatically when you published the library **Library** (every time you publish an update, the new version will be added to the history with your descriptions from the update notes). Finally, below that is an expandable list that contains all the autosaves that Figma has done from time to time.

Version history allows you to go back in time with just one click, and you can see what you've ever previously done in your file. In addition, from here, you can access many new options by clicking the **...** icon next to the current save point, as shown in the following figure:

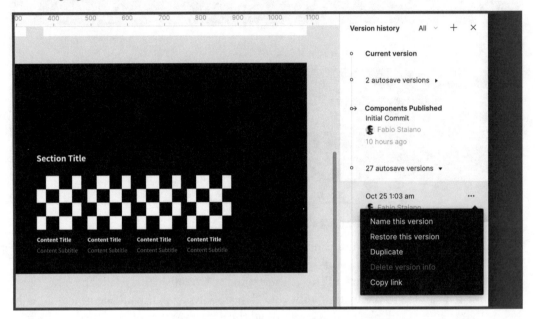

Figure 7.49 – The history version options

From this menu, you can give a name to a specific save point (to make it more recognizable), or you can click **Restore this version** to bring the selected version back to life. If you're not working on the file alone, you'll see not only your personal editorial history but everyone else's (you can change this by filtering out only your history by clicking the **All** drop-down menu at the top of the sidebar and choosing **Only yours** instead).

> **Note**
>
> It is important to know that for **Drafts** and free Team plans, version history will be limited to 30 days. Upgrading to the paid plan gives you unlimited access to version history.

The autosave function is great and prevents you from losing anything, but if you want to be twice sure that everything is saved correctly, Figma lets you do it manually, and it's very easy! In the **Version history** panel with the current version highlighted, just click the + icon in the upper-right corner, then give it a name and description, and that's it! From now on, you can return to that specific save point at any time. You can also access it, bypassing the **Version Control** panel, by using the *Command + Ctrl + S* (macOS) or *Ctrl + Alt + S* (Windows) keyboard shortcut.

All the collaboration, sharing, and history features in Figma are great and very easy to operate. Of course, you will use them mainly in teamwork, and right then, you will discover even more of their potential, so it will become a part of your daily design workflow.

Summary

This chapter was full of information and practical guides for designing our project. Some of the steps were already familiar to you – for example, adding a new layer to a frame, setting up auto layout, and changing properties of elements according to styles. But at the same time, there has been a lot of new information to take in, in possibly the most difficult subject on your journey. As always, don't worry if you feel overwhelmed – components and variants are huge, very complex topics, and no one really masters them right away!

It was a really rich chapter, and you not only learned about components and variants, but also greatly advanced our project by building the Home and Content Detail views – the most important screens of the application – using all the advanced features that you learned about in the previous chapters and this one. Also, now you know how to work with the library and even how to publish it for use in other team files. Plus, you explored multiplayer mode. Finally, you discovered version history and saw how you can restore and save your work at any stage of your design.

In the next chapter, you will learn how to design for different platforms so that our application can be opened on large screens without falling apart.

8

User Interface Design on Tablet, Desktop, and the Web

In the previous chapter, we made significant progress in designing layouts for our mobile app by completing two more views and we also created some important reusable components that are now easily accessible from your library. According to the brief that was defined in *Chapter 2, Structuring Moodboards, Personas, and User Flows within FigJam*, our application should run not only on smartphones but also on tablets and desktops, so in this chapter, you will learn what you need to do to make your design responsive and how to make it look good on large screens. You already know about functions that prevent your interface from breaking when resizing, such as constraints and resizing. It is true that if you apply them correctly, you can avoid many unwanted problems while scaling your layouts. However, this is not enough to make your design fully responsive, especially if you are creating a product for different platforms, as in our case.

So, in this chapter, you will discover many important tricks on how to optimally scale an application to larger devices without risking and impacting the functionality behind the design elements and/or interrupting the UX. You will start by testing your mobile interface on different smartphone models, and then move on to customizing it for tablets and the web, while making improvements to your design. As usual, you'll be guided by how-tos, but this time you'll have more room to work on your own using provided illustrated examples and tips. So, open up Figma and get ready for new challenges!

In this chapter, we are going to cover the following main topics:

- Discovering responsive design
- Adjusting the interface for tablets
- Adjusting the interface for the web and desktop

Discovering responsive design

In this section of the chapter, you will be introduced to the concept of **responsive design**, which is very important to know about and keep in mind when designing any digital product. You'll learn all the basic techniques on how to make your interface design as flexible and responsive as possible. This is a huge topic to learn, but you will start with simple things, such as adding missing elements and making sure the app looks good in different screen resolutions on your mobile device.

So, as you know, on the **Hi-Fi** page, you designed your application for streaming video within one specific screen size of a mobile device, which is the iPhone 11 Pro / X. But, as mentioned earlier, it's important to make sure your product looks decent on all major device resolutions it can be used on. To do this, you don't have to create new views from scratch. Instead, you focus on the ones you have so that they are perfect for any screen size.

Even when a design is done neatly and accurately, there may be some minor aspects that might seem insignificant but turn out to be important in the later stages of the work. From time to time, for example, you work with constraints and then resize frames to see if everything looks good, but while concentrating on other features, that aspect inevitably fades into the background. Don't worry, this is absolutely normal when you are learning and it is not easy to take things into account at the beginning, but with experience, it will become smooth and natural to anticipate what needs to be implemented in your design. For now, let's just take a step back to fix the missing points.

In the following sections, you will learn how to quickly check whether constraints and everything else in your layouts are set correctly, by scaling the frames to a size similar to other smartphone devices.

Design to code with fluid layouts

You should never forget that your design will eventually be implemented in code, so it makes sense that design and development are related to each other. Developers, like designers, look for ways to create scalable interfaces that easily adapt to multiple screens and resolutions without too much trouble. It is for these purposes that new programming languages such as **React**, **SwiftUI**, and **Flutter** were developed, and designers more or less follow the same path, creating responsive interfaces with fluid layouts and breakpoints.

To better understand these new concepts, you will start with the current **Hi-Fi** interface. If you copy the **Login** frame, make several – temporary – copies, and then use the frame presets, you can easily test the same view on many other similar smartphones:

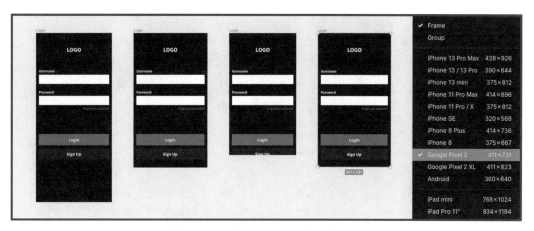

Figure 8.1 – Testing on similar devices

As you can see, on the larger **iPhone 13 Pro Max**, as well as on the smaller **iPhone 8**, and even on **Android** devices, this interface does not break but adapts to these screen sizes. This is due to a combination of resizing rules and constraints that you applied to your interface in *Chapter 6, Creating a Responsive Mobile Interface Using Auto Layout*, so all the elements resize their width according to the selected device. With this kind of testing, you can easily check if there are any issues that need to be fixed for resizing and/or constraints. What's more, it's a nice way to see how your layout changes across different devices.

Now you know how to quickly and easily check if your layout looks good on different mobile devices. Keep in mind that Figma has many basic popular presets for this, and that's usually enough, but if you need to test for a specific screen resolution that isn't listed, you can always manually enter its width and height in the appropriate fields. In addition, the **Login** view is pretty simple, in which the elements are simply resized to fit the parent frame. But this does not mean that other views and the elements within them act in the same way. Let's go ahead and see how to test more complex views.

So, if you are happy with how your **Login** view looks in different presets, you can remove all the test screens and repeat the same process with other views. For complex views, such as the **Home** view, created with **Auto Layout**, switching to a preset frame from the list will discard **Auto Layout**, and you may have some problems with this frame. To avoid this, manually resize the parent frame by entering the same height and width values as the presets of the smartphone models on which you want to test. In the following screenshot, you can see how the **Home** screen adapts to different sizes:

Figure 8.2 – Home screen resize testing

If done correctly, you should see a result similar to the one shown in the preceding screenshot. Also, you won't see as much re-adaptation here as you would in the **Login** view, since the **Home** page is composed of scrollable rows that stay the same across all smartphone frames.

This is how fluid layout works. After you finish quick resizing and testing, clean up your workspace (or restore a previously created save point in **Version History**). Now let's get down to creating a few elements to complete the design of our mobile interface. Immediately after that, you will discover breakpoints in the tablet section.

Mobile-first

Now let's go back for a moment to the reason why we started our project with mobile app design. Since, nowadays, more and more development frameworks are created primarily for mobile devices, the first design version of our application was mobile. What's more, it's always a lot easier to design a smaller interface and then fully scale it than to do the opposite – create a large one and then struggle to shrink the elements to fit on a smaller screen.

Before you start making your application fully responsive, there is still something missing in the mobile interface, so now you are going to polish and complete the **Home** and **Content Detail** views by adding navigation elements.

Navigation elements allow the user to easily move from page to page at will. For our application, you will create the typical bottom tab bar that you can find in most mobile applications. Apart from the **Login** and **Sign Up** views, all other screens in our application will have a tab bar. This time, you don't have many views in your file, but it is still better to create components for the navigation elements, as this is what you will be doing in your future, more complex projects. So, now go to the **Styles + Components** page and follow these steps:

1. In the **Navigation** frame, create a new **Text** layer and type Home. Apply the **Small Title/16px/Bold** text and **Pure White** color styles to it.

2. Using the **Ellipse** tool, draw a 38 x 38px circle directly above the text, remove the **Fill** and apply a 3px **Pure White** stroke. This will be your icon's placeholder. As a result, you should end up with something similar to the following screenshot:

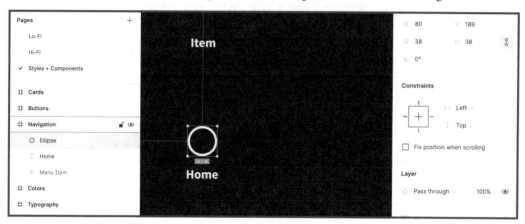

Figure 8.3 – Structuring an icon's placeholder

3. With the **Ellipse** layer selected, press *Shift + A* to wrap it in an **Auto Layout** frame. The frame is necessary because the icons you will choose could have different sizes or ratios, so it is better to wrap them in a container. Rename this frame to `Icon`, set **Alignment** to **Center** and, most importantly, set **Horizontal** and **Vertical Resizing** to **Fixed** to lock its width and height:

Figure 8.4 – Creating an Icon wrapper

4. Now select both the **Icon** frame and **Home** text layer, and enable **Auto Layout** with the *Shift + A* keyboard shortcut. Rename this frame to `Tab Item` and change **Alignment** to **Center**:

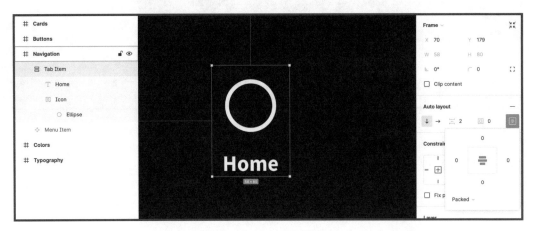

Figure 8.5 – Preparing Tab Item

5. Select **Tab Item** and, once again, press *Shift + A* to wrap it in another **Auto Layout** frame. Rename it to `Tab Bar`. Make sure **Direction** is set to **Horizontal** and change its **Fill** style color to **Secondary**.

6. Using the *Command + D* (macOS) or *Ctrl + D* (Windows) shortcut, duplicate **Tab Item** three times and change each label as in the following screenshot:

Figure 8.6 – Creating Tab Bar

7. Customize each icon as you wish by replacing each ellipse with the actual icon and setting **Horizontal** and **Vertical Resizing** to **Fill container**. You can draw icons with the **Pen** tool or use the svg / png icons you may already have (you can use a free set of icons in *Google Material Icons* at this link fonts.google.com/icons). Later, in *Chapter 12, Discovering Plugins and Resources in the Figma Community* , you'll discover a plugin that makes finding icons incredibly easy right in Figma.

The tab bar seems to be done, doesn't it? But don't forget that it has to adapt to different screen resolutions. So, let's try manually resizing it to make sure everything is fine. Once you stretch it, you get something like this:

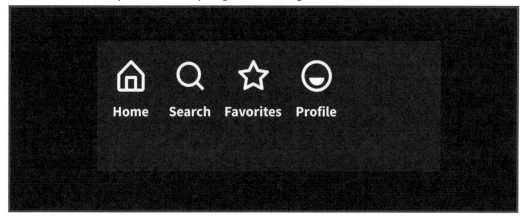

Figure 8.7 – Testing the tab bar resizing

This is not what you want your tab bar to look like in a real interface. Don't worry – you can fix it in a few clicks.

8. First, select the Tab Bar frame, then, in the **Alignment and Padding** panel, set the **Space between** option, as shown in the following screenshot:

Figure 8.8 – Alignment and Padding on the tab bar

9. Great, now you can finally move on. Select the tab bar and convert it to a component so it can be easily reused in any view you need.

For this exercise flow, you are only designing the main views that relate to the **Home** page, so you can simply change the **Fill** color style of both the **Home** text label and its **Icon** color to **Accent** to make it clear which tab item is selected. If you want to push yourself even further, you can follow the best practice by creating variants of this component so that you have an **Active** state for each of the tab items as in the following example:

Figure 8.9 – Tab Bar variants

Your new component is now included in your assets and ready to be added to the **Home** screen on the **Hi-Fi** page. But before proceeding with that, you need to make a small adjustment. Since the tab bar is a static element and does not scroll with the rest of the page content, the current **Auto Layout** structure of the **Home** frame is not appropriate for it. Follow these steps to fix its **Auto Layout** settings and properly add tab bar elements to the view:

1. Select the **Home** frame and disable **Auto Layout**.

2. In order not to lose all the advantages of **Auto Layout**, select all the inner layers of the **Home** frame and press *Shift + A* to wrap everything in a new **Auto Layout** frame, which you will rename to `Container`. This way, no customized **Auto Layout** settings will be lost.

3. Manually resize the container to fit the screen width (375px), add 16px padding
    to **Left** and **Right**, and finally set the **Left and right** constraints so it scales
    correctly later.

4. Now that the structure is set up correctly, you can proceed by inserting an instance
    of the new Tab Bar component by dragging it from the **Assets** panel and dropping
    it into the **Home** frame. Make sure the Tab Bar is placed outside the container,
    as shown in the following screenshot:

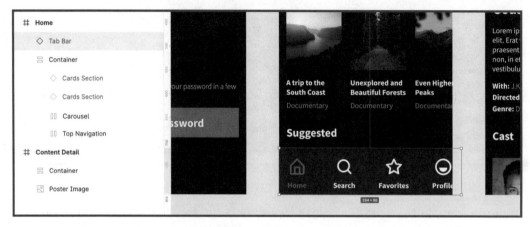

Figure 8.10 – Inserting the tab bar

5. Change the width of the tab bar to fit your screen. Change its **Left** and **Right**
    padding to 16. Then set its constraints to **Left and right** horizontally and to
    Bottom vertically. This will ensure that when your screen resizes, the tab bar will
    not change its size accordingly and stick to the bottom of the screen:

Figure 8.11 – Fixing the tab bar

That's all. The tab bar has to be added now to the **Content Detail** page. You can do this by simply copying the element from the **Home** view and pasting it in the **Content Detail** screen, but remember to disable **Auto Layout** for the parent frame first. Moreover, to make the interface consistent across all views, the **Content Detail** screen will need a top navigation bar, since this is an internal page, and the user must somehow return to the previous screen. The final result should look something like this:

Figure 8.12 – Overview of the result

It is also better to create a component for the top bar as it could be used for every internal view of the application. In addition, you can place the **Add to Favorites** button in the upper-right corner, as you can see in the preceding screenshot.

As you can see, it is very important to properly apply those features that can make it easier to scale your interface to other screen resolutions on mobile devices. This way, you set up your fluid layout once, and it will do the rest of the work itself, with the possible exception of minor additional corrections on your part. Thus, you can consider the mobile structure complete. It just remains to polish things a bit later when you work on the interactive prototype (that is, set the actual fixed behavior for the tab bar).

Well, you already know what a responsive interface is and why it is so important to make sure that all your layouts follow this principle. You have tested your views on various mobile presets, and you have also created and added a new scalable tab bar component to your library. Now that you've started diving into the topic, let's move on to a bigger task and scale our app interface to fit a tablet!

Adjusting the interface for tablets

In this section, you will take a step further and learn how to design your tablet app using ready-made Hi-Fi mock-ups for your mobile app. You will discover the best methods for adapting your design to significantly higher resolutions so that it looks great in all views, from simple to complex.

In the previous section of the chapter, you saw how a fluid layout adapts to different mobile resolutions, so it was pretty easy to properly configure our interface for each smartphone model in the presets. But just because our interface can scale automatically doesn't mean it will look good on larger devices, such as the iPad, without additional adjustments. Want to see a practical example?

The following screenshot shows the **Login** screen of the app immediately after switching to the **iPad** preset, without additional changes to the originally existing interface design:

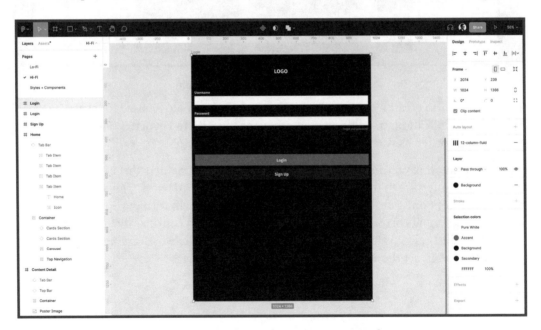

Figure 8.13 – Testing the Login view on iPad

This is not what you want the user to see on the iPad, is it? Would you use an app that looks like this? Always ask yourself this question to deeply understand if something is wrong with your design. Don't worry, in this section, you will learn about another concept of responsible design, namely **breakpoints**, that can help you solve this problem.

Introducing breakpoints

As you already know, a fluid layout is great when working with similar devices that are only slightly different from each other. But when you decide to move to other platforms instead, you need to stop and think about how to optimize everything in a special way. A breakpoint is the width of the screen at which a crucial and explicit design change occurs, a real leap between different UI views.

So, to ensure that your design is perfect for every device and every platform, you'll create your first breakpoint, which is a parallel, yet separate, user interface specifically designed for tablet layouts. Obviously, unlike a fluid layout, a breakpoint actually doubles the layouts that need to be managed, and therefore it's important to set additional breakpoints only when needed. To decide how many breakpoints you need to have, refer to your UX research results, which should include the types of devices and platforms your product will run on.

It's time to scale our interface and make it as enjoyable for a tablet as it is for smartphone screens. The first thing to do is to duplicate all views. The best way to organize parallel flows is to create separate pages for each platform so you can name them appropriately. But now you are maybe using the free plan and at the moment you may have reached a maximum of three pages per file; therefore, this time you can store everything on one **Hi-Fi** page. So, let's select and duplicate all four of our views. With multiple selection active, you can then click and drag the handles between frames and position them farther apart to make room for much wider interfaces, as shown in the following screenshot:

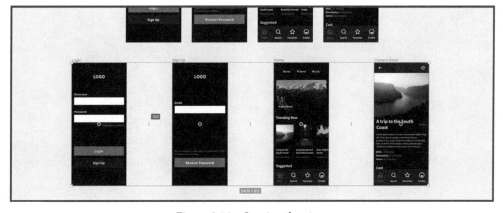

Figure 8.14 – Spacing the views

When you're done, select all of the screens and switch to a new frame preset by clicking **iPad Pro 11"** in the list of presets:

Figure 8.15 – Testing all the views on iPad

If each element has the correct constraints and resizing rules, the preceding screenshot should represent the result you get. If something went wrong, don't panic, just check which container frame is configured incorrectly and fix it, especially in the **Content Detail** view, which you did almost yourself as an exercise. Don't worry if this view is not the same as in the image, it will take months of experience to remember the important steps regarding resizing and constraints aspects. The good news is that you can always fix it in a few clicks without breaking your work. Also, right now, you will understand how important it is to work with fluid layouts. If, for example, your **Content Detail** view has **Fixed** width settings and no constraints, it would look like the example on the right compared to the correct one on the left of the following screenshot:

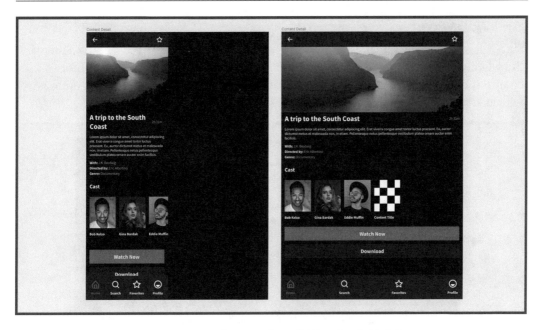

Figure 8.16 – Content Detail page without (left) and with (right) constraints

Take your time and make sure everything looks right. Keep calm if something doesn't work out at first. Check and fix all your **Resizing** and **Constraints** settings in the smartphone interface, and then duplicate and rescale the correct one to avoid any problems in the future.

When the base is ready, the next step is to decide what needs to be changed to improve the tablet layout. Let's take a look at, analyze, and work on each screen individually.

A – Login view

Since the smartphone screen is not too large, it is convenient to use full-width elements. But when you start scaling this interface to tablet size, the elements should be more compact. In the following screenshot, you can see one of the possible redesign options with examples before (left) and after (right):

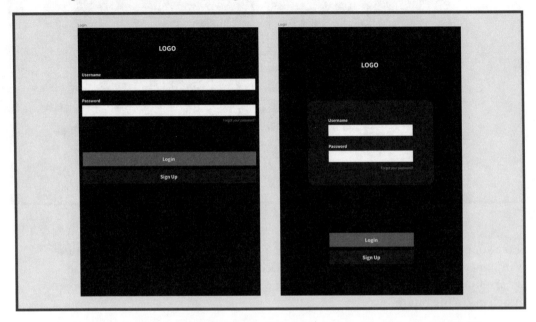

Figure 8.17 – Login view with fluid layout (left) and with a breakpoint redesign (right)

In the redesigned example, the left and right padding of 224px has been added to both text fields and buttons, so each element is better distributed over a larger space. In addition, a card has been added to make the form section even more compact and pleasant to the user.

Try to recreate the example breakpoint yourself. You don't have to go into the details; use the image as a guide and pay more attention to the **Auto Layout**, **Constraints**, and **Resizing** settings.

> **Note**
>
> When you're done, don't forget to test your interface by temporarily resizing it to make sure **Resizing** and **Constraints** are set correctly. For example, in this way, you may notice that **Button Group Constraints** needs to be changed to **Bottom**.

Great, you've just created a breakpoint view for tablets! Now you know why this is needed when scaling up for a larger screen and what it might look like in reality. Let's move on to the **Sign Up** view.

B – Sign Up view

The **Sign Up** view has elements very similar to the **Login** frame, so the adjustments will be more or less the same. Here's a screenshot comparing the design before and after:

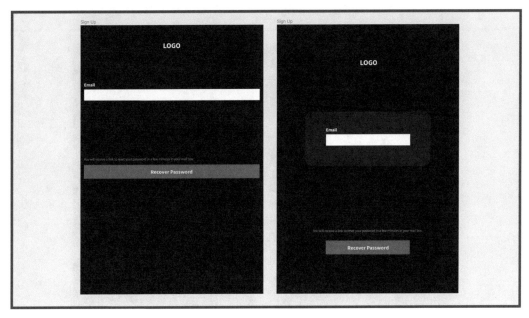

Figure 8.18 – Sign Up view with fluid layout (left) and with a breakpoint redesign (right)

Nothing fancy, but still way better than the unedited fluid version.

Again, follow this example to design the breakpoint view yourself. To be consistent, stick to the same values for padding, text field, and button width that you applied for the **Login** screen.

C – Home view

Unlike the two previous pages, the **Home** view requires more work as it has more complex elements, so you need to make the following changes:

- Change each carousel item's size to 700px (width) x 320px (height).

- Add more elements to the **Cards Row** component (on the **Styles + Components** page) to simulate the scrolling behavior.

- Add **Left** and **Right** padding of 164px to the **Tab Bar** element.

Here is a comparison of the default scaling interface (left) and the configured one (right):

Figure 8.19 – Home view with fluid layout (left) and with a breakpoint redesign (right)

As you can see in the example on the right, the carousel is more impactful, there are enough items in the cards row to simulate scrolling, and the tab bar is more compact and accessible.

There is one more thing you can do better in your design before proceeding. Now that you know how to simplify the process by creating complex nested components, it would be great – and really helpful for what's coming next – to convert the top navigation to a component. To do this in the best way, follow these steps:

1. Go to the **Home** frame (smartphone) and select the **Top Navigation** frame:

Figure 8.20 – Selecting the Top Navigation layer

2. Copy the layer with *Command + C* (macOS) or *Ctrl + C* (Windows) and paste it with *Command + V* (macOS) or *Ctrl + V* (Windows) in the **Navigation** collection on the **Styles + Components** page.

3. Convert it to a component:

Figure 8.21 – Creating a Top Navigation component

4. Copy your new component.

5. Go back to the **Login** view (smartphone), select the **Top Navigation** layer, then right-click and choose **Paste to replace**:

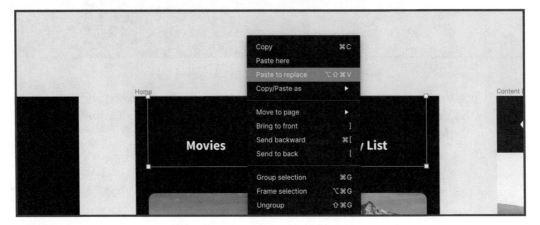

Figure 8.22 – Paste to replace function

6. Repeat the last paste action on the top navigation bar in the tablet **Login** frame.

Great, you just created a more flexible view, and now, having **Top Navigation** as a component makes it easier and faster to make more complex changes.

D – Content Detail view

Now that you know the tricks and have practiced scaling correctly, you can also experiment with the **Content Detail** view, which is not too difficult to adjust correctly. For example, you can dedicate more space to the main poster image. Also, since the buttons are really too wide, you can change the **Button Container** auto layout **Direction** to **Horizontal** so that both buttons are on the same row, as shown in the following screenshot:

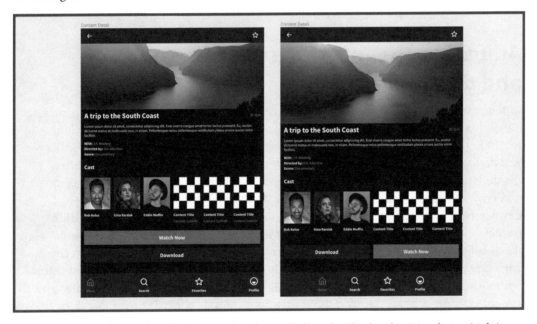

Figure 8.23 – Content Detail view with fluid layout (left) and with a breakpoint redesign (right)

Note that in the preceding example, the positions of the **Download** and **Watch Now** buttons have been reversed because, in the case of multiple actions on the same line, users tend to consider the action on the right more as the main action leading to the next step. For most users, this direction of movement is natural, and the same concept applies to horizontal scrolling, where left leads backward and right leads forward.

Well, the adaptation of our interface for tablets is complete. As you may have noticed, only one specific iPad model was used for this, but since each layout is still fluid, the design will automatically adapt to all devices with similar screen sizes. Also, only portrait mode was taken into account (that is, when you hold a tablet vertically), but it is also possible to customize the app for landscape mode if needed.

To summarize, you now have two parallel flows in your file: one for mobile, the other, which is a breakpoint, for tablets. There is one more set of layouts left to add, which targets browsers and the desktop. Since computers are fundamentally different devices than portable smartphones and tablets, this will be very different from what you have done so far. But since you already know the basics of responsive design, it shouldn't be too hard for you to complete this task, so let's get on with it!

Adjusting the interface for the web and desktop

In the previous section of the chapter, you created the interface of the tablet app, making it look like a native mobile app as much as possible. The next step is to move to bigger resolution screens, namely desktop and browsers. You always have to remember that web and desktop applications are completely different platforms. But aren't browsers part of the desktop, as well as smartphones and tablets? Let's clarify this point. Today, as stated earlier, development has really changed a lot. Year after year, application and website development have become more and more intersecting, and now thanks to scalable frameworks and programming languages, it is really difficult to draw a clear line between the two. So far, you have worked on the interface as if it were an application, but the application itself can be easily rendered in a browser and turned into a web application, with most of the functionality still present. A practical example is YouTube or any other similar platform that can be accessed from a smartphone, either from a browser or from its own standalone application.

It is always efficient to work in a hybrid way, since the final product will be absolutely scalable and available for any platform. Plus, now modern browsers have evolved significantly and are capable of supporting even the most complex content. But when designing and developing, it's important to know that browsers are still limited in some of the more integrated device features, such as personalized notifications or, trivially, the ability to use them offline, which is critical in some cases. Thus, from a design point of view, it is always correct to remember that technologies must be selected initially and based on user needs and product requirements.

So, for the current project, let's define that you need to deliver a native app design with a mirrored web app accessible directly from the browser – from desktop to mobile.

Scaling up to the web and desktop

Regardless of whether your application is launched on a large screen – in a web browser or in a standalone application – in both cases, the user experience will be very different from what you have seen so far. First, when using a computer, the user will be much more focused than when using a mobile device. Also, there is no touchscreen – except in the rare cases of desktop and laptop computers with touchscreens – but there is a mouse or trackpad, both instruments of very high precision. In addition, the cursor can move through objects without any actual click/action, and that adds an extra state to the UI elements. This and more should be considered when setting up a design for desktop. But don't worry, this section will walk you through the process step by step with hands-on exercises and detailed explanations of each adjustment solution.

Before you start working on scaling, there are a few other things to consider. Until now, you have strictly respected your layout grid as there was not much horizontal space – especially on smartphones – and you needed to use it as efficiently as possible. On huge screens with large aspect ratios, this problem no longer occurs. Instead, you may even have the opposite problem – you have to distribute a small amount of content in a wide space at the risk of creating an unpleasant look. So, depending on the amount of content, you can use two different types of basic containers: fluid or boxed. You can see the grid difference between the two in the following screenshot:

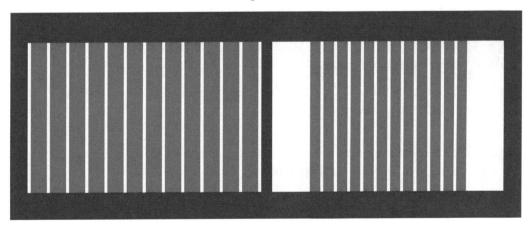

Figure 8.24 – Fluid (left) and boxed (right) layout

You already know what fluid is, as you've followed this method so far by creating containers that scale content based on the size of the parent frame. The boxed type, very common on desktop websites, makes everything more compact so that the elements are not too far apart. Imagine browsing the website on a 65-inch TV. It would be an incredibly large interface. Here's what happens to our app **Login** page if you enlarge it to a similar resolution with a fluid layout:

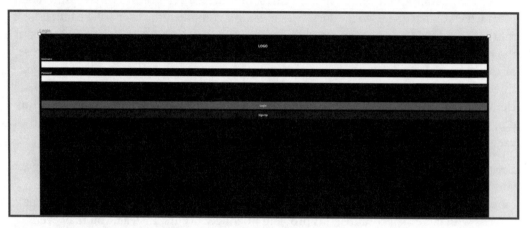

Figure 8.25 – Scaling our Login view on a TV

It is impossible to imagine a worse interface for this page, right? But you can fix this by setting a fixed-size container inside the frame. For example, you can set up an inner container of 960px, which is the standard width of the base size for a computer screen. This width will remain the same regardless of the monitor size, and the content will always be compact and centered. With this in mind, it's easy to figure out that the **Login**, **Sign Up**, and **Content Detail** pages will be boxed, while our **Home** screen can stay fluid to make the most of the screen width and display the full catalog of digital content.

Once scaling types are defined, duplicate your tablet views – you will use them as a starting point for fully scaling the interface.

While you'll be using tablet layouts as a starting point for scaling them up to desktop/the web, it makes sense that on a larger screen we can display even more of our app's content. Follow these steps to find out how best to do this:

1. Select the **Login** frame and, in the **Frame** presets list, this time you can select **Desktop (1440 x 1024 pixels)**.

    To work better with boxed layouts, you can also create a new layout grid style by setting **Type** to **Center** and doing some math to get a 996-pixel grid. You will learn about some helpful resources that can help you to make the process easier in *Chapter 12, Discovering Plugins and Resources in the Figma Community*.

> **Note**
>
> Every value field in Figma supports math operations. This is incredibly handy because you can, for example, calculate the width in the layout grid properties by entering `996/12 - (gutter value)`.

By now, you should know how to properly configure the elements in the interface, so use this section as an additional exercise on scaling. On the desktop/web interface, you have a lot more room to use, so you can certainly add more elements to the composition to make it look less empty and visually better. Just remember not to radically change the entire structure as it is necessary to keep things reusable. For reference, you can use the following screenshot where an additional side image was added on the **Login** page:

Figure 8.26 – Redesigned Login view for desktop
(photo by Gabriele Stravinskaite on Unsplash)

Of course, this is just one of the many possible design options for this page. So, feel free to play with this view as much as you like and customize it your way. Just keep in mind that all of your pages must be consistent and have the same styling, so here is what the **Sign Up** page might look like if it had a structure similar to the **Login** view example:

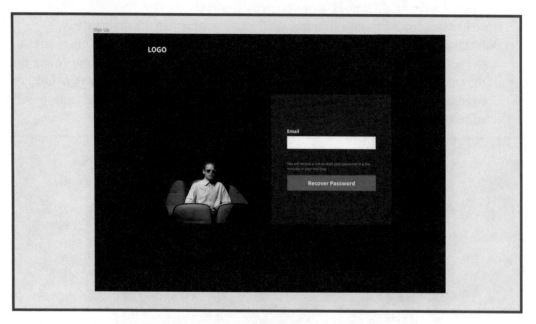

Figure 8.27 – Redesigned Sign Up view for desktop

Your next task is to work on the **Home** view, and here you will need to make some important structural changes.

2. Duplicate the **Home** tablet frame and swap the frame to the **Desktop** preset. Then, remove the bottom tab bar – you won't need it here, since this is a typical mobile-oriented navigation element, which is completely irrelevant for navigating a website or desktop application. Instead, you need to move the functionality behind the tab bar to a different location, and your best bet would be to create a new, redesigned top navigation.

3. Go to the **Styles + Components** page and create a new component, which should look like the following screenshot:

Figure 8.28 – Creating a desktop Top Navigation component

If you have any difficulties creating a new **Top Navigation** component, here are some tips:

- You can start by duplicating the mobile **Top Navigation** component and building a new one from it. This ensures that any possible future changes you may make to the mobile navigation will automatically be applied to this new element as well.

- The red circle you see in the preceding screenshot represents a placeholder for the current user profile picture.

- The main frame must be set to **Space between** so that when you scale, each element will have its own even position. In addition, the **Search** and **Profile** icons must be on the same side, next to each other, so they need to be framed together.

4. When you are satisfied with the result, select the element, rename it to Top Navigation - Desktop to distinguish it from mobile, and click on **Create component**.

5. Now, on the **Hi-Fi** page, go back to the desktop **Home** view and select the current **Top Navigation** layer.

6. With the selection active, click the component name in the right panel. This action will open the **Swap component** dialog box, and from there simply select **Top Navigation - Desktop** to instantly replace it:

Figure 8.29 – Swapping components

Done! As a result, you should have a nice **Home** screen desktop version of our interface as in the following screenshot:

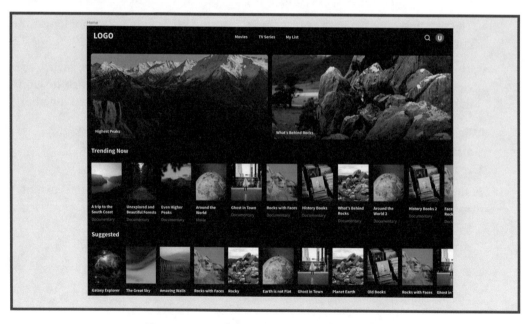

Figure 8.30 – Redesigned Home view for desktop

> **Note**
>
> If you want to quickly insert images on all cards in your interface, press *Command + Shift + K* (macOS) or *Ctrl + Shift + K* (Windows) to open the dialog. Select a bunch of images and click **Open**. Now you can simply click each field to quickly insert all the selected images.

Let's move on to the last view, which is the **Content Detail** page. Since it doesn't contain a lot of information, using a fluid layout would not be as functional, but since the **Home** screen is still fluid, it's impossible to pretend to be switching back and forth from fluid to boxed and vice versa. So, the best solution in this case is to create a hybrid page by wrapping **Content Detail** in a kind of invisible card. You can see how it looks in the following screenshot:

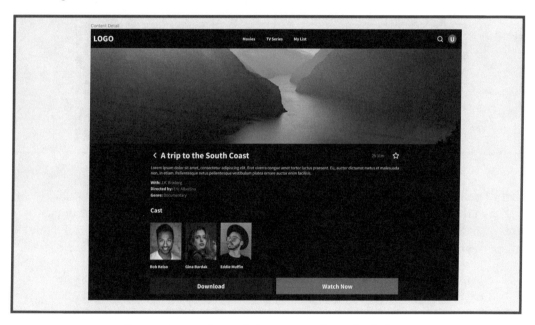

Figure 8.31 – Redesigned Content Detail view for desktop

It makes sense (remember to insert navigation back and the ability to add content to favorites in this view), but it could still be improved. For example, you can present **Content Detail** as a pop-up card that opens directly on top of the **Home** view:

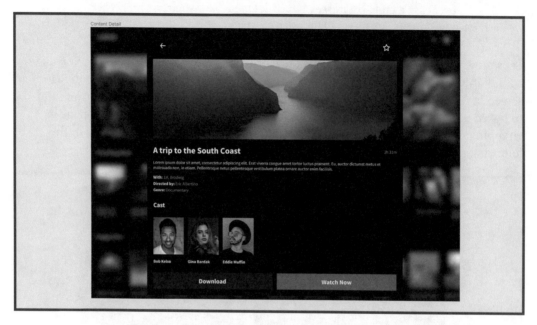

Figure 8.32 – Improved Content Detail view for desktop

Looks much more interesting, doesn't it? Moreover, it greatly speeds up navigation through the content, since the user always stays in the **Home** view and opens popups on top of it. It is much easier to create such a structure than you might imagine. Follow these steps:

1. Duplicate your **Home** view, rename it to `Content Detail`, then select the **Container** frame and add a **Layer blur** effect to it, changing its value to `22`:

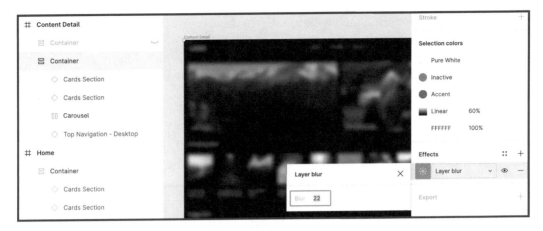

Figure 8.33 – Adding Layer blur to the inner container

2. Now just select the **Container** frame in the tablet **Content Detail** view and copy and paste it into the newly created **Content Detail** desktop frame. Add a **Secondary** background color to it, bring the **Image Poster** here as well, and add a **Top Bar** for the **Back** and **Add to Favorites** elements. That's all. Remember to set both **Constraints** to **Center** so that when you scale the interface, the popup stays exactly in the center of the page.

It's completely up to you whether you stick with the simpler, hybrid-styled **Content Detail** page or try something more advanced. Feel free to experiment and you may eventually come up with your own solution.

Polishing details

In this chapter, you've created many new views, and they're all still on the same page, so your workspace might be a mess by now, especially if you haven't had a chance to take care of moving and grouping frames. Of course, if you have one of Figma's paid plans, you can put the Hi-Fi frames of each platform on a separate page, but in any case, there is a great way to immediately recognize your elements – rename each frame correctly.

Let's start with your smartphone mock-ups. Go to these frames and rename them by adding `Mobile` to the name, for example, `Login - Mobile`, `Sign Up - Mobile`, and so on. You can do this faster by selecting all frames and using the keyboard shortcut *Command + R* (macOS) or *Ctrl + R* (Windows), which will launch the **Rename Layers Modal** window, allowing you to rename multiple layers at once. There are many options for renaming layers, but for this specific purpose, you need to first click **Current name** and then type ` - Mobile`. In the same way, you can add `Tablet` to the tablet frames and `Desktop` to the desktop frames. Try to keep them visually separate in your working area, and stick to the correct order of the views, as shown in the following screenshot:

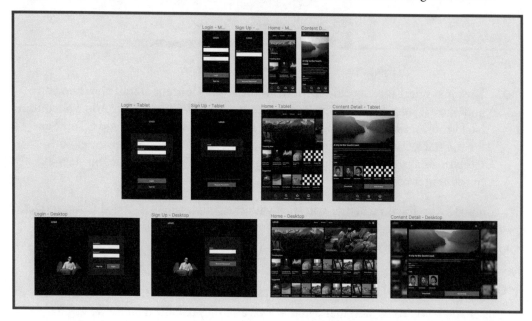

Figure 8.34 – Overview of the workspace

So, the base of the application interface for the different platforms is finally complete. As you can imagine, if you are going to design and structure a complete application with every required page, the flow can instantly become much larger and more complex, so organizing, renaming each layer, and keeping your workspace clean is very important.

For even smarter organization, you can make each file more recognizable at a glance among all your files in the Figma welcome screen. To do this, you can set a thumbnail using any frame in the file or by especially creating a new one for this purpose. Let's set up a thumbnail for our project. To do this, you should right-click the **Home - Desktop** frame and select **Set as thumbnail**:

Figure 8.35 – Setting a file thumbnail

Now open the Figma **Home** tab and you should see the frame image you just selected to preview the file:

Figure 8.36 – Thumbnail result

If you wish, you can create a new frame with a design of a suitable cover image to make it even nicer and more recognizable. It can also happen that you do not see the installed thumbnail. In that case, just close and reopen Figma to clear the cache.

Well, adjusting the interface for desktop and the web was pretty tricky, wasn't it? And now you can understand why it is set aside from applications for mobile devices and tablets, which means that it requires a more thorough analysis. As you can see, you even had to rethink the anatomy of one of the pages and make it hybrid or even a popup. In addition, you always need to redesign the navigation for the web due to the different ways of interacting with the computer. Again, it's okay if you made some mistakes or didn't fully understand something; you always have the opportunity to come back to the difficult points and try again. Plus, the more you get into design, the more you pay attention to details while using your smartphone, laptop, or any other device. So give yourself time, and those tasks that seemed difficult to you will not be so after a while!

Summary

Responsive design is one of the principles that a designer must always stick to when working on any interface. An app or website you create might have a great user experience and a stunning user interface, but if it's not properly adapted for all the resolutions and devices it needs to run on, your good work will be diminished all at once. And in this chapter, you have done everything to prevent this from happening with your application. You have completed your mobile app interface by creating additional reusable components and making sure all layouts are fluid by testing the views in different smartphone presets. Also, you have adjusted the design of your app for tablets by redesigning a couple of views specifically for this platform, that is, creating a breakpoint, so now you know when and why it is worth doing it. Finally, you've learned how to scale the interface correctly for desktop and the web while maintaining the harmonious and consistent look of your designs across all platforms. It was a lot of work, but you successfully completed all the tasks!

So now that you have a static user interface for multiple platforms, you might be wondering what comes next. You can be sure that the next stage of the design will be just as fun and interesting because you are going to make everything dynamic! Well done if you're thinking about prototyping the functionality that Figma has turned into pure magic. You will soon learn how to make your components interactive and also bring all your views together by creating a dynamic flow with smooth transitions between screens and cool animations of some elements in your layouts. This, and much more, you will explore in the next chapter, after which you may even feel like a wizard!

Part 3: Prototyping and Sharing

In this final part, you will make your prototype live and interactive using triggers, transitions, and interactive components. You will also learn how to test, publish, view, and export your project.

In this part, we will cover the following chapters:

- *Chapter 9, Prototyping with Transitions, Smart Animate, and Interactive Components*
- *Chapter 10, Testing and Sharing Your Prototype on Browsers and Real Devices*
- *Chapter 11, Exporting Assets and Managing the Handover Process*
- *Chapter 12, Discovering Plugins and Resources in the Figma Community*

9

Prototyping with Transitions, Smart Animate, and Interactive Components

In the previous chapter, you adapted the design of your app for tablets and desktops, making it responsive, which was a big step forward. Now, on your **Hi-Fi** page, you have not one, but three beautiful flows, and you may be wondering what comes next. Now is the perfect time to move on to prototyping – an important and interesting stage in a designer's work. Think of this as you needing to package what you just created in order to present it in the most impressive way possible. However, you should also keep in mind that prototyping can be very helpful not only for others, but also for you, and it often happens that while building an interactive flow or seeing it in action, you realize that you need to fix something. Don't worry if this ever happens, this is completely normal, as designing is not a linear process.

In this chapter, you will learn about the important prototyping features in Figma and apply those that are needed to your interface. There are a lot of them, but you will start with the basics, then move on to more advanced ones. You will find that creating a dynamic flow with impressive animations and cool tricks behind the scenes is a very exciting journey, and the results can be amazing! As before, in this chapter, you will find guides on how to best implement some of the techniques in your interface, as well as suggestions and ideas for self-practice. It might sound challenging but with everything you've learned about Figma, it will be as fun as it is useful for you!

In this chapter, we are going to cover the following main topics:

- Mastering transitions and triggers with prototype animation presets
- Animating with presets and smart animate
- Structuring interactive components
- Creating interactive overflows and overlays

Mastering transitions and triggers

You have reached the point where we can say that the main interface design of our product is complete, and even from the static layouts, it is very clear what your application is about. However, the design is not complete yet, as there is still some work to be done. In this section of the chapter, you will take the first step into a new stage of work on the application. Before we dive into this new topic, let's summarize what you should have in your design file so far.

First things first, you should have a flow for a mobile app that contains four views – **Login**, **Sign Up**, **Home**, and **Content Detail** – plus two more parallel flows for tablet and desktop, the interface you have created by redesigning and scaling your screens for smartphones. Of course, we didn't create all the views that such applications might actually contain, as some of the design steps would take longer to be fully ready for development, but it was a great start that allowed you to learn about and practice with basic and advanced Figma tools and features.

When you work on real projects, you will have to devote much more time to the UX phase and, possibly, come back to it more than once in order to dive deeper into analysis and research, especially if the product is more complex. Therefore, the whole process of designing a real application may not be as smooth and purely phased as the current one, and it will take a lot more effort to get to the prototyping stage. However, suppose the static design you have now is approved, and we can go further and make the interface come alive with **transitions** and **triggers** for a start. You are already quite familiar with the functionality of the **Design** tab in the right sidebar, which allows you to work on the visual part of the interface. In this chapter, you will discover the **Prototype** tab, which is also present in the right sidebar, as shown in the following screenshot:

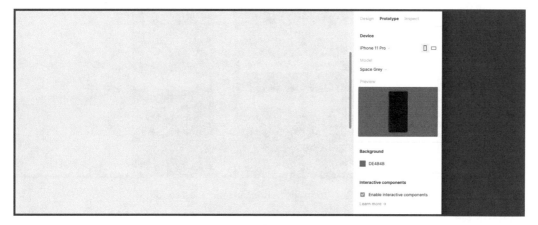

Figure 9.1 – The Prototype tab

If you open the **Prototype** tab without selecting any items on the canvas, you will see general prototyping settings for the current file. Make sure the **Enable interactive components** option is enabled (you will explore and try out this feature later in the chapter) and get ready to learn and apply your first **Prototype** functions in Figma. In this section, we'll start with the basic ones, namely transitions, which allow you to switch from one frame to another using triggers and animations that make this navigation more natural.

Moving between frames with transitions

All views of our interface for different platforms still exist separately, are not connected with each other, and do not interact. In *Chapter 2, Structuring Moodboards, Personas, and User Flows within FigJam*, you built the user flow in FigJam and stuck strictly to it until now, but the app layouts themselves are not interactive, therefore, they do not represent a flow altogether, as if it were a real application.

What you need to do now to get one step closer to an interactive prototype is to connect views to show Figma which paths users can follow and how they should actually proceed. This is what you will use transitions for.

Let's begin by selecting the **Login - Mobile** view – obviously this will be your starting point and the very first user step when the application is launched for the very first time, then switch the tab from **Design** to **Prototype** in the right sidebar as shown in the following screenshot:

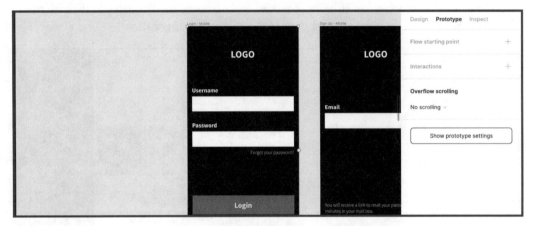

Figure 9.2 – Prototype options for the selected frame

You will see that with active selection, the context in the **Prototype** tab has now changed, and overall, it looks completely different from the **Design** tab. You can no longer find editable properties of forms and texts here, but a number of settings dealing with flows and user interaction. What's more, you may have noticed that there are some changes to your canvas now – a new indicator, a small round marker that appears in the middle of your chosen frame, to the right of it. It's called a **Hotspot**, and it's thanks to this handle that you can implement your first frame-to-frame transitions in a few clicks.

Click and hold the hotspot, then drag it into the **Sign Up - Mobile** view to draw a connector that links the two views, from the source where the hotspot is located to the destination:

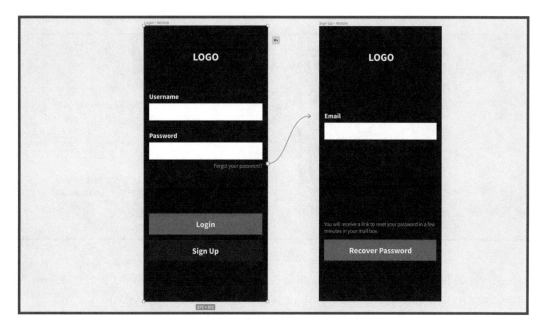

Figure 9.3 – Creating a connector

This way, you can be sure that after performing an action in the **Login** view, the user can switch to the **Sign Up** view, which sounds logical. But don't you think that there is still something wrong with that? In fact, you don't want the entire **Login** view to generate the transmitting action, but only a part of it, or rather a specific element, which is the button. So, if instead of clicking on the entire **Login - Mobile** view, you only select the **Sign Up** button, you will see that it now has a hotspot as long as the **Prototype** tab is open. Each element (as long as it is inside a frame) has a hotspot, no matter if it is nested or external.

Since the **Sign Up** button will take the user to the appropriate view, you can remove your previously made connector by clicking it and simply pressing the *Backspace* key. Then set the right transition by selecting the **Sign Up** button in **Prototype** mode and creating a connector to the **Sign Up** - **Mobile** view as shown in the following screenshot:

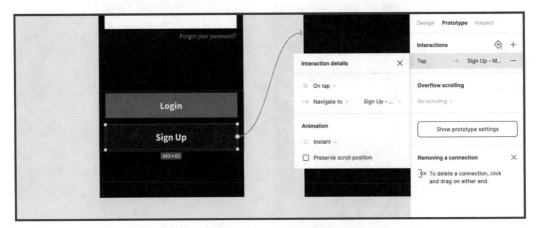

Figure 9.4 – Connecting the Sign Up button

Great, you've just made the **Sign Up** button element interactive by linking it to another view! And immediately after this action, near the right sidebar, a dialog window will automatically open, which displays the default configurations for the newly created connection, as you see in the preceding screenshot.

Right now, you have an interaction that is triggered **On click / On tap**, which means that you will need to click or touch an item, and this allows you to navigate to the destination page, in this case, the **Sign Up** - **Mobile** one. That's enough to get the flow working, and you'll see exactly what it looks like when you play the prototype by clicking the **Play** button in the top bar (in the next chapter, you will learn more about this function).

Another important option that you can see in the same dialog is **Animation**. By default, it is set to **Instant**, which means that after you click the button, you will immediately switch to the **Sign Up - Mobile** view without any transitions or animations. In many applications, this is actually the default behavior for navigating between views, but in certain cases, such as when using the native iOS development framework, you may want to move between views with right-to-left or left-to-right navigation, depending on the direction of flow.

Let's try to change the **Animation** parameter. Whenever you switch to **Prototype** mode by selecting the corresponding tab, you will see all the connectors on the canvas that you previously configured for your elements. This means that you can access the interaction parameters of any element by simply selecting any connector that you might want to edit. So now select the one you created, and all the options will immediately be visible again. Click the **Animation** drop-down list:

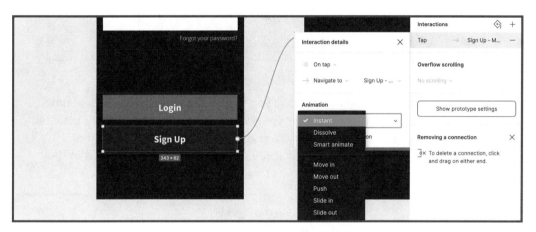

Figure 9.5 – The Animation drop-down list

Aside from **Instant,** there is a huge list of different **Animation** options available: **Dissolve** is a simple dissolving transition between views, and **Smart animate** is something more complex but powerful and you will explore it in detail later in this chapter. Next, you can see the **Move**, **Push**, and **Slide** animations block, and to better understand each of them, here's an illustrative example:

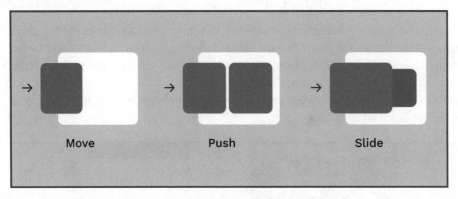

Figure 9.6 – Move, Push, and Slide animations

Using these different transition types allows you to give the user a better idea of how the flow is occurring, or to simulate some specific behavior such as modals or activity views. Now select your connector and try changing **Animation** from **Instant** to **Move in**, and once you do, many new advanced settings will appear as shown in the following screenshot:

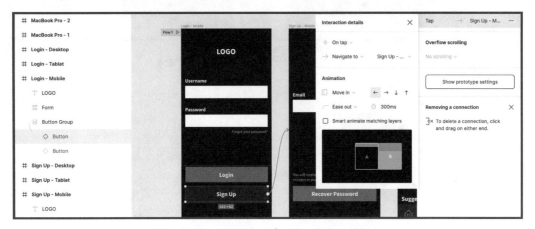

Figure 9.7 – Animating the Sign Up transition

As you can see, here, you can set the **Direction** and **Timing** parameters for **Animation**. But that's not all. If you want to customize your transition in a deeper and more complex way, you can click on one of the **Ease** options, which set the acceleration of the transition between the starting point and the destination, simulating the principles of physics by applying mathematical rules. To get a better understanding, imagine you are throwing a ball: its trajectory on a time and speed scheme will not be linear, due to traction and friction. And this is exactly what you can see here, a set of rules that will make your animation even more natural, appealing, and emotional:

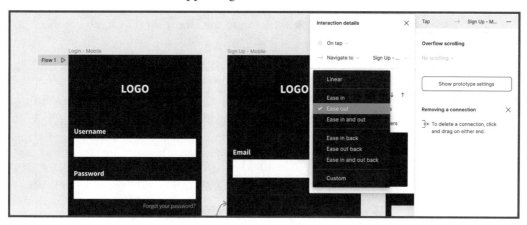

Figure 9.8 – Animation's Ease options

If you want to go even further, instead of **Ease** parameters, you can create an animation in **Custom** mode, which gives you many additional options for creating your own easing curves by setting **Time** and **Speed** values:

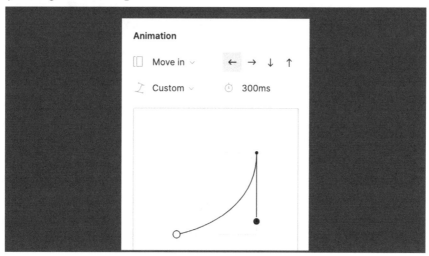

Figure 9.9 – Custom easing

> **Note**
>
> The small preview window right below the graph editor is a cool and quick way to check what your animation looks like without even launching your prototype. You just need to hover over it to see it live.

We'll keep it simple for our app and use mostly **Instant** transitions, but if you want to test out all the different ways to animate your frames, feel free to do so. Let's connect all the views together by following these steps:

1. Make the transition from the **Login** button to the **Home** view as shown in the following screenshot:

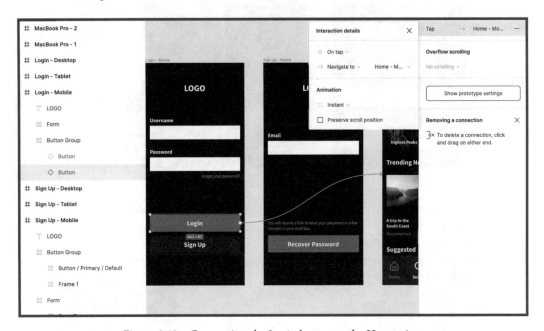

Figure 9.10 – Connecting the Login button to the Home view

2. Connect the **Recover Password** button in the **Sign Up** view to the **Login** view, then change **Animation** to **Move out** and **Direction** to **Down**. Thus, you simulate confirmation of the end of the password recovery process, after which the current view is discarded, returning the user to the **Login - Mobile** page:

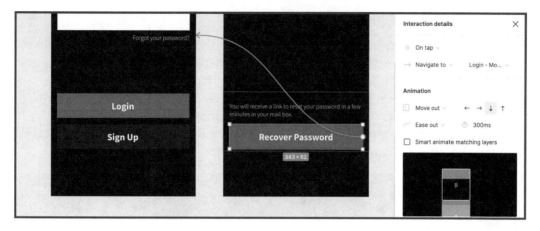

Figure 9.11 – Connecting the Recover Password button

3.   Finally, select one of the cards in the **Home - Mobile** view – not the entire frame, but an individual **Content Card** – and link it to the **Content Detail - Mobile** page:

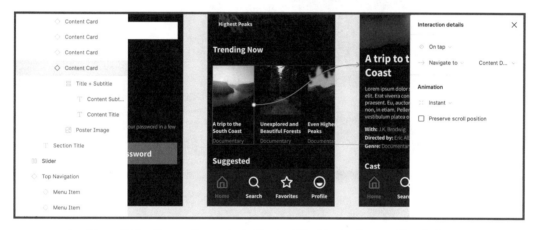

Figure 9.12 – Connecting a single Content Card to the Content Detail view

Great, now all your views are connected, and you have your first flow, so you have already completed the first iteration of the interactive and usable prototype that you will very soon see in action. It was quite fast and easy, right? Later, in the *Structuring interactive components* section of this chapter, you will continue to work on this with a few more details, but before moving on, repeat the same steps for the tablet and desktop interfaces, creating similar flows.

Exploring triggers

You've learned how to switch frames using transitions and, in this section, you'll explore triggers in Figma. You've already used one of the basic triggers, which is **On click / On tap**, but from an interaction perspective, there is still a lot to discover. You will get many completely different results using triggers, but first, let's get to know all of the ones available in Figma and how you can activate actions/animations on elements. So, click on the **Login** button connector and then open the drop-down list of available triggers by selecting the current option, namely **On click / On tap**:

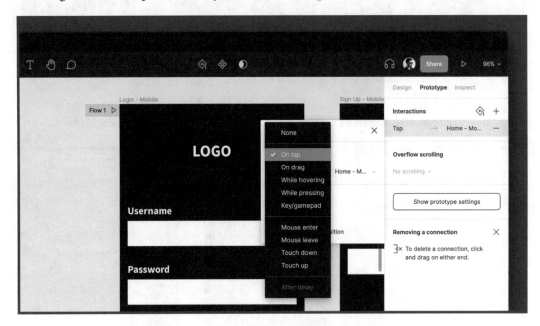

Figure 9.13 – List of available triggers

In this drop-down list, you can see a whole new set of ways your elements can interact. Let's take a closer look at each of the triggers to better understand the difference between them in the following sections.

On click / On tap

This is the default one. It launches an action after clicking/touching an element. It includes both mouse cursor and touch input.

On drag

Once this trigger is set, the interaction begins when the user clicks and drags the selected item. This is the right trigger to use if you need to simulate behavior such as sliders, drawers, or any slide gesture. It works best in combination with smart animate features, which you'll learn about in the next section of this chapter.

While hovering

This option triggers some kind of action while the user's mouse hovers over a hotspot, so as soon as the cursor leaves it, the user will return to the previous state. You could see this interaction in tooltips, image previews, and more, but remember that like any hover action, it is not supported on touchscreens.

While pressing

In this case, the user gets the interaction after clicking (or touching) and holding. Use this option to simulate social media app-like reactions or any other specific settings/menus. As with **While hovering**, this trigger returns you to a previous state after you release your click or finger.

Key/gamepad

This trigger is very special and powerful, although an underrated one. In fact, it allows you to associate an action with a specific key on your keyboard or with a key combination (for example, *Press A to Continue*). Moreover, it is possible to use gamepads (Xbox One, PS4, and Nintendo Switch Pro controllers are officially supported, but other pads may work fine as well) and associate actions with their keys. With this feature, you can prototype not only applications designed for consoles (see, for example, streaming services also available on Playstation and Xbox), but even games!

Mouse enter / Mouse leave

This set of actions is used to trigger an interaction when the mouse cursor enters or leaves a specific area. They are two separate and different triggers, but unlike **While hovering** and **While pressing**, both do not return the user to the previous state when the interaction ends.

Mouse down / Mouse up

With these triggers, the user can activate an interaction whenever a click (or touch) starts with **Mouse down**, or the user releases it with **Mouse up**.

After delay

This trigger is similar to a timer. As soon as the delay ends, the interaction begins. It can be very helpful in some cases, but it should only be used when really needed, otherwise your prototype will play on its own. It can only be applied to top-level frames, and it's very useful, for example, to simulate an app splash screen.

These are triggers that you can use to make your design not only dynamic but simulate maximum interaction with a real product. It is very important to remember all possible user actions with your design elements and reflect them in the interactive prototype. Now that you know what transitions and triggers are in Figma, it shouldn't be difficult for you to quickly build an interactive flow and make it pretty convincing with just these functions. But still, there is one more thing that can make your prototypes even more outstanding, and this is such a huge and interesting topic: smart animate. Let's dive into this!

Animating with smart animate

In this section, you will discover **Smart Animate**, a feature that is very easy to use but takes some time to master. Having a clean, organized workspace with the correct name for each layer is extremely important for this feature to work properly. For this reason, to avoid any problems the first time you use smart animate, you will not apply this to your interface, but instead, test it on other separately created frames for this purpose. It would be great if you go even further and not only do the suggested exercises from this section but also experiment yourself. Since smart animate is a huge topic to explore and we can't cover all its possibilities in this chapter, it is highly recommended that you devote enough time to your own practice, and at some point, you will definitely discover more ways to use this amazing feature. And, when you feel more confident and ready to move on, you can apply smart animate interactions to the current project wherever you see fit.

What is smart animate?

All of the animations and transitions you've seen so far are already excellent and effective prototyping tools of all kinds. However, in some cases, it may happen that you have to simulate much more complex behavior of your elements, which is not similar to anything that is present in Figma presets. This is where smart animate comes in.

With smart animate, you can easily create your own animations by specifying starting and ending points, and Figma takes care of the rest. What smart animate does behind the scenes is keep track of the layer names and hierarchy of elements that need to be animated and, if there is a match between the start frame and end frame, it will handle the transition between them as best as possible.

Let's take a look at a practical example to better understand how this works. In our current interface, in the **Home - Mobile** view, we have a tab bar and top navigation that can guide the user to other views. In those target views, the tab bar and top navigation will still keep the same position. If you set the **Move in** transition from the **Home** view to the **Search** view, and then take a hypothetical snapshot in the middle of that transition, you get the following:

Figure 9.14 – Overlapping two views

The target screen will overlap the entire **Home** view, whether it contains the same elements or not, which would be bad practice, not at all like any real application. You can fix this very simply by leaving the **Move in** effect but enabling **Smart animate matching layers**. It is a minor version of smart animate that can be embedded directly in all other animation methods as shown in the following screenshot:

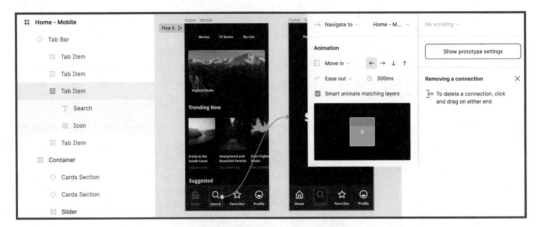

Figure 9.15 – Using smart animate with a Move in animation

With **Smart animate matching layers** enabled, the animation will run as normal, except that each matching layer in two views, such as **Tab Bar** and **Top Navigation**, will stay in place without switching between views. In other words, Figma recognizes the matching layers within two views, then determines what has changed and applies the appropriate animation between the frames.

Smart animate can be applied both to entire elements and components and individual layers inside a component or group. Of course, the full functionality of smart animate doesn't end there. There are many other aspects that it can dynamically change, such as **Position**, **Scale**, **Opacity**, **Fill**, and **Rotation**, and this will be the next thing for you to learn about with a few visual examples.

Getting advanced with smart animate

Imagine doing some complex animations in your interactive prototype for things such as sliders, swipeable cards, interactive graphics, and more. It might sound like a difficult task, but smart animate solves a lot on its own. Let's say you want to create a toggle that is known to have two states: **ON** and **OFF**. Let's see how this works dynamically. First, create a frame with a styled toggle element inside (you can use the example from the screenshot below with two rectangle shapes grouped together). Then duplicate the entire frame – so you will have it exactly with the same names of the inner layers. Be aware that the duplicated parent frame may have a different name, but the inner elements that you want to animate must match the names of the inner layers in the frame you want to connect to. Finally, customize the second toggle state by repositioning the smaller rectangle and coloring it however you like, or use the example in the screenshot:

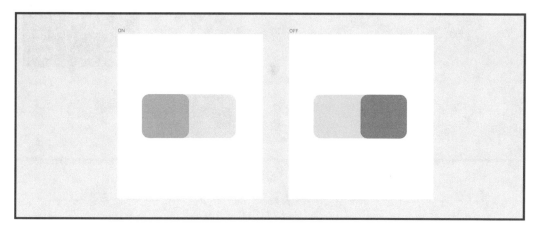

Figure 9.16 – Drawing two toggle states

To link these two toggle elements, you need to switch to **Prototype** mode and then create a connector from the first frame to the second one. The right trigger for this case would be **On drag** and in the **Animation** section, **Smart animate** must be selected, as shown in the following screenshot:

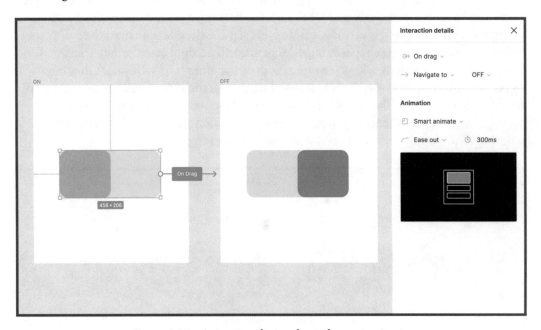

Figure 9.17 – Animating the toggles with smart animate

> **Note**
> It is also possible to add more than one connector between the same elements. For example, if you want the animation to run both **On tap** and **On drag**, just draw an extra connector, or click the + button in the upper-right corner of the **Interaction details** section.

To make the toggle complete, create a connector with the same properties, but this time in the opposite direction – from the second frame to the first. This way, you can turn it on and off as many times as you like. To see what it looks like, you can run the prototype by clicking the **Play** button in the top bar and try switching it on and off. The result is incredible: even if the two states are actually different frames, the animation makes them act as if they were the same element, and your **Toggle** gradually changes its color and the position of the element's slider, like magic.

Everything you just learned is just the tip of the iceberg. The possibilities of smart animate are endless with all the supported properties. You could even combine more animations in a flow to achieve greater results, such as this mail app:

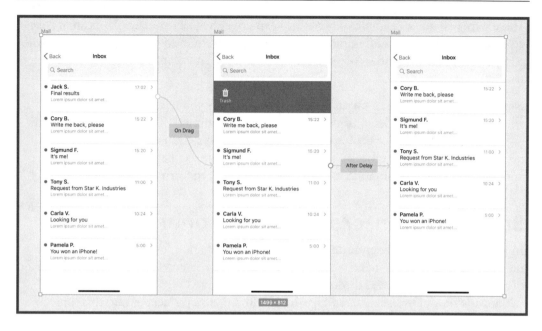

Figure 9.18 – A more complex smart animate and triggers example

Here's what happens in this prototype scenario: when you drag the first email, a trash can row appears indicating that that email has been removed, and immediately after that, with an **After delay** transition, the list automatically scrolls up. Note that if you are in **Prototype** mode, when you hover over an object, Figma will highlight identical elements in other frames, so you already know how smart animate will affect your interface:

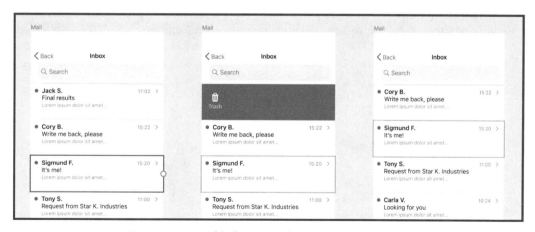

Figure 9.19 – Highlighting one element and its duplicates

These were just quick examples of what you can do with smart animate. You can of course go further by using and adding more complex elements, or even combining them all with components, variants, and so on. The only limitation of smart animate is your experience with it!

Now that you know how to use the features Figma offers you to create a dynamic flow with smooth transitions, cool triggers, and impressive animations, it's time to learn how to prepare your layouts for prototyping, manage them in a clean and efficient way, and optimize your workflow process. There is one feature that can help you with all of this, and that is interactive components, which you are about to learn about!

Structuring interactive components

In this section, you will be introduced to Figma's newest and most powerful feature, namely interactive components, which were recently officially released, after a long period of beta testing. It was a breakthrough that radically changed the way designers work, making the flow of projects incredibly simple. How? Let's dive deeper into this topic to find out about it.

What are interactive components?

As you've seen, making a prototype interactive and navigable in Figma isn't all that difficult, but if you want to create a flow with complex, detailed animations, you have to duplicate many frames, sometimes repeating entire views over and over again. For example, imagine you need to create and then show in your prototype hover states for all buttons present in our streaming app interface. Sounds intimidating, doesn't it? And it still wouldn't be the worst thing you can imagine since our application is not that complicated!

Let's see how it would look if we wanted to display a hover state for one button:

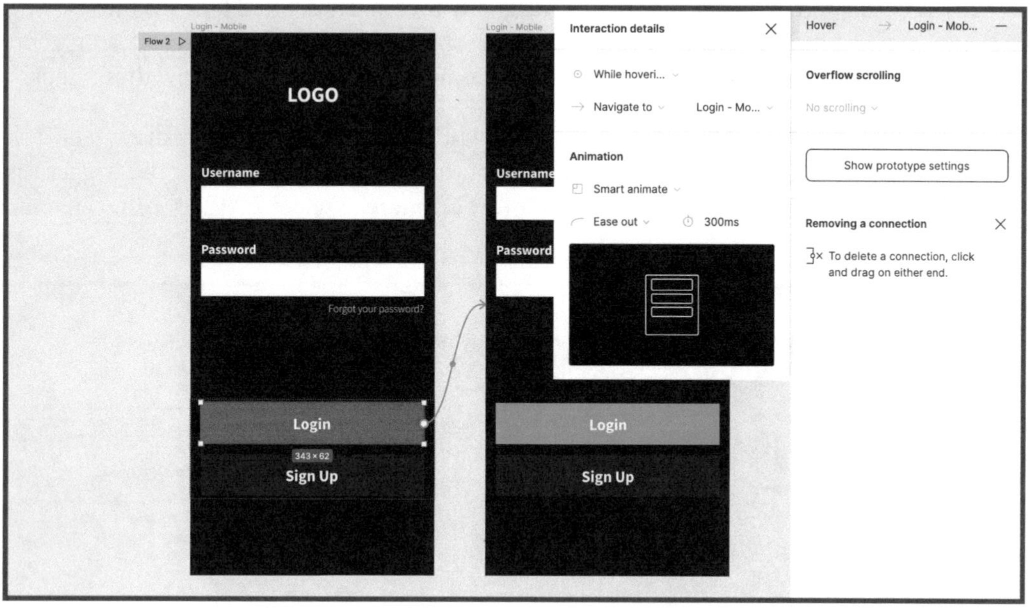

Figure 9.20 – Duplicating views to animate button states

Wait, you also have secondary buttons that have a hover state as well! And what, again an extra flow? Of course, it would be irrational to have an excessive number of views, so designers prototyped only a critical part of the flow, abandoning all other possibilities in favor of a cleaner workspace and also to save time. This caused a lot of problems, such as limited user testing and leaving developers with a larger gray area to fill in.

Fortunately, these difficulties are now gone since Figma introduced interactive components, which, in simple terms, allow you to set interaction rules directly to the main components so that all subsequent instances inherit not only a component's properties but also its animation and triggers. To better understand the concept, let's take a practical look at it.

Creating interactive components

Let's start with something simple and convert your previously created buttons into interactive components by adding animation directly to the main components using your already structured variants. Go to the **Styles + Components** page and follow these steps:

1. Select the **Primary Default** button and – while in **Prototype** mode – draw a connector that has the **Primary Hover** button as its destination. Set the trigger to **While hovering** and make sure that **Smart animate** is selected. The settings in your dialog should match the following:

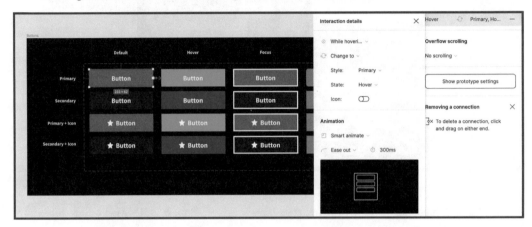

Figure 9.21 – Connecting the Default button with the Hover button

2. Select the **Primary Default** button again and create another connector, but this time, with the **Primary Focus** button as the destination. Set **While pressing** as the trigger:

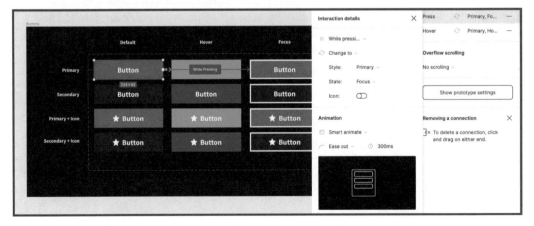

Figure 9.22 – Connecting the Default button with the Focus button

3. Repeat the same process for the **Secondary** button (and, if you created variants for buttons with icons, also for them), connecting the **Default** state with **Hover** and **Focus** and setting the right triggers:

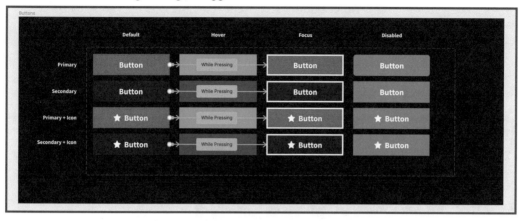

Figure 9.23 – The final outcome

Done, you've just made your buttons interactive! You have just set all the basic interactions right inside the component blueprint, and now wherever you use that particular component, it will have **Hover** and **Focus** states in each of its instances, so you don't have to duplicate any of your views. Want to see it in action? Run your prototype and play with your buttons! You can see that each button in the interface now has interaction states, and it works for both desktop, which requires **Hover,** and mobiles and tablets, which require **Focus** states:

Figure 9.24 – Previewing the Hover state on a button

Interactive components are an incredibly powerful feature that takes prototyping to a whole new level and allows you to avoid huge increases in views in your flows. But not all interactions need to be set right inside the component. For example, the **Login** button, while having states like any other button, still needs to be pressed to bring the user to the **Home** view. This is what makes this particular button different from others in your interface, because obviously each of them has its own destination views. Don't worry, because interactive components do not interrupt flow interactions that you might have already created or that you might want to create. And all of your previously set transitions from buttons to specific views will still work correctly:

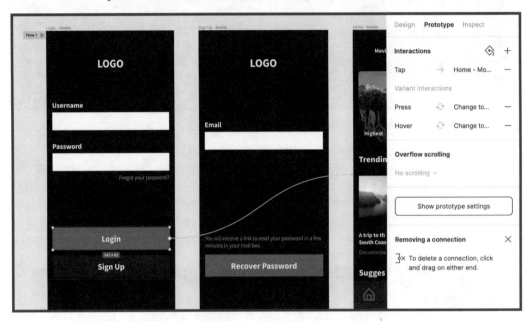

Figure 9.25 – Individual and variant interactions

When you include interactive components in your prototype, the **Prototype** sidebar will show your flow interactions as well as variants interactions. By combining these two, you can reach a completely new level of your workflow optimization since it will become much easier to manage, plus you can make it as close as possible to the real product that will be released.

Just like you created interactive components for your buttons, you can with any other element that you previously converted into a component. For example, if you want to make the tab bar interactive, instead of changing its states in each separate view, you can add triggers for it right in the variants as follows:

1. Select each **Tab Item** individually and create a connector to the corresponding active state variant (that is, the **Search** tab should be linked to the variant with an active **Search** icon, and so on). Set **On click / On tap** as a trigger and **Smart animate** must be selected:

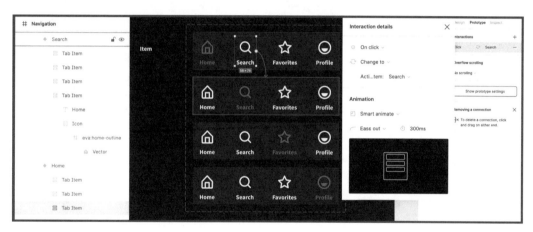

Figure 9.26 – Making the tab bar interactive

2. Proceed to the next variant, and then to the rest in sequence, connecting each **Tab Item** (except the active ones) with the corresponding **Tab Bar** variant. The final result should look like this:

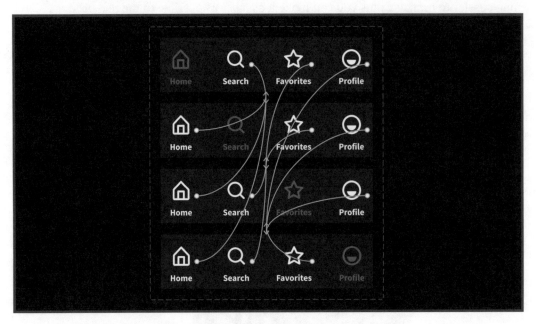

Figure 9.27 – The outcome of our tab bar prototyping

It might look pretty messy, but all the connectors remain in the component set and don't appear in the UI flow itself, so in the end it won't be that annoying.

Well, now you know about the concept of interactive components, but there is a way to optimize your prototyping even more. In the previous section, you built the main flow by adding transitions. This flow follows one direction, not letting the user return from the **Content Detail** to the **Home** view, for example. This is not how our app is going to work and there is actually a back arrow for this action, but for now, this is just a design element, not an activated one. Of course, you can easily fix this by simply adding a connector back to the **Home** view and that will work too. But in fact, **Top Bar** is used in many other views, and you would have to connect each of its instances over and over again. What if you could simplify it by setting this interaction to the main component, which will return the user to the previous view, whatever it is?

To do this, go to the **Top Bar** component on the **Styles + Components** page and follow these simple steps:

1. In **Prototype** mode, select **Tab Item** inside the **Top Bar** component as shown in the following screenshot:

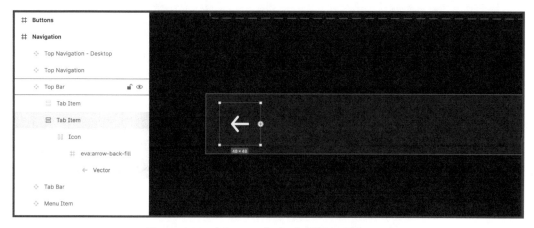

Figure 9.28 – Selecting the back Tab Item element

2. Add an interaction by clicking the + button on the right sidebar.

3. Set the trigger to **On click / On tap** and the action to **Back**:

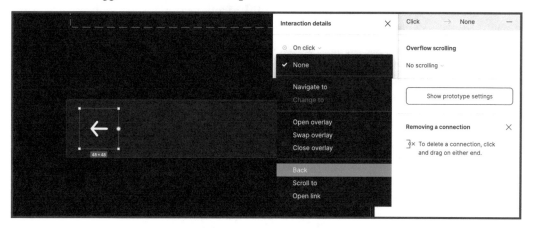

Figure 9.29 – Setting the Back action

And that's all! In just a few clicks, you have assigned a *go-back* command to all instances of the component. If you look at your interface right now, you will find that the **Back** action is automatically applied to **Mobile**, **Tablet**, and **Desktop** frames too:

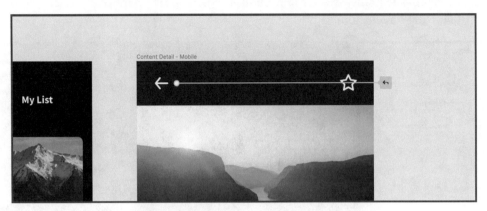

Figure 9.30 – The outcome on our frames

To make the **Content Detail** view even better, it would be a good idea to add interaction to the **Add to Favorites** icon as well. You can start converting the star icon to a component, after duplicating it from the **Top Bar** component, and then create a **Filled** variant of it. Replace the star icon in the top bar with the component you just created. Then you just need to add the **On click / On tap** interactions in the newly created variant to switch from **Default** to **Filled** and back. In the following screenshot, you can get a more specific overview of what you need to achieve:

Figure 9.31 – Making the Favorite button interactive

Great job! You've just taken your prototype to a whole new level, and now you don't have to worry about displaying the states of your buttons in your layouts and letting the user return to the previous view when needed. Remember, it's always a good idea to make your design as close to reality as possible to better present and test the interface. And, as you've seen, Figma can make it easy to achieve that goal so that you can reflect even the smallest interaction details in your flow, which can really make a difference. Our next topic will be about other features, namely overflows and overlays, which you will also need to add, and it will complete your prototyping work.

Creating interactive overflows and overlays

You have now reached the point where your application interface is almost finished and most of the prototyping is done. However, there are a few more important details that you need to add. And in this section, you are going to do that by creating scrollable views and setting interactive overlays on top of all other elements.

Making our view scrollable with overflows

As you know, some of our views contain a lot of content that goes beyond the initial vertical space, hiding what is outside the original device viewport. If you remember, in order to see and manage those elements that were outside the parent frame, you had to turn off the **Clip content** function. But this is not the case in playing your prototype, because the interface must reflect the real resolution of the device. So, in order to observe views that are too long and do not fit on the screen, we must scroll through them. For now, you haven't implemented scrolling in your views yet, so this is what you will do right now.

It might sound like a huge task, but Figma makes it very easy to solve this problem. As a starting point, you are going to apply scrolling on mobile, and then you just need to do the same for tablet and desktop. Since our **Login - Mobile** and **Sign Up - Mobile** views do not contain long content, they do not require scrolling. However, you should keep in mind that some views might perfectly fit smartphones with bigger screen resolutions, such as an *iPhone 11*, with everything inside, but they would not necessarily be displayed the same way on much smaller screens, such as the *iPhone 6*. So, in this case, scrolling might still be needed. Therefore, it is extremely important to test your interface on different devices, as you did in *Chapter 8, User Interface Design on Tablet, Desktop, and the Web*.

You will now start with the **Home - Mobile** view, which certainly requires the user to scroll down to see all of the content. So, open the file and do the following:

1. Select the **Container** layer and manually change its height to the top of the tab bar. It is important that the content exceeds the **Container** limits, otherwise, the view will not scroll:

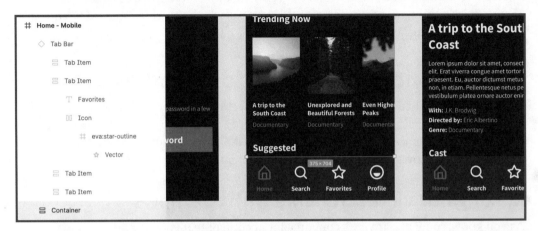

Figure 9.32 – Selecting and resizing the Container element

2. Switch to the **Prototype** mode and – with **Container** selected – change **Overflow scrolling** to **Vertical scrolling** as shown in the following screenshot:

Figure 9.33 – Changing the Container behavior to Vertical scrolling

By setting this option, you simply told Figma that your interactive prototype can be scrolled vertically. Moreover, since **Container** does not include **Tab Bar**, this element will automatically remain at the bottom of the frame when scrolling through the content of the view itself. Alternatively, you could apply scrolling behavior for the entire **Home** frame, but then you must enable the **Fix position when scrolling** option for your tab bar (you can find this function in the **Design** tab under **Constraints and resizing**). This option is actually very good in many situations, allowing you to lock an element at its current position even when the whole view is scrolling:

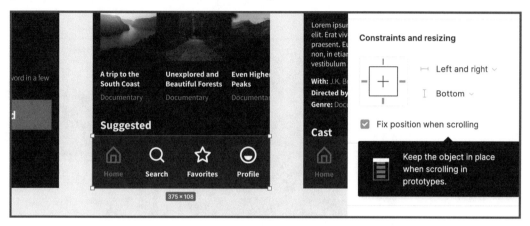

Figure 9.34 – The Fix position when scrolling option

The next view that needs scrolling is our **Content Detail - Mobile**. Repeat the steps for this screen and make sure everything except **Tab Bar** is in the **Container** layer (if you don't have one, you can always select the needed elements and frame the selection to create a new container), and then change its behavior to **Vertical scrolling**. To ensure that the scrolling behavior will work fine across the entire screen, even if the parent frame is resized, set the **Container** vertical constraints to **Top and bottom**.

The scrolling work is not completely finished yet, as there is still something to do. Both the **Home - Mobile** and **Content Detail - Mobile** views also have a set of sliders and rows that require horizontal scrolling. The procedure for working on this is almost the same as the one you have already done:

1. Select a row you want to make scrollable.

2. Resize its width to match the outer frame width.

3. Switch to the **Prototype** mode and this time set **Overflow scrolling** to **Horizontal scrolling**:

Figure 9.35 – Changing the Carousel behavior to Horizontal scrolling

> **Note**
>
> Since your **Cards Section** is a nested component, you cannot manually resize and change its behavior in layouts. To make it scrollable, go to the **Main Component** on the **Styles + Components** page and apply the changes. Alternatively, you can detach its instances to get a simple frame with a row of **Content Cards** inside, and then resize it directly on the canvas.

Great, you're done for the mobile views, and now they are scrollable! As you've seen, doing that in Figma is very fast and easy, so you can easily add scrolling behavior to tablet and desktop screens wherever it's needed.

Creating interface overlays

Prototyping in Figma offers many ways to make your interface come alive and covers most of the possible user interactions in apps, websites, and even games. All of the prototyping features you've used so far are essential to professional dynamic flow building. But there is another simple, but no less interesting, addition that needs to be implemented in our prototype, namely **overlays**. Just like interactive components, overlays are very useful when you want to keep your flows clean and have a limited number of frames in your work area. Overlays are great when you want to add additional elements to your prototypes, such as popups or tooltips, without duplicating additional views for this purpose. Let's jump right into practice to better understand this new concept.

Go to the **Styles + Components** page, create a new frame and rename it to `Overlays`. Here, create a simple **Dropdown Menu** like the example shown in the following screenshot and then make it a component:

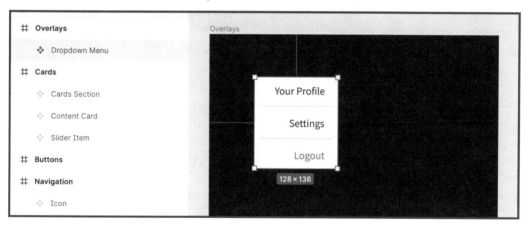

Figure 9.36 – Creating a Dropdown Menu component

Now go back to the **Hi-Fi** page and drag an instance of the component you just created from the assets. Place it directly above the **Home - Desktop** frame, but this time not inside it as shown here:

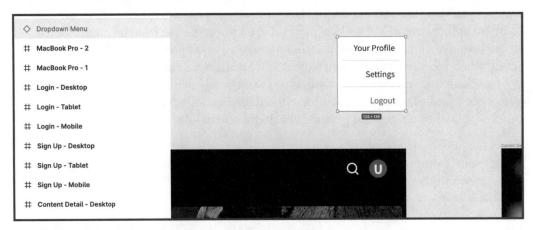

Figure 9.37 – Placing an instance of Dropdown Menu in the Hi-Fi page

Why does it make sense to put it there? The fact is that it must exist as a separate frame, which, after you set the appropriate parameters, Figma will use as an overlay element to open it on top of all the items to which it will be attached. In our case, it should appear when clicking on the **Profile** icon, so select the icon, switch to **Prototype,** and create a connector from it to the dropdown menu. Set the trigger to **On click / On tap** and set the action to **Open overlay**, then enable the **Close when clicking outside** option to allow the user to easily dismiss the overlay. Moreover, you can check the **Add background behind overlay** checkbox to add a solid color behind the overlay and make it even more readable:

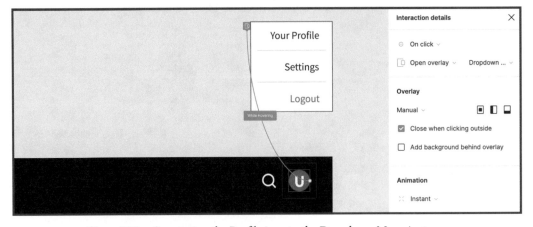

Figure 9.38 – Connecting the Profile icon to the Dropdown Menu instance

Okay, now there are a bunch of new options to manage the overlay. Here, you can make it appear exactly in the center of the screen (for example, for modals, popups, alerts), on the left border (for example, boxes, menus), or even at the bottom (for example, smartphone keyboards), but in our case, it should have a very specific position, so click the **Overlay** position drop-down list and select **Manual**. A transparent clone of the **Dropdown Menu** element will appear in the **Home - Desktop** frame, which you can drag across the screen to drop in the exact location where you want it to be displayed. Place it just below the **Profile** icon as in the following screenshot:

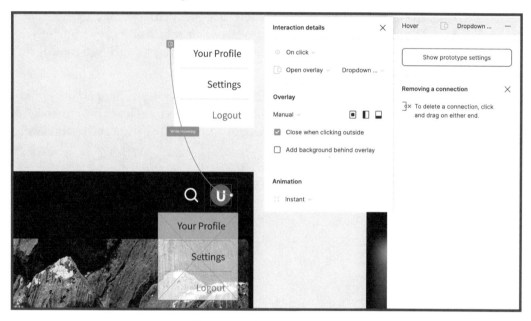

Figure 9.39 – Manually moving the element where we want it to appear

As you work on any prototype, keep in mind that the user flow doesn't necessarily mean switching from one screen to another, as there might still be some interaction happening on one screen. And thanks to Figma's overflow and overlay features, you can now present all content in your views with working scrolling and implement dropdowns, alerts, tooltips, and more in your prototype without having to create additional views to do so. Finally, we can say that the design of our application has come to life, as you will see for yourself in the next chapter!

Summary

This chapter was your first step into the world of prototyping in Figma, which is just as important a design phase as UX research and UI creation. You have learned how to connect views to each other to build dynamic flows using transitions and triggers, and when combined with smart animate, this can give outstanding results. You have also learned how to create interactive components that significantly simplify your workflow, making interactions within frames so much better. In addition, you have discovered that each view, depending on its intended use and the content inside, can be prototyped differently, since the user can stay on the same screen longer, scrolling the content or performing additional interaction with some active elements. And Figma brilliantly takes this aspect into account, offering you overflows and overlays, which you have also successfully implemented in your interface.

Now that you know enough about basic and advanced prototyping techniques in Figma, you can dive deeper into this topic, and in the next chapter, you will learn how to make your three flows – that is mobile, tablet, and desktop – ready for sharing and testing across multiple devices.

10
Testing and Sharing Your Prototype on Browsers and Real Devices

In the previous chapter, you learned how to prototype your interfaces in Figma using a variety of techniques for interaction, transitions between views, and animation of the elements. You also converted static layouts to live flows for the interfaces of all three devices, which was a pretty challenging but interesting task, and you learned a lot along the way. As a result, you not only linked all screens together but also made some components interactive, as well as adding missing elements to the application. At some points during this practice, you ran the prototype to make sure everything was set up correctly, and this is absolutely the right strategy, since constant monitoring of the prototype is necessary to prevent errors.

However, we intentionally did not go deep into the study of the prototype launch function, since this is a rather large topic that requires a separate study. And this is what this chapter will be about. Here, you will learn not only how to run a prototype, but also discover many new Figma features that allow you to share your work, collect feedback, effectively prepare the interface for testing, and much more. In this chapter, you will also learn how to run the prototype on a real device and make it better by structuring the flows in the file.

In this chapter, we are going to cover the following main topics:

- Viewing and testing your interactive prototype in Figma Presentation view
- Exploring the Figma app and its Mirror functionality to view and test a prototype in real time
- Sharing your prototype with others
- Working with feedback and reviews

By the end of this chapter, you will be able to view and test the interactive interface you created in Figma directly on small devices such as tablets and smartphones, as well as providing access to your prototype in a variety of other ways.

Viewing your interactive prototype

You've come a long way to the point where you can say that the design and prototyping for your application are complete, and now it's finally time to see the result. In this section, you will discover a whole new set of prototype parameters and learn how to properly configure them for a dynamic preview of your interface right in Figma. For a more realistic viewing experience, you'll learn about using device presets that come with Figma, and if you want to go even further, there is the Figma mobile app – a standalone product that allows you to test the app's design right on your smartphone or tablet. But let's take everything in order, and first, we will take a closer look at the **Prototype** tab and how to run it.

Running the prototype on desktop/the web

Although in the previous chapter you created a whole flow connecting views to each other and using interactions and **Transitions**, so far you have only seen the static version of the application design (with a few minor exceptions). Now, it's time to view the dynamic version of the prototype, but first, let's see what settings are available for it. With no layers selected on the canvas, switch to the **Prototype** tab to see the general prototyping options:

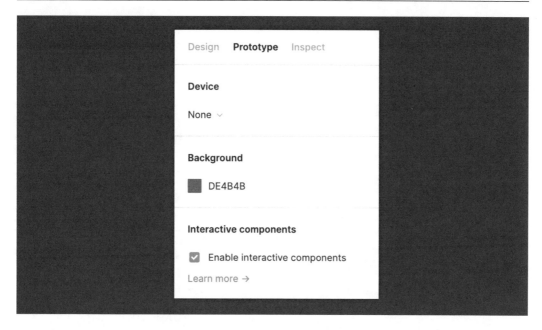

Figure 10.1 – General Prototype options

You are already quite familiar with this tab, but let's take a look at it once again and see what else you can manage with these parameters. The first section you see is the **Device** selector, where you can choose from a list of device presets for how the prototype will be framed:

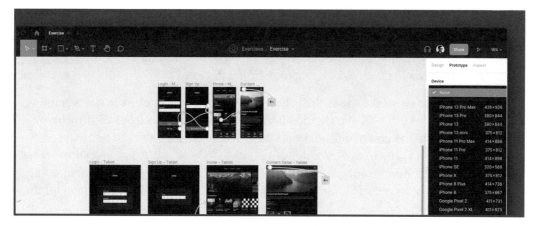

Figure 10.2 – Device selector

It is important to understand that choosing one of these real device mock-ups will not affect the actual resolution of the interface you are about to run. To better understand this aspect, select **iPad Pro 11"** from the list and launch your prototype for mobile devices, and this is what you will see:

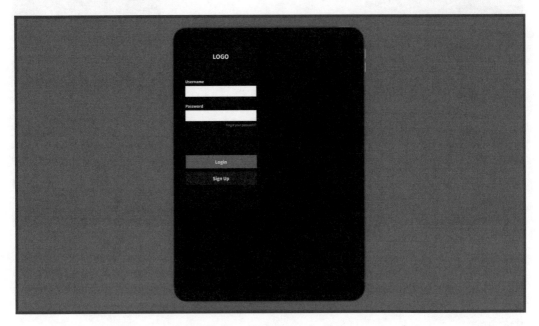

Figure 10.3 – Selecting the wrong device for the current resolution

In the preceding figure, you can see that the view does not match the preset, and whenever you have something like this (they do not fill all the space, as in the preceding example, or on the contrary, they are cropped and you do not see all the content), you can fix it right in the **Device** selector by switching to the right device.

In this case, since you worked with the **iPhone 11 Pro** preset frames from the beginning, to see the interface at its best you should also select **iPhone 11 Pro** from the **Prototype** list. After choosing the preset, a **Model** selector will appear just below, in which – if available – you can even change the color of the device. Once you've got everything set up, you can finally run your prototype. To do this, you should select the initial mobile frame (**Login - Mobile** view) and click on the **Present** button – the one with a **Play** icon on the right side of the top bar. As a result, you will get a fully functional prototype:

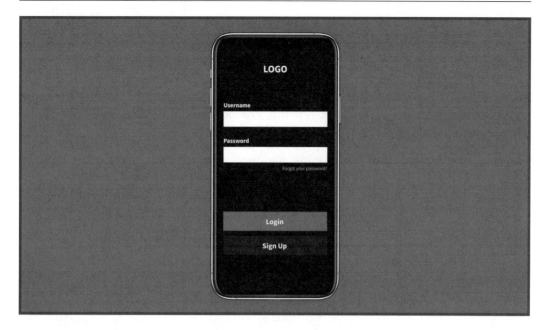

Figure 10.4 – Playing a prototype

As you will have noticed, the prototype opens in a new, separate Figma tab (or browser tab if you're using a web app) and this dedicated specific space is called **Presentation view**.

> **Note**
>
> In the general **Prototype** settings, you can also customize the **Background color** of the **Presentation view**, which is the surface on which the device is displayed. In addition, you can change the **Orientation** of the device to be able to show the prototype in both **Portrait** and **Landscape** modes.

It's amazing how impressively realistic your interface looks when framed in a device mock-up, so it's a great way to present it to your customers or stakeholders. However, when you are still in the internal testing stages, using a specific preset can be limiting and inconvenient. For example, if you want to quickly switch between interfaces with completely different resolutions in order to test versions for mobile devices, tablets, and desktops in real time, you need to go back to the settings each time and manually select the most appropriate preset to display your interface right.

To avoid this problem, you can use the last two options from the device list: **Custom size** and **Presentation**. The first, **Custom size**, allows you to set a custom width and height value that will be used for each prototype you run. The second, **Presentation**, which is much more useful and simpler, shows the prototype in full, whatever its actual size. In the last case, you will not have any mock-ups for the layouts, but you will always see the entire proper screen size. For now, let's switch to this **Presentation** mode as it is most suitable for our current testing phase.

Now that your **Presentation view** is set up and ready to use, we can finally try our mobile prototype interactively. In the **Presentation view** tab, you can easily share your prototype and leave comments, and you will learn more about it in the section *Sharing your prototype with others*, dedicated to this topic. But for now, let's focus on the view settings. In the top-right panel, click **Options** and a dropdown will appear with a whole bunch of new options, as shown in the following screenshot:

Figure 10.5 – Prototype view settings

From this menu, you can fix any viewing issue you may encounter. Here, you can choose to display the interface of the desired size while maintaining the original interface size or filling the entire screen as much as possible. If you want a much cleaner, non-distracting way of presenting, you can turn off the **Show Figma UI** option, and the entire Figma interface will be hidden. Make sure the **Show hotspot hints on click** option is enabled, as we'll use and talk about those soon in this section. You may also notice that some of the options are grayed out, but don't worry, once you start working with **Flows** and **Comments**, all of these options will be enabled.

Now, let's try to navigate the frames to see that everything that you have done in the prototyping works in a dynamic way. You can use the *Left* and *Right* arrow keys on your keyboard to move through all the frames in the file, but this will be similar to viewing a slideshow presentation. What if, instead, we want to actually test all the interactions that you implemented earlier? This is very easy to do. You just have to click where the **Hotspots** were set in our design. Remember the elements you linked using **Connectors**? They are now clickable!

In our design, you can test the interaction right on the very first screen. Just try hovering over the **Login** button and it will immediately change its state to **Hover** as this is the interactive component you created earlier! If everything is right, the **Sign Up** button should act the same way:

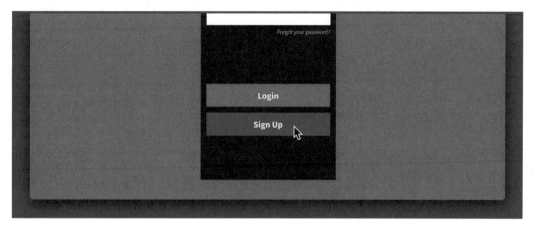

Figure 10.6 – Testing the hover state

Continuing your testing, let's now click on the **Login** button, after which you will be taken directly to the **Home - Mobile** page, as this is the exact scenario set up during the prototyping phase. Now that you are on the **Home** page, you can see it live with all of its scroll behaviors, both horizontal and vertical, and it works great, as if you had it on a real device. Here, however, you might get a bit confused about continuing the flow, since you haven't made every card clickable, and therefore it becomes problematic to determine which one to click on. Don't worry, in that case, there are **Hotspots hints** to help you see all the interactive areas. To see them you just have to click anywhere on the screen (even outside the interface outer frame) and Figma will highlight all the **Hotspots** on the current page in blue for a second, as shown in the following screenshot:

Figure 10.7 – Blinking blue Hotspots

Hotspot hints are certainly very useful for the prototype creator, but they also make it incredibly easy for any external viewers to follow the flow.

> **Note**
>
> You can quickly restart your prototype from the beginning at any time by pressing *R* on your keyboard. What's more, if you go back to the design file and do some visual editing or adjustments to the prototype settings, you won't have to reload the **Presentation view** as the prototype will automatically update in real time.

With these simple navigation techniques, you can now easily view your entire interactive prototype on mobile, tablet, and desktop pages. Take a moment to quickly test all the views to see if everything is working well and, if necessary, fix any small bugs that you might find. For example, remember to test opening the dropdown menu you created for **Home - Desktop**, the one that appears after clicking the **Profile** icon, and see if it works and opens in the right place. When working on real projects, it is best to test interactions as you work on them by keeping the **Presentation view** open next to your file. This way, you can directly check if the transition from page to page is done correctly and the animation of the elements performs the way you want. You can always change something for the better in your prototype if you feel like it is necessary.

Now that you know how to launch and navigate your prototype in **Presentation view**, let's see how to do the same thing, but this time right on your smartphone or tablet!

Running the prototype on a smartphone/tablet

Undoubtedly, viewing your prototypes in Figma is an easy, quick, and practical way to present and test your interface. And when using mock-ups in prototyping, it might look almost the same as in real life ... but it's still an unrealistic experience of interacting with a product, don't you think?

This becomes more evident when testing, for example, mobile interfaces on your laptop or desktop computer rather than on smartphones. Specifically, we have hover states for our button, which are not presented on a real mobile device where the user interacts with the touchscreen. So, what if we want to test our application directly on smartphones and tablets?

Yes, Figma has a solution to this problem – the Figma mobile app, which is available in the **App Store** (iOS) and **Play Store** (Android). This is what the Figma mobile app looks like on a device:

Figure 10.8 – Figma mobile app in dark and light mode

So, what can this app actually give you? In fact, it is a standalone portable viewer for your projects that allows you to access all designs directly from your portable device. Of course, this app cannot replace the Figma desktop or web app, as it only allows you to view, not edit your files. But its main advantage is that you can run an interactive prototype right in the app, so your mobile interfaces will look and feel as real as possible in the Figma mobile app, and your tablet views in the tablet app version accordingly.

> **Note**
>
> The Figma app requires you to be signed in with the same credentials you use with your Figma desktop/web app in order to access all of your files and connect to the **Presentation view** in real time.

If your smartphone or tablet is running an iOS or Android operating system, find and download the Figma app from the store, and then log in with your account. The first thing you will see is a list of your recent files, and if you find and enter our project, it will look like this:

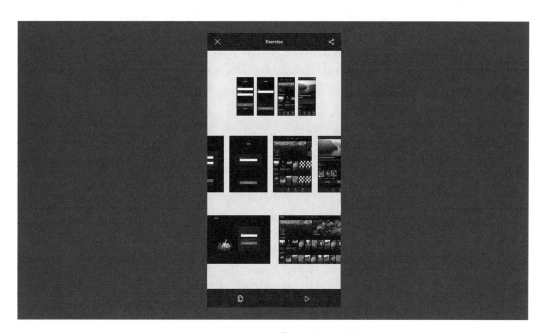

Figure 10.9 – Viewing a file on the mobile app

On this file page, you can see the tab bar with only two tabs. On the first, you can freely move, pan, and scale the layouts, and on the second, you can run the prototype directly from your device.

> **Note**
>
> If you want to restart the prototype or exit this mode, tap and hold anywhere on the device screen to bring up the quick actions menu.

This app has another incredibly useful feature, namely Mirror. There used to be an app of the same name, also from Figma, the only purpose of which was to reflect the frames that you select in Figma on the screen of your smartphone. Now, this feature is built into the Figma app, and from here you can constantly view your frames and interactions between views directly on your device in real time. To try this, exit your prototype and go to the **Mirror** tab. In the following screenshot, you can see its initial state:

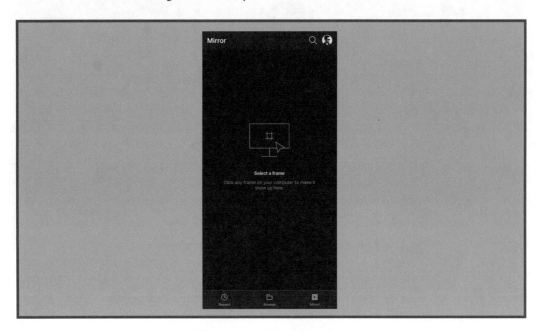

Figure 10.10 – The Mirror tab

Now you can simply open any file on your desktop or web Figma and select the frame you want to view. The app will automatically recognize your choice and update the prototype on your device in just a few seconds. With this fairly simple yet powerful tool, it becomes incredibly easy to design interfaces while constantly monitoring how they appear on the actual target device. This way, you can always check the actual sizes of the elements, transitions between the pages, interactions, and the states of each element. However, don't expect a hassle-free experience, since some interactions may work differently from the desktop counterpart.

The Figma application lets you view and test all your frames regardless of their size, since they will always adapt to the width of your device screen. Of course, if you test on a real device that you are prototyping for, it will be a better and more natural experience.

As you can see, Figma makes it as efficient as possible to test your prototypes by inviting you to not only view your product in Figma with all those fluid interactions and cool animations but literally test it with your fingers in the Figma app!

Take some time to explore this app, especially in collaboration with Figma itself, playing around with the Mirror feature, and once you're ready to move on, you'll learn how to share your prototype in the next section.

Sharing your prototype with others

Now you know how to view and test your prototype in Figma, in the **Presentation view** and right on your device. It is possible that in the course of testing, you discovered something that you wanted to fix in the design or in the transitions between screens. This is absolutely normal, since prototyping should be primarily useful for you, in order to identify and correct inaccuracies or change something. If everything is in order and you are happy with your work, it is time to move on to the next step, which is to show your prototype to other people, who could be colleagues, friends, clients, or stakeholders. So, in this section, you will learn the best practices on how to share your prototype with others in Figma.

Linking the prototype and managing permissions

In *Chapter 7, Building Components and Variants in a Collaborative Workspace*, you learned how to share your design files by sending email invitations and giving others either full collaborator rights (with an editor role), or limited access to third parties (with the role of a viewer, without the possibility of editing). Thus, it makes sense that everyone you invite will have access to the prototype as well, since access to the project automatically provides the ability to play and view your prototypes.

However, there are times when you only want to share an interactive prototype without showing your design files, even in read-only mode. This feature is also provided in Figma. To do this, while in the **Presentation view**, you should click on the **Share prototype** button in the upper-right corner:

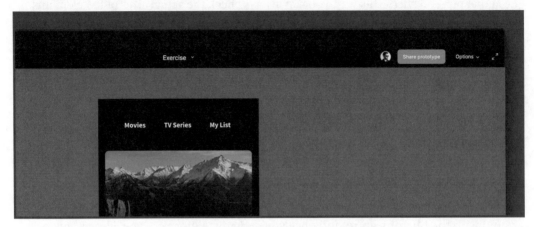

Figure 10.11 – Share prototype button

This will open the sharing options dialog box, which you have already seen in the previous chapters. If you already have co-editors and/or viewers listed, they can view and try the prototype, but at the same time see (or even edit) the original file. To give someone access only to the prototype, you should paste their email address and click on the **can view** dropdown menu item. You will see that you now have an additional completely new option, namely **can view prototypes only**:

Figure 10.12 – Viewing permissions

> **NOTE**
> The **can view prototypes only** option is available only for Professional teams and Organizations.

You can also assign this option to someone you previously added as an editor or reader, thus changing their permissions. By setting the **Anyone with the link** rule to **can view prototypes only**, you can then click on **Copy link** in the lower-right corner and send the generated link directly, which you now have on your computer clipboard. Whoever gets it can only access the interactive prototype, but in no case will they be allowed to see what is behind it.

Embedding the prototype

In **Presentation view**, just like in the design file, you will also find the option to create an embed. But what does this incorporation consist of? How is this different from what we can do with the file itself? And how can this be useful? Now you will receive answers to all these questions, point by point. Go ahead and click on the **Get embed code** option at the bottom of the same sharing dialog in **Presentation view** and you get something like this:

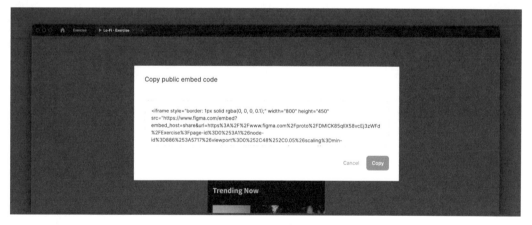

Figure 10.13 – Embed code

This is HTML code that you can just **Copy** in a block, and once you do it, you can paste it into any website or application that supports HTML blocks. For example, you can use it on your personal website to create an interactive portfolio of products, or in documentation to display interactive examples. What you do is entirely up to you.

> **Note**
>
> An embedded prototype can be public and accessible to anyone who sees the page or application that includes it, or private, and this will require the user to be signed in and have the right permissions.

Let's take a look at how it works so you can better understand how useful it can be. The easiest way for us is to test it right in FigJam. Copy the embed code of your prototype, then open any FigJam file, select the **Media** option in the bottom toolbar, and paste the frame block into the link box. That's all. You now have a fully working Figma prototype right on your FigJam board:

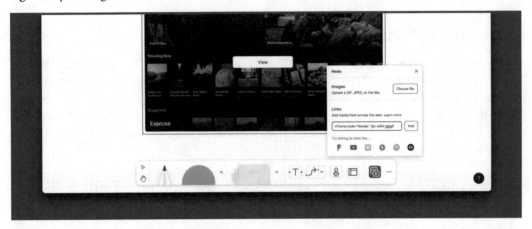

Figure 10.14 – Using an embed prototype on FigJam

Note that embedding a prototype (using the **Share prototype** button in the **Presentation view** tab) and embedding the entire file (using the **Share** button in the main design workspace) will give you different results. In the second case, once your code is embedded and pasted anywhere, you can only view and navigate but not edit anything:

Figure 10.15 – Embedding a Figma file in FigJam

Keep in mind these two functions, which may seem like they are the same but are completely different. However, each of them can be useful because you can immediately provide access to the structural composition of your file or just the prototype. Plus, it's a good way to let anyone who's not familiar with Figma see your work, and it doesn't even require account creation (as long as you give access to your embeddings with public permissions).

That's all you need to know in order to share your work the way you like, setting whatever accessibility rules for any occasion possible. Sharing in Figma is a generous feature that goes beyond the app itself and makes it easy to implement, show, and present your designs and prototypes to anyone. But in most cases, you will be sharing your work to get feedback and reactions from customers, target users, or stakeholders. Once again, Figma has made it easy to collect feedback and collaborate with others in an easy and fun way, and in the next section, you'll learn about all the tools and tricks and how to do it.

Working with feedback and reviews

At this point, you have gone through the main stages of the design workflow. Our interface is designed, interactive, shareable, and completely ready for the stage of user testing, review, and comparison. However, collecting feedback is a very important part of a designer's job, and you should take it seriously. Other people may see and appreciate your design in a different way, often unexpectedly, so it can be challenging at times. It is also very important to know how to analyze comments and see what is behind them – a simple note about the style or a whole UX case. So, don't be afraid to ask the right questions, respond, empathize with user needs, and try to take criticism as an opportunity to look at your work from a different perspective and possibly make it better. It can be overwhelming at first but don't worry, it all comes with experience, plus, Figma can help you make collaboration and communication with others a greatly organized and fun process. You will learn all about these techniques in the current section.

Viewers and comments

When we're on the Team plan, or when your file is shared with other collaborators, each of you can use the appropriate **Add comment** function to add notes and feedback anywhere in the workspace. In the following screenshot, you can see what an example comment might look like:

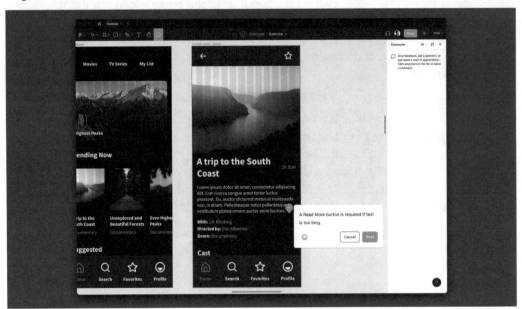

Figure 10.16 – Inserting a comment

When you activate the **Add comment** mode, the right sidebar will allow you to view, scroll, respond to, and resolve (if the requested change has been made) all comments from all contributors on the current page:

Figure 10.17 – Comments panel

Figma recently rolled out a new update for comments and they became even more readable. In addition, now you can also use reactions or directly tag someone from your team who can help solve a specific problem. Don't hesitate to try out those new features!

During the phase of collecting feedback, it often happens that for some reason you do not want to provide access to the source of the file, but still want someone to be able to view the design interface and share their opinion and leave feedback.

This can be a common case where customers or stakeholders need to see the product and leave feedback or suggest corrections that need to be made. In this situation, you can simply provide a link to the prototype only (keep in mind that the prototype always starts with the view that you see in front of you when you create a shared link), and from the **Presentation view**, even those who do not have access to the original file will be able to insert comments using the appropriate tool on the top bar:

Figure 10.18 – Add comment function for viewers

Remember that even if someone only intends to leave comments in your file or prototype, and nothing more, a Figma account – any, even a Starter one – is required. Thus, there will be no unpleasant surprises such as anonymous and unwanted comments.

All reviews collected in this way will be automatically added to the list, which is available from the design file, and whoever has edit rights will see a badge on the icon, indicating the presence of new comments:

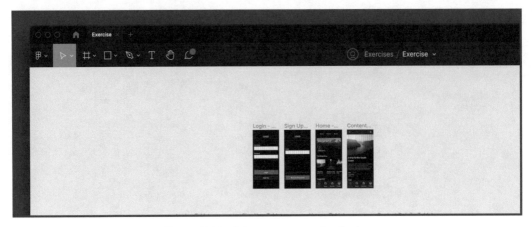

Figure 10.19 – New comments alert badge

In summary, comments can be used in two different and equally useful ways. First of all, for internal use, for collaboration between everyone who works on the interface design so that they can communicate, suggest, review, and keep track of what needs to be fixed. And also at critical stages (such as completing a wireframe, interface, or interactive prototype), to collect feedback and reaction from customers and stakeholders. In this way, all parties will be involved to avoid any problems and misunderstandings in the development process.

Structuring flows

Since you have three different flows for multiple devices, you need to switch between interfaces, which may not be so easy and fast. In complex projects, you can have even more dynamic flows, and often at first glance, they can look almost the same. In such cases, it is quite easy to send the wrong link by mistake, and as a result, the recipient will see the wrong prototype. How can you avoid this confusion?

To solve this problem, Figma has created **Flows**, a function with which you can label, structure, and manipulate your flows in a file. To see exactly how this works, let's implement **Flows** for our prototypes, and to do this, follow these steps:

1. Temporarily exit the **Presentation view** and return to the **Hi-Fi** page. From here, switch to the **Prototype** tab and select the first view of the mobile flow, that is, **Login - Mobile**.

2. In the upper part of the panel, you will find the **Flow starting point** option. Click the + button and the first **Flow** will be added:

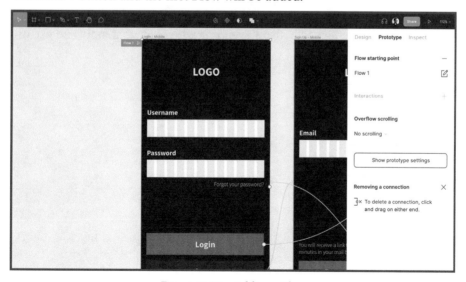

Figure 10.20 – Adding a Flow

3. From now on, Figma will know that the **Login - Mobile** view is the starting point for one of our user flows. By default, this flow was named Flow 1, but to make it more specific, you can rename it to Mobile Flow simply by clicking on the name and entering a new one.

4. Then click the **Edit** button and add a **Description**. This way, you will make everything clear even to those who are not involved in the project, but they will only see the finished prototype, so that they can quickly get the idea:

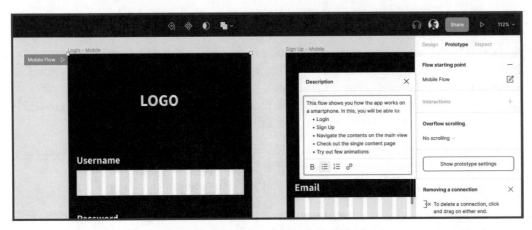

Figure 10.21 – Setting a description for a Flow

Repeat the same operation for the tablet and desktop flows, giving them the appropriate names and descriptions. When you're done, you can see and explore all the flows you've created in the project in the right sidebar (you shouldn't have active selections in the canvas to see a list of your flows). From here, you can even run a prototype of a specific flow, or copy a link to it, which will direct everyone who receives it, only and exclusively, to this flow:

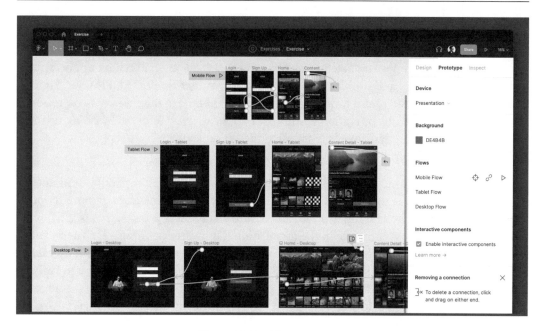

Figure 10.22 – Flows overview

In addition, from now on, a new left sidebar will be available in the **Presentation view**, which allows you to navigate between the different flows in real time with a single click, as well as to read their descriptions so you already know what to expect:

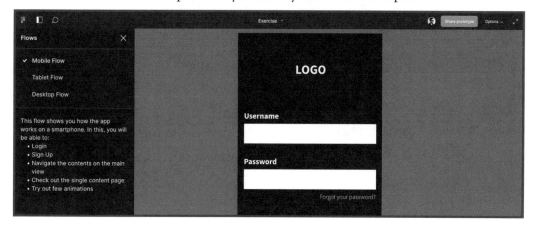

Figure 10.23 – Presentation view with Flows

Flows are a great addition to the prototype feature that makes your interactive interfaces more organized and easier to manage. As long as you use appropriate names and clear descriptions, even in a file with multiple flows, it will be easy for you and your teammates to navigate.

Advanced user testing

User testing of a product – and at different stages of design – by those who represent the target audience is an important step for every project, as well as an excellent opportunity to detect critical issues and problems long before the product is released. **Flows** in Figma are also an undoubtedly useful function for this case, as you can offer a user two or more flows to perform the same operation within your application or website. By doing this kind of comparative analysis, you can investigate user behavior more deeply, as well as identifying bugs and problems.

In fact, when prototyping very large and complex applications, it is impossible and not very efficient to provide users with the entire prototype, consisting of a huge number of possible paths, and tell them to try it. So, it is best to structure real tasks, that is, a list of goals that the user must complete in the application. Only after defining all of them, you can then create specific prototypes for these purposes and provide the user with this set of flows from various parts of the application. For example, the first flow might be to register a new user and log into the application, the second to select and view streaming content, and so on. In this way, the flow description can be strategically used as a numerical step-by-step list that the users must be able to follow on their own.

However, there may be circumstances when **Flows** in Figma aren't enough, for example, when there is no way to closely observe the testing phase or to interview each individual user to determine their satisfaction with the user experience. In this case, there are some very interesting alternative tools that you can use alongside Figma for creating user tests and user research. The most famous is definitely **Maze** (www.maze.co):

Figure 10.24 – The Maze tool

Maze is an extremely interesting tool with a free plan that allows you to send real structured tests to a significant number of people. It allows you to try out different flows of your prototype by asking the users to complete the assigned tasks, and finally have them fill out short surveys you can prepare in advance, so you can gather ideas and opinions and analyze the general level of satisfaction. Obviously, the prototypes you'll be using in Maze can be created in Figma, and in fact, it will be enough to use the link to the Figma prototype when requested by Maze.

As you know, one of Figma's greatest strengths is its powerful collaboration features, and perhaps this section has made you even more convinced of this by seeing how easy it is to leave and manage comments. You will use comments a lot when working in a team, and as you've seen, Figma is still developing them to make them even better. You also learned about another easy-to-use but very useful feature, namely **Flows**, and even implemented them in your prototype, so now everything is better structured and understandable. And if you ever need or want to go further with user testing, you can always refer to external tools such as Maze, which in collaboration with Figma can give you better user testing results!

Summary

Perhaps this chapter was special for you because, here, you finally saw the live result of your work. You've surely discovered a lot of pleasant surprises – you had already implemented amazing prototyping techniques before this, but it might have been impressive to see how it all works in practice. And even if you found something that didn't work as planned, don't worry, you now have enough experience to correctly identify the source of the problem and fix it quickly. In the future, you will find such errors earlier, because now you know how to monitor and test a prototype in real time, both in the Presentation view and in the Figma application.

Apart from that, you also learned how to share your prototype, embed it to give easier access to it, and let others comment and share their opinions right in Figma. You also learned how to structure your prototype better using Flows, and now your prototype is even better prepared for user testing.

In the next chapter, you will be exploring the **Inspect** panel, and you will learn how to export assets and prepare your design files for further development.

11
Exporting Assets and Managing the Handover Process

At the moment, you have successfully completed the stage of building a prototype of our interface, which you configured and tested in Presentation view and possibly within the Figma mobile application. You have come a long way to get where you are, all the while mastering Figma and comprehending the principles of the design working process. Therefore, we can safely say that your future projects will be easier in terms of working with Figma since you can now not only use all the necessary functions of this design tool but also the more complicated ones, since real projects require much more detailed work at each stage of interface design.

Speaking about working on *the really* complex products, you need to understand that there is a large team of professionals behind each product, and designers are one of the key players, involved in frequent communication with their colleagues. And this aspect is just as important as what you have studied so far. You can create excellent layouts with a strong user experience, but if things are never fully developed or are released with serious problems due to misunderstandings in the team, your work will instantly turn out to be meaningless. To minimize these kinds of issues, Figma has a set of functions for quickly exporting and preparing assets for handover to developers. This is what this chapter will focus on, and beyond that, you will also learn how to make your design files easily accessible and understandable to both you and others.

In this chapter, we are going to cover the following main topics:

- Exporting from Figma
- Exploring the **Inspect** tab
- Handing the project over for development

By the end of the chapter, you will have learned how to distinguish Figma's save and export formats, export assets and code snippets, and apply best practices for smooth handover to the development team.

Exporting from Figma

At this point, you have a pretty clear overview of the exact work behind analysis, design, interactive prototyping, and product testing. Now you will focus on the very last stage – working on the handover of all resources and assets, which happens after you have made sure that your design is absolutely ready for it. The first thing that you need to know about is the Figma tools: these allow you to prepare and export the file and individual elements to everyone who will then work on the actual development of the application or website. There are several ways to do this, as well as several formats that Figma offers for it. This and more will be presented to you in this section of the chapter.

What formats are supported?

First, we need to define an important difference between saving and exporting in Figma, as well as other design tools. By clicking on **File** in the menu bar (desktop version only) or on the **Figma** logo in the upper left corner and then **File**, you can save a local version of the project:

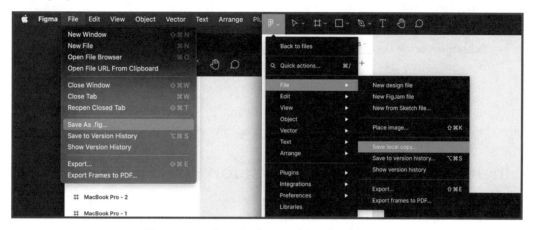

Figure 11.1 – Save As .fig… and Save local copy…

This will be a real backup of the source of the project, which you can store locally or possibly share with third parties by transferring the product from one account to another on a permanent basis. Thus, saving is equivalent to working with source files that support the ability to open and edit whatever you have created in Figma (excluding file comments, rules/permissions, and version history – these won't be included in the saved .fig files). Exported assets, as opposed to saved assets, will be completely independent of Figma, and therefore, when you export part of a project or the entire project, you create a copy that is no longer native to Figma.

The export option is available from the same **File** menu, just below the save options. The first function, **Export…**, allows you to specify your choice, and you will explore it in more detail later in this chapter. Another option, **Export frames to PDF**, exports a single PDF file containing all the frames of the current page, even if they are of different sizes. **PDF** (**Portable Document Format**), as you probably already know, is an extremely versatile format type, but above all it is absolutely compatible with any system, old or new. This format is very convenient as it can collect text, fonts, vectors, and images.

In addition to PDF, Figma allows you to export some of the most common formats, such as these:

- **Portable Network Graphics** (**PNG**) – a lossless raster format that keeps eventual layer transparency.

- **Joint Photographic Group** (**JPG**) – a compressed raster format that gives a smaller file size but reduces quality.

- **Scalable Vector Graphics** (**SVG**) – a vector format that can be scaled without loss of quality since it is based on numeric values and coordinates. It is not pixel-based and does not work with bitmaps.

Now, after this brief overview of the formats available in Figma, let's move from theory to practice and learn how to export single and multiple assets.

Single- and multiple-assets export

Besides the function of exporting an entire document or entire pages of a file, you can also export only some parts of a design and collect assets used in a composition to pass on to the development team or for any other purpose. This operation can be performed by selecting items individually or in bulk according to your needs. Let's start by exporting a single element.

It happens quite often that you need to provide the development team with a set of icons used in your design, so now you will try to simulate this action with a single icon. To do this, go to your **Hi-Fi** page and follow these steps:

1. Open your layouts and select any icon, such as the star, provided in our **Content Detail** view. Pay attention to the right panel, where the **Export** section will appear, which is currently inactive. To activate this feature, click the + next to it.

2. Now Figma will show you some of the options available for exporting this single asset. Since this icon is vector, you can choose the **SVG** format to keep it editable, or alternatively, you can save its bitmap but preserve transparency by choosing **PNG**:

Figure 11.2 – The Export section

3. Next to the format selector, you can see the scale setting. Click **1x** to open a list with some asset scaling presets.

   There are several choices with different letters at the end of each value. Values with an **X** at the end act as a multiplier, and those with a **W** and **H** set the object to a fixed width and height, respectively. For example, if you now choose **2x**, the icon will be proportionally twice its current size and therefore heavier in terms of file size. This may be required to avoid visual artifacts and blurring for some devices that actually have a higher pixel density with the same screen. You can also enter your own scale value in this field.

4. When you're done, just click the **Export** (+ *Layer Name*) button, choose where to save this individual asset, and confirm, and your file will appear right there in just a few seconds.

Note

You can add more than one **Export** option to each item by simply clicking the + button in the appropriate section on the right sidebar. This allows you to easily export the asset in different formats with one click, or export in the same format but at different scales, such as **1x** and **2x**.

However, after you have exported an icon, you will notice that the export settings remain active with all fields filled in, which is certainly handy if you want to re-export the same icon later. But what's even more useful is the ability to customize the export options directly during the design process, so that all the elements will be immediately ready for the export phase. Thus, you can preconfigure the export parameters for you and anyone else who would like to export assets from the file, even with view-only permissions:

Figure 11.3 – Export section for users with view-only permissions

One of the main benefits of this feature is that developers can remain autonomous in exporting assets directly from Figma. And this is not the only advantage of this.

If you set the correct export options for each asset (for example, **PNG** format with **1x** and **2x** scales – for each icon, for all card images – **PNG** and maybe some full parent frames in PDF to have a quick preview of the interface), each element will be ready to be extrapolated from Figma, and you can even do it with one click. Exactly for this purpose, there is the previously mentioned **Export...** function, which you can find by clicking the Figma icon menu at the top left and choosing **File**. To access it faster, you can press *Shift + Command + E* (macOS) or *Shift + Ctrl + E* (Win) and a bulk export window will appear. This dialog collects all the assets on the current page with relative settings set for each and performs a bulk export:

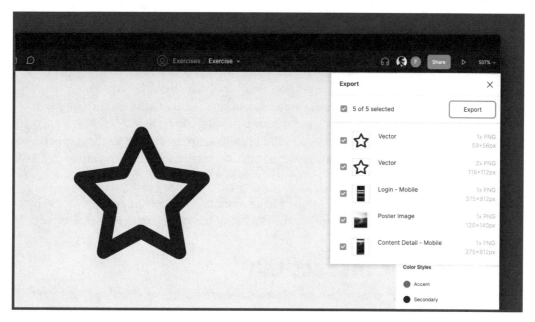

Figure 11.4 – Bulk exporting assets

As you can see, the list is presented as checkboxes, so you can optionally also deselect some of the assets that you do not want to export at the moment. Alternatively, you can select one or more items on your canvas, and then run the **Export...** function, and the window will contain only those selected items. It also works for selecting a single layer that can contain multiple assets inside. For example, if you select the **Content Detail** frame and then open the **Export** dialog box, it will show only the exportable assets contained in that view.

Let's recap all the possibilities Figma offers you for your assets and files. So, there are five formats – **FIG**, **PDF**, **PNG**, **JPG**, and **SVG** – for saving or exporting the elements you want. The first one is for downloading a local copy of your file, and its further use can be exclusively in Figma. Other formats are easy to open outside of Figma and are completely independent after export, so you can share them without any special restrictions. Each format has both advantages and limitations, and your choice depends on your needs and the goals of that export. Also, you can export items individually or in large quantities, as well as exporting the same item in several formats and scales with one click, if you have configured everything correctly beforehand. Finally, you have learned how to make it easier to work with elements that you might need to share by setting all the **Export** options for them right at the interface design stage. Moreover, in this way, you open up the ability to others to freely save these elements from Figma, even for viewers.

Take the time to explore export functions a little more on your own if you need to. When you're done, you'll move on to exploring the last tab of the right panel, namely **Inspect**.

Exploring the Inspect tab

As you can see, the right panel contains a huge number of functions, settings, and tools. It took you several chapters and a lot of practice to get to know it at a good level. All that's left for now is the last tab of this panel, namely **Inspect**, and in this section, you will fill this missing gap and explore it in detail. The main peculiarity of this tab is that, unlike **Design** and **Prototype**, it is also available to those with only view permissions, so it is a great tool for developers and external collaborators. This is what this tab looks like without any active selections:

Figure 11.5 – The Inspect tab

It basically consists of two parts: one is dedicated to **Styles** and **Interactions** and the other is about **Code** snippets, and now we will dive into both.

Styles overview

Let's start right off with part of a complete overview of the entire **Styles** library, which you can see in the **Inspect** panel with no active selections. This is a complete collection of **Grid**, **Text**, **Color**, and **Effect** styles present in the current file. This overview makes the **Inspect** tab incredibly valuable, especially when you consider that it is visible even without file edit permissions.

> **Note**
> If you have set any interactions on a particular frame before, in addition to styles, the **Inspect** panel will display an overview of the transition properties.

By clicking on the **Edit** button (it appears when you hover over any listed style name), regardless of the style's type, you can view its detailed information, that is, the associated parameters and any descriptions you added during the style creation stage, which helps you understand when it is best to use each style:

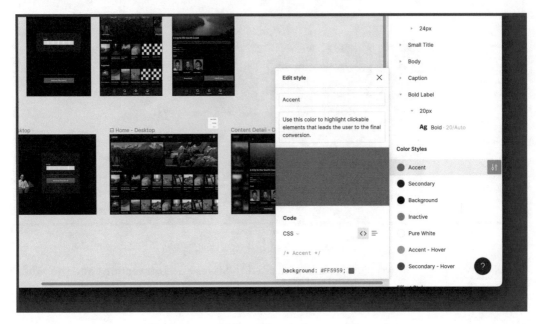

Figure 11.6 – Adding a description to a color style

The **Inspect** tab can not only display information about the entire file as a whole but also, above all, about individual layers as well. Let's now see what will happen in the **Inspect** tab if you select any item on your canvas. Click on any layer and Figma will show you a quick summary of all properties applied to it. For example, after selecting a **Button** element, **Inspect** looks something like this:

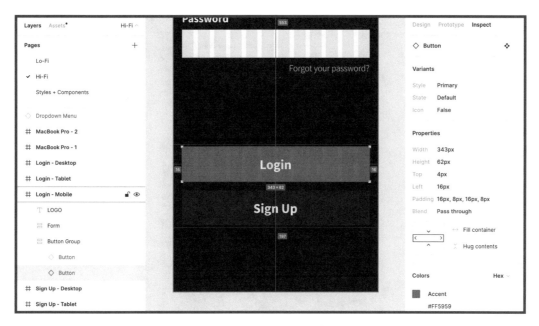

Figure 11.7 – Inspecting a button

Of course, there is no new information that you cannot get in the **Design** tab, but what **Inspect** does is organize it in a simple way, and, above all, this summary is available to anyone with access to the file. This way, you can get information for each individual layer in the file, from the simplest to the most complex. And, as you might have guessed, depending on the type of item selected, the summary will contain different properties. Here's what you'll see about a **Text** layer, for example:

Figure 11.8 – Inspecting a Text layer

Remember that the **Inspect** tab is for informational purposes only and is read-only, regardless of your file permissions. This means that it is impossible to change any value here or adjust any settings, except for the name and description of the styles in the library (for editors).

Design to code

As a designer, you will most likely rarely use the **Inspect** tab, as it is primarily intended for developers. Of course, the property summary can be useful in other cases as well, but its main purpose is to provide the development team with all the values they might need to write the actual code. At the beginning of your journey, it was mentioned that Figma may seem limited in comparison to, for example, Adobe Illustrator, but the truth is that these products are slightly different and complementary. In Figma, the limitations are dictated by a specific need, namely the ability to easily convert everything we design into code. All elements you create in Figma are automatically converted to the best, mostly web, rules using the latest **HTML5** and **CSS3** standards. So, if, for example, you can't find a specific filter or effect in a code snippet, it might not be possible to reproduce it in HTML and CSS, so Figma won't reflect that.

Does this mean that what designers create in Figma is already automatically turned into a complete and functional web product? No. For these purposes, there are, for example, plugins that export entire interfaces in HTML/CSS, React, and other programming languages, but this way is still recommended exclusively for really basic products such as quick landing pages or simple testing prototypes. In this context, automatic systems never guarantee high quality as with what we can achieve with targeted development.

However, what is really useful in the **Inspect** tab is the ability to select specific items and inspect, copy, and use the same properties for different purposes. For example, after clicking on any **Button** element, the following will be displayed immediately below the summary of properties:

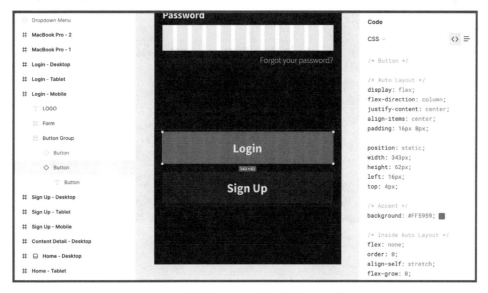

Figure 11.9 – Code snippets for the Button element

In the **Code** section of the **Inspect** panel, **CSS** rules are set by default, as this is the most useful and commonly used option. **CSS** stands for **Cascading Style Sheet** and is a style rule sheet that combines the structure created in HTML (which serves to create the "skeleton," the foundation of your layout) to structure and style a website or web application. What is especially remarkable about it is that the highest-quality code is achieved here when using **Auto Layout** at the design stage. In fact, **Auto Layout** corresponds to a 1:1 **Flexbox** web system and therefore allows you to already have at your disposal all the rules you need to create the prototyped layout. If you didn't use **Auto Layout**, values would be suggested with absolute value coordinates in **Frames**, which should be avoided where possible, as this results in unresponsive interfaces. The **CSS** rules that we have access to range from color rules to rules about text, effects, sizing, and positioning. Each property and function presented in the **Design** tab is equivalent to a rule that you will find here later.

As you can see, the **Code** section can make web development a bit easier. But what if instead of a website, we need to develop mobile applications? It is also possible to get the code for these purposes, just click on the **CSS** option and a dropdown will appear where you will find both the **iOS** and **Android** options and thus access small snippets – based on the selected level – of the code in Swift and XML respectively:

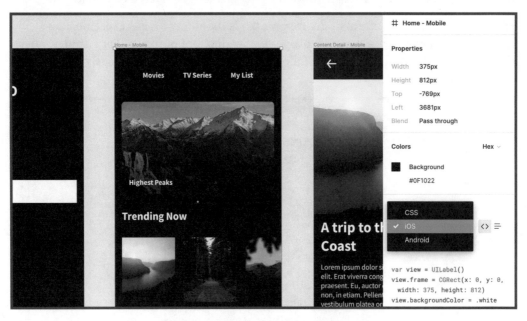

Figure 11.10 – Switching to iOS and Android code snippets

But nowadays, these specific mobile languages, including SwiftUI and Flutter, are constantly undergoing major changes due to their rapid development, and therefore are less interesting and useful than their CSS counterparts.

Now you can see why the **Inspect** panel is made primarily for developers who typically use Figma to get the information they need to write code. But still, this does not mean that you should not explore this tab and just ignore it in your work, because the better you know its functionality and capabilities, the better you will be in communicating with the developers on your team. A good exercise would be to study **Inspect** as a viewer to see how things look through this lens. To do this, you can open your file in incognito mode in your browser using an extra Figma account and the generated shared link. It may be that you come across new discoveries and surprises!

In the next section, you'll learn how to make your design project in Figma even more development-friendly, and you'll find out why it's important to keep it that way even if the product is already on the market.

Handing over the project for development

Your journey was as exciting and interesting as it was intense, wasn't it? You have gone through the important steps in designing a generic product. Of course, all phases have been minimized to keep the overview for you as complete as possible. Nevertheless, we can say that at the moment, you have keys with which you can approach any other projects on your future path, which will be devoted to the creation of real products, and therefore the designs will be much more detailed and elaborate. In addition, it is likely that you will be a part of a whole team working on a complex digital product, and it will also be a very interesting journey in which you will combine tools that you already know and discover new, more advanced features.

So, does our work really end here? Can we really consider the project closed? Of course, even after testing the product, getting approval, and providing the developers with the necessary resources, there are still very few cases where a designer actually "stops" working on something that has been created. So, what will happen next?

Of course, there are no universal answers to this question, and it all depends on the type of your job and whether you are a freelancer or an in-house designer. But while there can be many scenarios, this section will give you a general overview of how things usually work if the designer is part of the team that manages the entire product or a part of it.

What's next?

In the early days of digital technology, professionals were only hired to design a product, and once it was developed, it was no longer necessary to maintain a working relationship. Often, designers were not even providing the source files of the project; instead, they were only sending representative images of how the product should look in the end. Year after year, the value of digital products increased, companies began to invest more and more in them, and with that, the approach to design and development completely changed.

A digital product today represents a full-fledged ecosystem. Research and analysis are its foundation, and the design and prototyping phases are constant aspects that make it come alive as the product will always be updated and improved. This is what defines a successful product – one that is built based on flexibility, modularity, and continuity in its development.

And for this reason, more and more companies and agencies are no longer starting with the product itself, but with a **design system**, or rather, a system of building blocks that helps create one or more products with scalability in mind. We have also built the foundation for a modest design system, chapter by chapter, by structuring typography, colors, grids, and components. The design system grows with the product; it is constantly expanding and evolving through the creation of new blocks and may even contain more abstract aspects of the product, such as tone of voice, accessibility, inclusivity, and more. In addition, the design system can be used to create a range of products that fit together to provide more than one service without making the user feel pushed into an unfamiliar environment.

Speaking of design systems, we must differentiate it from **UI kits**. This comparison would require a separate book, and we won't go into too much of it, but you should have an idea of the main principles of both. A UI kit is a collection of design elements such as components and styles, and at this point, you might think that this is quite the same as a design system. However, there is a fundamental difference between them, which is important for you as a designer to understand. As mentioned earlier, a design system grows in parallel with the product and includes both standard and specific elements created exclusively for it. Moreover, a design system can go further and provide rules for more aspects, such as the means of communication with the user, tone of voice, and others. Apart from the design team, other professionals can contribute to it, such as copywriters, psychologists, marketers, and so on. UI kits usually have little to do with a specific product, although a UI kit can also offer a set of text styles, colors, grids, and components, all of which can be easily reused for various apps or websites, perhaps with some style customization or other minor changes. A UI kit is often used as a quick way to create generic digital products, or as a starting point for building and customizing your own design system.

Thus, a UI kit can speed up the initial process, but as your product gets more complex, you run into tough constraints, so it is worth investing in the creation of a design system.

Documenting, reiterating, and improving

It is normal that while a project is growing, improving, and developing, the composition of the team that works on it may change, and the number of professionals can also increase. At these times, project files and resources are frequently and repeatedly passed from hand to hand among other designers and developers. You should never underestimate this aspect and always take it into account in your future work process. What you can do is organize your projects, files, and folders, always clear them of useless items, and rename layers, styles, and components in the best way. However, this is not always enough. Especially when you are working on a product that has a design system based on styles, components, and variants, it is very important that they are all clear, transparent, and documented.

But what exactly does this mean? Well, you can make it easy for anyone new to the project by specifying when to use each library item specifically. Thus, if you go to the **Styles + Components** page and select any element – for example, **Carousel Item** – you can add a code snippet for it, or perhaps indicate the use case in a few words or sentences for this component:

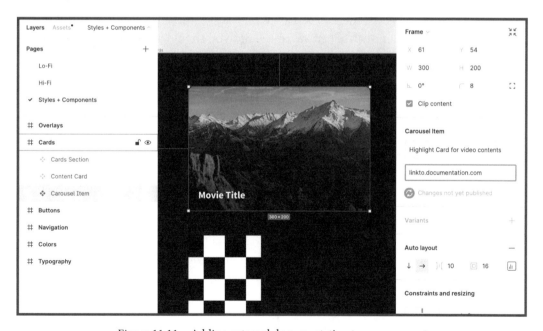

Figure 11.11 – Adding external documentation to a component

For more complex cases, you can add a direct link to any more extensive documentation that can be created in an external platform, such as **Notion**, **Zeroheight**, or even in a separate Figma file, depending on the needs of the project.

In addition to components, it is best to apply accompanying information to styles as well, where you can describe the purpose of a specific typography or color. In larger projects, even text styles, colors, and spacing are converted into so-called **design tokens**. In fact, thanks to design tokens, Figma styles can be converted to code in real time and, in the case of some changes, they are automatically replaced in all instances of them in the actual source of the application. This is a very advanced concept, but it's worth exploring with the developers on your team.

As you can imagine, there is always room for improvement for any product, which is great because you, as a designer, can strengthen your skills, get new ones, and grow professionally. And even when you've created a mature product with an incredible design system (which itself takes years of work), there will always be something to change, develop, and improve. This is due to the fact that user needs are constantly changing, technology is developing at a tremendous speed, and standards are often revised. Therefore, it is useless to try to create the perfect product right away, as you risk never going into the release phase. When you feel that a product is well designed, it's important to launch it to market, study user reactions, conduct market research with your target audience after launch, and see if everything is working as expected. Your preliminary analysis may seem perfect in theory even after a few tests, but in practice it may fail due to unforeseen events or miscalculated variables. But you should always use this as an opportunity to take advantage of the new data that the market is providing to solve critical problems.

That way, even when a product is doing well in the market, the designer's job is never over, and you will continually repeat the design process and try to improve what you already have. There will always be many questions and problems to be solved. Is there any way to improve the conversion rate? Can it be influenced if you move a button or change its color? At this point, there is a great way to get useful data – an **A/B test**, that is, creating another version of the interface that will be compared with the current one and presented to a group of people belonging to the target audience in order to understand whether it will perform better or worse in the market. Large companies conduct such experiences in an expensive way, releasing slightly different versions of the same product. You can see for yourself by opening the Facebook mobile app on your device and on a friend's one: do you have the same interface, the same icons, the same arrangement of the elements on the tab bar? Probably not. As you can see, the designer always has something to do, and design in general has a huge impact on the life of the product and its users.

As you can see, being a designer means always being ready to take on challenges, knowing that there is always a way to improve the user experience and meet the users' needs on a deeper level. It's also important to empathize not only with your audience but also with your teammates by giving them your files in an organized and understandable way. Thus, it will be much easier for you and other designers as well to navigate through documented and descriptive resources rather than through something messy, especially if you need to create a design system, which is almost inevitable and is indeed necessary if your product is constantly evolving.

Summary

In this chapter, you discovered that Figma can not only be an efficient and fast design tool but goes beyond that, considering the needs of other team members who might work in collaboration with designers. Thus, you learned how to export a whole file or its individual elements from Figma in several possible formats, as well as how to set up elements for subsequent export while still at the active design stage. Also, you have finally explored the functionality of the last tab of the right panel, namely **Inspect**. In addition, you learned about what a design system is and how to document and assign descriptions for styles and components in your projects so that everything is well organized and easy to use.

In the next and final chapter, you'll see how to extend Figma by discovering the amazing Figma Community, where you can explore hundreds of cool UI kits, templates, and plugins from creators around the world. Using Figma Community resources, you can not only speed up and optimize your workflow but also find inspiration to create something amazing yourself!

12
Discovering Plugins and Resources in the Figma Community

In the previous chapter, you completed the interface design of our video streaming application by learning about exporting assets and preparing files for further development work. Of course, in real life, your design routine will be full of other aspects that this book cannot cover, but now you clearly understand how product design begins, what stages it consists of, and when we may (or may not) call it completed. You should understand, however, that in reality, things can be different. Thus, in some cases, you could work in a team of designers who are engaged in only one separate feature of a huge digital product, or you could get a job in a company that has already launched projects, and you will need to work on improving them from the design side. Yes, you will have many challenges on your way, but as you gradually overcome them, you will open up tremendous opportunities for learning something new, and you will be growing professionally and personally.

Another reason why you shouldn't worry too much and take more risks is that now designers prefer to be open, share experiences with each other, and support and guide beginners. This happens in a variety of ways – meetups, conferences, open talks, mentoring, and more. Figma also does a lot to unite designers around the world by providing them with a whole platform for sharing entire resources, namely the Figma Community, and you will learn all about this in this chapter, which will be special not only because it is the last chapter, but also because it will not be devoted to the interface of our application. Therefore, for the activities offered in the chapter, you only need your drafts, so open up Figma and get ready to dive into the world of the Figma Community!

In this chapter, we are going to cover the following main topics:

- Exploring the Figma Community
- Finding useful resources
- Extending Figma with plugins

By the end of this chapter, you will be able to freely navigate the Figma Community, find and duplicate helpful files for personal use, and select and install plugins for your needs that can help you improve your workflow.

Exploring the Figma Community

As you know, Figma was created from the very beginning as a collaboration tool. It was revolutionary not only in terms of the concept of the design tool itself but also for encouraging designers to share and communicate with each other. The fact is that in the beginning, unlike developers, designers remained reserved and rarely opened their resources for public use. However, today we can finally say that designers are developing a strong sense of community, just like developers, so their mindset is changing and they are increasingly sharing their knowledge.

And it is for this reason that the Figma Community was created, a special public space within Figma itself that contributes significantly to the interchange between designers around the world. The Figma Community allows you to make your creations available to others in a very simple way and possibly inspire someone to do something of their own that way. Isn't that amazing?

So, in this section, you will explore the Figma Community and learn how to search and duplicate resources from it for personal use in Figma and FigJam, as well as how to publish your files.

Accessing and publishing to the Figma Community

It's incredibly easy to explore the Figma Community space. Just go to your Figma main tab – where **Teams**, **Files**, and **Projects** are located – and click on **Community** in the left sidebar, just below **Drafts**. And this is what you will see immediately after:

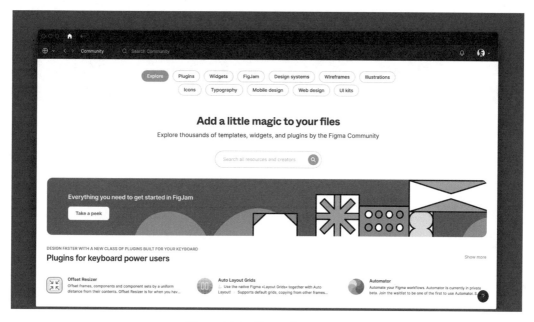

Figure 12.1 – Figma Community

This is your starting point in finding a wide variety of resources (most of which are free, but there are some that are view-only available and have to be paid for to be used) that other designers like you publish to a wider audience. You can freely explore the different categories available here or use the search bar at the top to look for something specific, such as files, plugins, or creators.

Let's start by talking about files, which are basically designs created in Figma. You can copy any of these to your drafts and start using it, but before that, you can explore it in the read-only preview by clicking on it in the Figma Community section. At the top right, you can see a **Duplicate** button, which allows you to copy this resource to use and modify it however you want:

Figure 12.2 – Duplicating a file

You, as a designer, can also contribute to the Figma Community, which is now a hugely important platform that depends on the efforts of each creator. So, if you ever create a resource that is useful to you, it is very likely that it will be useful to others as well, and you might consider making it available publicly to the Figma Community. This is easily achievable with the **Sharing** feature in Figma from any open file you want to publish. After clicking the **Share** button – as if you wanted to invite contributors to the file – in the tab at the top, switch to **Publish to Community**:

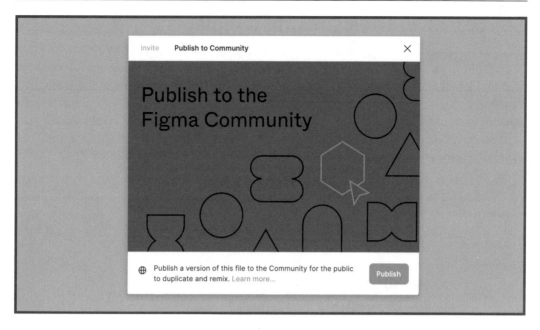

Figure 12.3 – Publishing a file to the Figma Community

From here, all you have to do is select the appropriate thumbnail, add the name and relevant details such as the description and tags, and validate the publishing. Right after that, your file will be available to everyone in the Figma Community.

> **Note**
>
> By default, every file published in the Figma Community will be licensed under a *Creative Commons Attribution 4.0 International License*, which means anyone can use, edit, and republish your file as they wish, simply by indicating the authorship. Be careful not to publish files that you have created under a contract with any client or company.

The Figma Community is an amazing place, and you will soon discover many valuable resources you can find for any purpose. At first, you may feel lost in all this diversity, which is growing more and more every day. Don't worry: later in this chapter, you will learn more about the different types of resources so you can easily navigate this space.

Starting off with FigJam and templates

So, now you know how easily you can duplicate Figma Community resources to your Figma, but in fact this space is not limited here, and it offers us many very useful resources also for FigJam, including extremely interesting templates that you can use in the very early stages of a project. By heading into the dedicated FigJam section of the Figma Community, you can find tons of starter whiteboards to kick off everything we did in *Chapter 2, Structuring Moodboards, Personas, and User Flows within FigJam*, in even less time. For example, you may want to build a user persona, and you just have to search for that. Here's a great example of such a foundation:

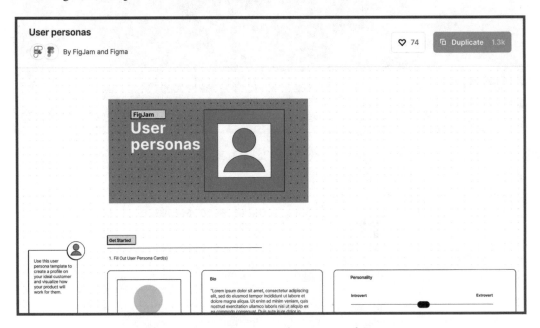

Figure 12.4 – User personas by FigJam and Figma

The amount of such amazing resources is endless, and you can get flowcharts, team agendas, empathy maps, or even ice-breaking activities and other cool templates to improve teamwork or just take a fun break for a few minutes all together. Take some time to explore these presets, paying attention to how they were created, and you will surely learn a lot from it. When you feel more confident in the Figma Community space, move on to the next section for some great examples of quality resources.

Finding useful resources

Now that you know how to find and copy files from the Figma Community for personal use, let's take a look at exactly which resources you might be interested in most. Since you saw how easy it is to publish to the Figma Community, there are now tons of resources out there, and it is sometimes difficult to know which are valid and which should be avoided. In this section, we'll take a look at some interesting resources to help you to know better how to navigate this incredibly valuable but equally risky space.

UI kits and design systems

Speaking of the most useful resources to be found in the Figma Community, the first to be mentioned are the many variations of **UI kits** and **design systems** created by professionals, large companies, or well-known brands. Using these files, you can start designing a new project not from scratch, speeding up and simplifying the initial process. This can be done in two ways. First, you can find those files that are real starter kits, consisting of basic elements and styles. This way, you will have a starting point for the subsequent creation of a custom library. Think of a package of essentials as a blueprint that is used to work faster and not to forget anything important. Here is a practical example of this kind of kit, **Design System (Starter Kit)**, which you can easily find in the Figma Community:

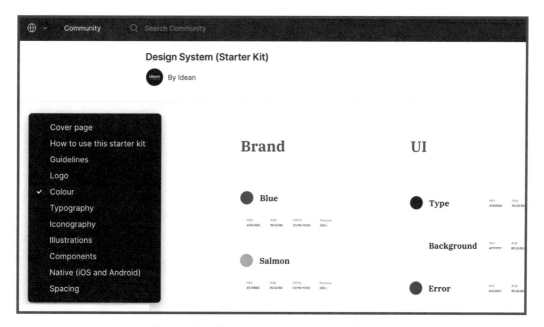

Figure 12.5 – Design System (Starter Kit) by Idean

The second way is to use kits that are part of development frameworks that not only offer a complete design system that can be customized but also a ready-to-use code counterpart for each style and element. One of the more representative examples we mentioned earlier is *Google Material Design*. You can find the official creator page in the Figma Community, which contains a whole series of open source files, including the latest version of their design kit:

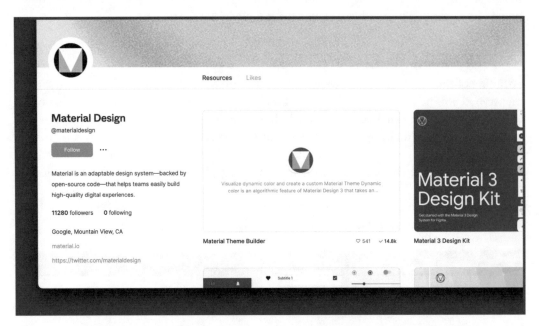

Figure 12.6 – The official Material Design account in the Figma Community

If you want to take a deeper look at this kit and its related design system, you can head over to the official `material.io` site to see the complete documentation on how to use it and how to implement every design element and every piece of code.

As you may know, Material Design is an Android-centric style, but what if you need iOS-styled components? Sadly, Apple still does not have official Figma kit files, but with the great potential of the Figma Community, this is not a problem. Therefore, you can easily find many unofficial but very good kits that strictly follow all the recommendations and code counterparts from `developer.apple.com/design/human-interface-guidelines`. Here's a good example that you can find as **iOS 15 UI Kit for Figma**:

Figure 12.7 – iOS 15 UI Kit for Figma by Joey Banks

This, like any other file, can be duplicated in your drafts, disassembled, modified, and examined in parts. You can just use the **Styles** and **Assets** libraries right away or have them as a complete reference for any complex work you want to do. In fact, one of the main methods of mastering every aspect of interface design is examining the source files of other professionals. This way, you can understand how everything is done, what is behind each decision, and how you can improve your design, or perhaps go further by adding something of your own.

Even more stuff

The Figma Community resources are limitless, and what you've seen is just the tip of the iceberg. In addition to UI kits and design systems, you can find just about anything for any need in the Figma Community space. Let's say you don't need a complete design system, but just a set of layout grids to copy and publish to your personal library – here it is, **UI Prep Layout Grids 4.0**:

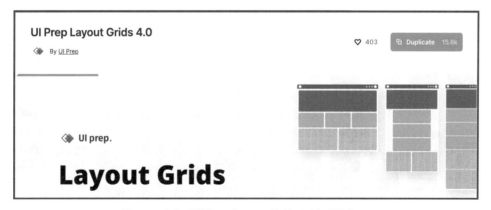

Figure 12.8 – UI Prep Layout Grids 4.0 by UI Prep

Or maybe you need a fresh gradient to test out some cool new combinations in your interface? No problem, you will find a lot of them, for example, **uigradients – Figma Style Library**:

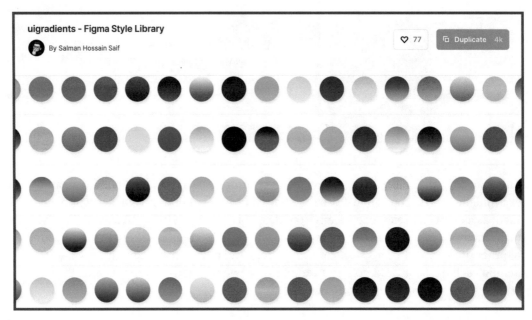

Figure 12.9 – uigradients – Figma Style Library by Salman Hossain Saif

Okay, we're done with styles, grids, and so on. Let's try something a little fancier and more specific, such as a set of cool travel illustrations, for instance, **[Orbit Design System] Illustrations**:

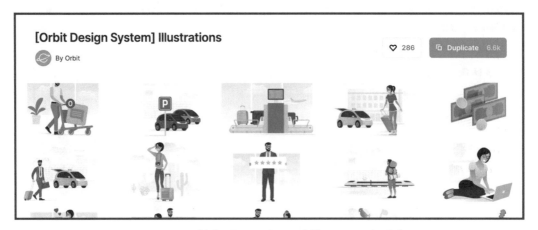

Figure 12.10 – [Orbit Design System] Illustrations by Orbit

As you can see, you just need to understand what you need and you can find it in the Figma Community. This could be icon kits, project presentation slide kits, or even avatar generators that make use of components and variants to create dynamic assets, such as **Avatar Illustration System**:

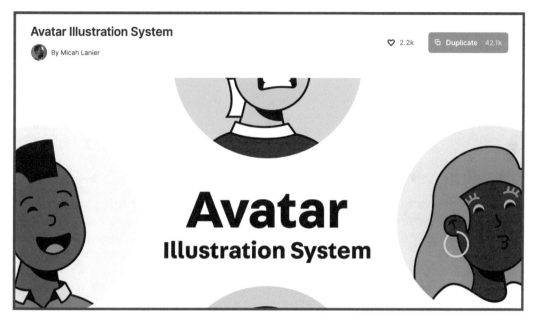

Figure 12.11 – Avatar Illustration System by Micah Lanier

This is all great, but as said at the beginning, you have to be careful not to run into low-quality files. It is best to duplicate and study the file well before moving on to actual use to see if it satisfies your needs properly. Plus, you can rely on the **Likes** and **Reviews** system – another effective way to avoid wasting time on resources that are poorly created or may be out of date and no longer maintained.

As you can see, there are a lot of designers in the Figma Community who volunteer to share their masterpieces with their peers, and this is a really great opportunity for you to ease some aspects of your workflow and get some tips from these files. It's perfectly okay to get help from the Figma Community because that's what it was created for, but try not to overuse its resources and find the right balance between using resources and creating projects with your own unique approach.

However, not all the Figma Community's resources are related to design itself; there is a whole section dedicated to extending Figma functionality, namely **Plugins**. If you've ever installed some of these in your web browser, you probably know how plugins can add a little extra to your usual experience. Well, plugins in Figma work in a similar way, and in the next section, you'll learn everything you need to install and start using them!

Extending Figma with plugins

You've now explored all the tools and features in Figma, from the basic to the advanced, and they're all great without exception. But while some of them can significantly improve the quality and speed of your workflow, you will still run into limitations in the case of even more specific personal requests or the need to further optimize some part of your work. Of course, this is a completely normal situation, in which many designers find themselves, and so in the Figma Community you can find such solutions for specific tasks, and these are plugins. Plugins are extensions for Figma and/or FigJam created by third parties that further empower your tools. So, now you're going to explore these incredible plugins in the Figma Community space, then learn how to install and manage plugins in your Figma account, and finally take a look at some of the ones that you might find useful in your design workflow.

Installing and managing plugins

It is extremely easy to add new plugins, and unlike what happens with other applications, they do not affect computer performance due to the web application nature of Figma. The plugin installation procedure is almost the same as for copying files – follow these steps to learn how to do it:

1. First, you search in the Figma Community space, select the plugin you want, and then, instead of using **Duplicate** like with files, you will use the **Install** button.

2. To make sure you are looking for the right type of resource, there is a very useful filter that limits searches to plugins only, hiding files:

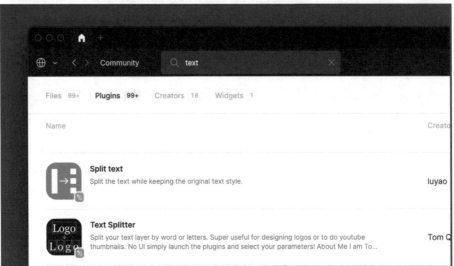

Figure 12.12 – Searching and filtering plugins

3. After you copy any file from the Figma Community, it will automatically open in a new tab in your Figma.

But after installing a plugin, nothing specific happens and your Figma seems to remain the same. So, where are all these extra features? How can you use them now? Since Figma plugins are now globally installed in your account, you can access them directly from any file and project. You can do this by selecting the appropriate option either by right-clicking anywhere on the canvas, or by using the main menu in the upper- left corner. Through this option, you can see all your installed plugins:

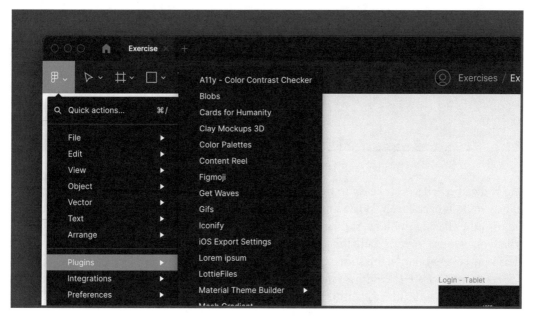

Figure 12.13 – Accessing your installed plugins

> **Note**
>
> To remove a plugin, simply open the list of plugins using the corresponding option from the Figma logo menu and click **Manage plugins...**, and this will bring up a dialog box with all your plugins, where you can delete or see the details of each of them.

Clicking on a plugin name in this list will open a new popup dedicated to the functionality of that particular plugin only. For example, if you open **Lorem ipsum**, a plugin that allows you to automatically fill selected text fields with placeholder content, you get a pop-up window (freely draggable around the interface) that allows you to configure all the parameters for the action of this plugin as shown here:

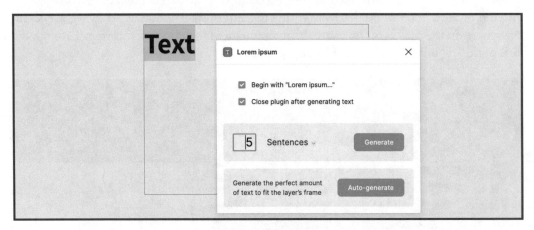

Figure 12.14 – Setting up the Lorem ipsum plugin

As you can see, it's pretty easy to find and run installed plugins in Figma, but there is a way to do it even faster. What's more, this method can also be applied to quickly access many other basic functions, not just plugins. All you have to do is remember a shortcut that you can use in your daily life, that is, *Command + /* (macOS) or *Ctrl + /* (Windows). For non-US keyboards, the shortcut may not work, and you can use *Command + P* (macOS) or *Ctrl + P* (Windows) instead. This shortcut opens a **Quick Actions** window through which you can easily find what you need on the fly. This way, you will be able to find all the options and functions presented in the menu under the Figma logo. So, instead of manually opening the **Lorem ipsum** plugin, you can do the same operation by simply using the shortcut and typing `Lorem`:

Figure 12.15 – Launching plugins with Quick Actions

Figma motivates designers to use **Quick Actions** more often by recently releasing the ability to use plugins without any additional dialog boxes. So, how can you use plugins like this outside of their interfaces? It is enough to use **Quick Actions** by simply specifying the parameters required by the plugin. Here's a practical example with **Unsplash**, another great plugin that lets you instantly select royalty-free images from unsplash.com, without ever leaving Figma. After having it installed, use the **Quick Actions** shortcut, find Unsplash, and instead of pressing *Enter* to launch it, press *Tab* to insert all of the following options:

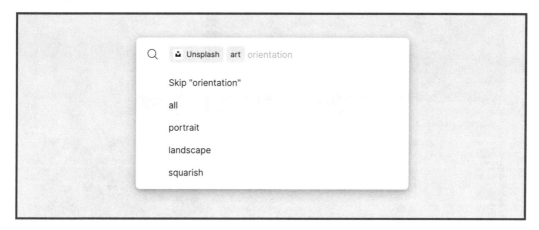

Figure 12.16 – Using the Unsplash plugin with parameters

Obviously, it is also possible to access this plugin through its dialog box by selecting **Unsplash** in the usual way. But it's clear that for power users who use keyboard shortcuts and keyboards a great deal and always try to optimize their time as much as possible, this is a very important turning point.

Now that you know about the possibilities to improve and facilitate your work in Figma with plugins, you might be feeling quite excited and want to know more about them. But since there are so many of them for all sorts of different uses in the Figma Community, let's set your starting point by looking at some of the specific plugins that can serve as your foundation.

Suggested plugins

As with file resources, there are a lot of plugins in the Figma Community, and at first it can be very difficult to figure out which ones might actually be useful and which ones should be avoided. In this case, you can also rely on reviews, as well as the date when the plugin was last updated – an indication that there is a developer or team behind the plugin who is still actively working on the project. However, if you are still feeling overwhelmed and unsure of where to start, there are a few guidelines for reliable plugins that can be very helpful in your day-to-day work.

Iconify

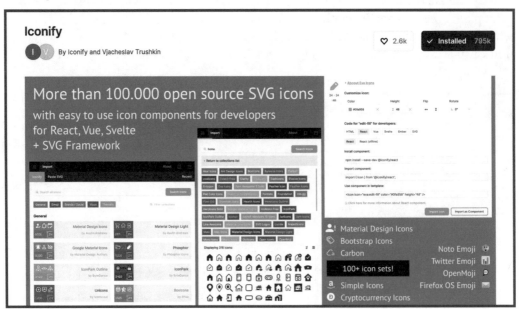

Figure 12.17 – Iconify by Iconify and Vjacheslav Trushkin

Iconify is a collection of the most famous free icon libraries currently available, which you can get with a few clicks right in Figma. To find an icon you want, you just need to enter a keyword or browse a specific library and import the vector directly into your file, ready to use.

Content Reel

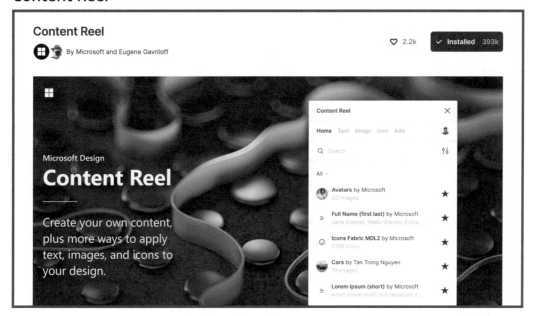

Figure 12.18 – Content Reel by Microsoft and Eugene Gavriloff

Content Reel is a plugin published by the Microsoft Design team that makes the process of filling placeholder content incredibly fast. Here you will find not only the classic *Lorem ipsum* but also entire collections of texts, icons, and images. All of this you can start using with one click to simulate a more realistic interface using libraries provided directly by the plugin (for example, addresses, phone numbers, or placeholder profile pictures). You can even upload your own personal content libraries from here.

Clay Mockups 3D

Figure 12.19 – Clay Mockups 3D by Hamish

Making great design projects is important, but it's just as important to know how to properly represent what you've been working on. This plugin will make this aspect much easier for you, as with it, you can easily create quick 3D mockups to represent the designs in your portfolio. Rotate the device as you like and in one click, display the interface that you created onscreen. It's incredibly simple, fast, and impressive!

Contrast

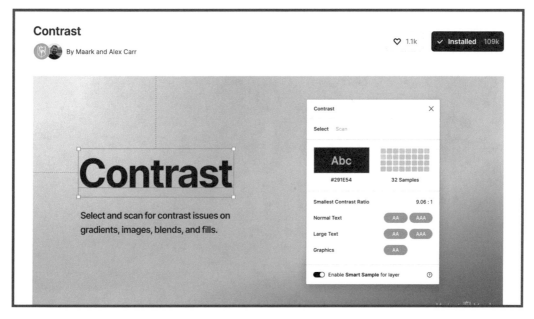

Figure 12.20 – Contrast by Maark and Alex Carr

Accessibility makes a huge difference in design, but it happens that among the many things that need to be done, this aspect is often overlooked. Thanks to this plugin, you can make sure that there are no errors in the contrast and readability of text in your files. To do this, you just need to select individual levels or scan all pages to see reports related to errors in the interface, according to the **Web Content Accessibility Guidelines** (**WCAG**).

Figma Tokens

Figure 12.21 – Figma Tokens by Abdul Wahid and Jan Six

This plugin can be thought of as advanced, but once you have to work as a team on a design system, it can make things easier. The plugin comes in handy if you need to work with developers to create a token system. Don't forget about this amazing tool, even if you are working on your own right now.

This concludes our short overview, although of course there are other interesting plugins you can find. However, there is no universal set of them for every designer, as they develop their own workflow over time. Therefore, it is better to choose plugins depending on specific personal needs, rather than installing too many of them and in a chaotic manner. For now, you can try and experiment with the preceding suggestions, but don't go too far in choosing new plugins – they will find you on their own when you have any specific request.

Summary

In this chapter, you have learned that Figma can be not only a cool design tool but an equally cool place to connect with designers from all over the world, exchange resources, and get inspired, all with the help of the Figma Community, which can be accessed very easily directly from Figma! How amazing is that?

Now you know what types of resources are represented in the Figma Community and how to search and filter them correctly. You have also learned about some examples of great files and plugins that can be your basis for a collection of useful resources. By combining all of this with your knowledge of Figma tools and functions, you can now optimize your work as best you can. Keep in mind, however, that no matter how good the files or plugins seem to you, it's always best to test the end result yourself to ensure that there are no inaccuracies.

Of course, there is still a lot more to explore in the Figma Community, and you will have many more incredible discoveries along the way. Who knows, maybe one day you might even want to share your creations there! That would be great, because it is very important not only to receive, but also to give, and sometimes giving turns out to be even more beneficial for you.

With this last chapter, you have completed your journey of learning the basic principles of creating interfaces with Figma, and we want to thank you for reading this book to the end. It was not easy, and there were many challenges on your way, so it is recommended to refresh your knowledge from time to time, referring to the chapters and exercises of the book that were especially demanding for you. And, when you're ready to move on, you'll discover dozens of ways to go beyond this book and improve your design skills.

Interface design is a rapidly evolving world, full of unlimited opportunities to create and improve products that people use every day. To become a true expert in your field, never stop learning and constantly putting your knowledge into practice, because this is the real key to success.

Index

Packt.com

Subscribe to our online digital library for full access to over 7,000 books and videos, as well as industry leading tools to help you plan your personal development and advance your career. For more information, please visit our website.

Why subscribe?

- Spend less time learning and more time coding with practical eBooks and Videos from over 4,000 industry professionals

- Improve your learning with Skill Plans built especially for you

- Get a free eBook or video every month

- Fully searchable for easy access to vital information

- Copy and paste, print, and bookmark content

Did you know that Packt offers eBook versions of every book published, with PDF and ePub files available? You can upgrade to the eBook version at packt.com and as a print book customer, you are entitled to a discount on the eBook copy. Get in touch with us at customercare@packtpub.com for more details.

At www.packt.com, you can also read a collection of free technical articles, sign up for a range of free newsletters, and receive exclusive discounts and offers on Packt books and eBooks.

Other Books You May Enjoy

If you enjoyed this book, you may be interested in these other books by Packt:

UX Design for Mobile

Pablo Perea, Pau Giner

ISBN: 978-1-78728-342-8

- Plan an app design from scratch to final test, with real users.
- Learn from leading companies and find working patterns.
- Apply best UX design practices to your design process.
- Create low and high fidelity prototypes using some of the best tools.
- Follow a step by step examples for Tumult Hype and Framer Studio.
- Test your designs with real users, early in the process.
- Integrate the UX Designer profile into a working team

101 UX Principles

Will Grant

ISBN: 978-1-78883-736-1

- Use typography well to ensure that text is readable
- Design controls to streamline interaction
- Create navigation which makes content make sense
- Convey information with consistent iconography
- Manage user input effectively
- Represent progress to the user
- Provide interfaces that work for users with visual or motion impairments
- Understand and respond to user expectations

Packt is searching for authors like you

If you're interested in becoming an author for Packt, please visit `authors.packtpub.com` and apply today. We have worked with thousands of developers and tech professionals, just like you, to help them share their insight with the global tech community. You can make a general application, apply for a specific hot topic that we are recruiting an author for, or submit your own idea.

Hi!

I really hope you enjoyed reading *Designing and Prototyping Interfaces with Figma* and found it in getting started using Figma to create amazing interfaces!

It would really help us (and other potential readers!) if you could leave a review on Amazon sharing your thoughts on *Designing and Prototyping Interfaces with Figma*.

Go to the link below or scan the QR code to leave your review:

https://packt.link/r/180056418X

Your review will help us understand what's worked well in this book and what could be improved upon for future editions, so it really is appreciated.

Best wishes,

Made in United States
Troutdale, OR
09/13/2024

22795952R10213